HOW TO DO BUSINESS WITH THE PEOPLE'S REPUBLIC OF CHINA

Philip Wik

an Entrepreneur Press book

Reston Publishing Company, Inc.
A Prentice-Hall Company
Reston, Virginia

Library of Congress Cataloging in Publication Data

Wik, Philip.
   How to do business with the People's Republic of China.

   "An Entrepreneur Press book."
   Bibliography: p.
   Includes index.
    1. China--Economic conditions--1976-   . 2. China--
Commerce. I. Title.
HC427.92.W54 1984   346.5107   83-24796
ISBN 0-8359-2919-1   345.1067
ISBN 0-8359-2918-3 (pbk.)

©1984 by **Reston Publishing Company, Inc.**
   A Prentice Hall Company
   Reston, Virginia 22090

10   9   8   7   6   5   4   3   2   1

Interior design and production: Jack Zibulsky

Printed in the United States of America

CONTENTS

FOREWORD, viii □

INTRODUCTION, xi □

Risks and Rewards, xi □ Purpose of this Book, xii □ Notes and Acknowledgments, xiii □

1 CHINA IN TRANSITION, 1 □

Before the Revolution (1839–1948), 2 □ Rehabilitation (1949–1952), 5 □ The First Five-Year Plan (1953–1957), 6 □ The Great Leap Forward (1958–1960), 7 □ Recovery (1961–1965), 8 □ The Cultural Revolution (1966–1969), 9 □ Readjustment (from 1970), 10 □

2 THE FOUR MODERNIZATIONS, 15 □

Agriculture, 16 □ *Grain, 16* □ *Irrigation, 17* □ *Fertilizer, 19* □ *Mechanization, 20* □ Industry, 20 □ *Light Industry, 21* □ *Electricity, 22* □ *Coal, 22* □ *Petroleum, 24* □ *Iron and Steel, 27* □ *Nonferrous Metals, 28* □ *Transportation, 30* □ Science and Technology, 32 □ Education, 34 □ *Computers and Telecommunications, 35* □ Defense, 39 □ *Intentions, 40* □ *Capabilities, 45* □ *Needs, 47* □ Summary, 48 □ *Agriculture, 48* □ *Industry, 49* □ *Science and Technology, 49* □ *Defense, 50* □

3 TRADING BLOCKS, 51 □

Sino-Japanese Relations, 51 □ Sino-Western European Relations, 52 □ Sino-United States Relations, 54 □ *A Short History, 55* □ *The Taiwan Question, 58* □ *Trading Opportunities, 60* □

4 MAKING CONTACT, 65 □

Appraising the Market, 65 □ *The Feasibility Study*, 65 □ *The National Council for U.S.-China Trade*, 67 □ *Research Centers*, 69 □ *Banks*, 70 □ *Service and Trade Organizations*, 72 □ *Other Organizations*, 73 □ *Online Databases*, 73 □ *Research Guides*, 74 □ *Newspapers*, 74 □ *Books and Periodicals*, 75 □ *U.S. Government Organizations*, 78 □ *The Corporate Intelligence Agency*, 80 □ Entering the Market, 85 □ *The Proposal*, 86 □ *Consultants*, 91 □ *Visa Formalities*, 92 □ *Customs*, 93 □ *Transportation*, 94 □

5 NEGOTIATING THE CONTRACT, 97 □

6 NAVIGATING THE BUREAUCRACY, 105 □

The Problem, 105 □ What China is Doing, 107 □ What You Can Do, 108 □ China's Trading Establishment, 111 □ *The National Party Congress*, 111 □ *The National People's Congress*, 112 □ *The Politburo*, 112 □ *The State Council*, 112 □ *The State Planning Commission*, 114 □ *The State Economic Commission*, 114 □ *The State Science and Technology Commission (S&T)*, 114 □ *The State Capital Construction Commission (SCCC)*, 115 □ *The State Machine Building Commission (SMBC)*, 115 □ *The State Agricultural Commission*, 115 □ *The State Finance and Economic Commission*, 115 □ *The Ministries*, 115 □ *End-Users*, 118 □ *Foreign Trade Corporations*, 120 □ *The China Ocean Shipping Company*, 137 □ *The China National Foreign Trade Transportation Corporation*, 138 □ *The China National Chartering Corporation*, 138 □ *The China National Import and Export Commodities Inspection Corporation*, 138 □ *The China International Trust Investment Company*, 139 □ *The China Council for Promotion of International Trade*, 140 □ *Professional Groups*, 140 □ *Delegations*, 141 □ *The Chinese Export Commodities Fair*, 141 □ *Local Administrations*, 143 □

7 LAW, 145 □

The Contract, 145 □ Trademarks, 148 □ Patents, 149 □ Copyrights, 150 □ Arbitration, 150 □

8 FINANCE, 155□

Banking, 155□Credit, 158□Pricing, 162□Payment, 164□Insurance, 169□Joint Ventures, 170□Countertrade, 179□

9 CHINA PROFILE, 185□

Land, 185□Climate, 186□People, 187□Religion, 188□Language, 189□Housing, 192□Food, 193□Money, 194□Transportation, 196□Telecommunications, 197□Pleasure, 199□

10 WILL IT LAST?, 201□

APPENDICES

    1 PINYIN CONVERSION, 213□
    2 ABBREVIATIONS OF CHINESE ORGANIZATIONS, 219□
    3 METRIC CONVERSION, 221□
    4 CHRONOLOGY, 223□
    5 OFFSHORE PETROLEUM REGULATIONS, 227□
    6 JAPANESE AND EUROPEAN TRADE AGREEMENTS, 237□
    7 U.S.-CHINA AGREEMENTS, 245□
    8 SAMPLE CONTRACTS, 255□
    9 FOREIGN EXCHANGE REGULATIONS, 271□
  10 TAX LAWS, 287□

SELECTED BIBLIOGRAPHY, 305□

INDEX, 317□

Figure 1
THE PEOPLE'S REPUBLIC OF CHINA

Source: *China: A Country Study*, Foreign Area Studies, The American University, Washington, D.C., 1981, xxii.

Figure 2
TOPOGRAPHY AND DRAINAGE

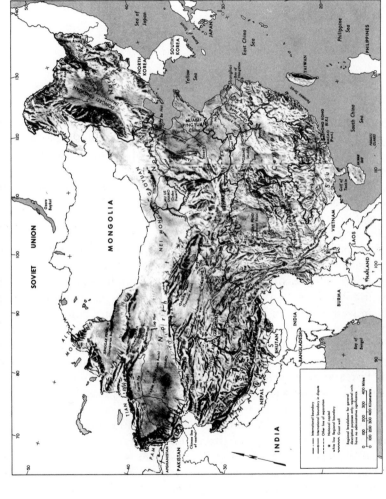

Source: *China: A Country Study*, Foreign Area Studies, The American University, Washington, D.C., 1981, 50.

FOREWORD

China, with a population over four times that of the United States—greater even than the combined population of the Arab nations—began to appear to Western businessmen, after Richard M. Nixon's visits there, as a potential world supermarket, eagerly awaiting the arrival of salesmen from the West. Imagine, the thinking seemed to go, a developing nation with nearly a billion consumers, each eager to acquire every conceivable consumer item that Western ingenuity could provide: automobiles, radios, television sets, etc.

The 1972–76 dream of a business euphoria has fallen short of reality as did the now laughable pre-1949 estimates of the Chinese market, when the prognosticators believed that the then 600 million Chinese constituted a potential bonanza for U.S. consumer imports. The reason for this shortfall is understandable in light of what we know about China today.

First, we know that while the typical Chinese consumer may be quite similar to his Western counterpart in his desires, the degree of "consumerism" reached in China will be dictated by the highly socialized, highly bureaucrat government. While the typical Chinese consumer may yearn for a television set or miniature radio, and may even be willing to go into debt—Western style—to acquire it, the chances are likely that the first television set or radio he buys will be manufactured in China and channeled into the marketplace through a system of allocations, the complexity of which only a highly socialized system is capable of devising.

The China of today is loosening some of the old restrictions and, through higher prices and tax incentives to agricultural producers, attempting to raise the standard of Chinese living; however, to suggest that business conditions in China resemble the flourishing entrepreneurial community of the United States would be misleading. Moreover, the per capita income in China is still quite low, although it is expected to increase despite a projected population figure of 1.5 billion by the year 2000.

Second, while many businessmen might have understood the fallacy of thinking that nearly a billion Chinese consumers were eagerly awaiting

American-made goods, they did not understand the difficulty of doing business at a time of cultural upheaval and with people traditionally accustomed to making decisions slowly. Now—to coin a new "Chinese" proverb, "With the wisdom of a thousand hindsights"—we know that there is only one customer in China: the Chinese government through its Foreign Trade Corporations (FTCs). Working through this bureaucracy takes good judgment, skill, and experience. We are fairly certain, for example, that China will continue to manufacture most of its consumer items, not only for internal use, but also to build an export business.

We know that the supposed shortage of raw materials in China was another fallacy. China has gas, minerals, and oil reserves that may rival those of the Middle East. It may be too early to predict how these resources will be developed in the long run, but an educated guess is that they will be used to maintain a program of foreign trade which will generate the cash for China's imports.

The Chinese people, particularly in the business community, are showing a great deal of Western-style enthusiasm, determination, and unity as they work to fulfill new goals. Among these goals are the modernization and mechanization of agriculture, and the development of gas, oil, and other mineral resources. If China is even moderately successful at reaching its goals to provide food, housing, clothing, and medical care for its people, China will experience a level of affluence it has never known.

Thus, China seeks an industrial revolution reminiscent of that of the West during the last century, but at this more advantageous time in history, many of the innovations, inventions, machinery, and technology are already at hand. When all of these ingredients are combined with the human and mineral resources that abound in China, the goal of a "complete industrial revolution from scratch by the year 2000" seems practical and possible.

Powerful factors motivating China to move forward economically are the threat from the Soviet Union and Japan's rise to unprecedented economic status despite a shortage of the natural resources that are so abundant in China.

Chinese officials have made overtures to the U.S. to form a China-U.S.-Japan triumvirate to gain world economic and military advantage over what China views as Soviet aggression. Supporters of the idea of a triumvirate cite its many advantages, including the opportunity to pool Chinese resources with Japanese and United States technology which, supporters claim, would fill a power vacuum in Asia and establish a strong second front against Soviet advances in such regions as Africa and the Middle East. Opponents of the triumvirate say that the United States and China are still too far apart ideologically to establish a viable relationship in the world of international politics. Washington has given the idea a cool reception so far. A triumvirate, however, remains at least a possibility for the future and one which, ideologies notwithstanding, may work to the advantage of those wanting to do business with China.

Despite past turmoils and political upheavals in China, there is currently agreement among various Chinese factions as to economic goals. Further, although Chinese officials have been oblique in their overtures, they have made it clear to friendly ears that they want closer ties with the West. It is also clear that China intends to "buy its industrial revolution" from the shelves and showcases of those nations in a position to provide China with buying-power generated through the development of its natural resources and export business in oil, gas, chemicals, petrochemicals, coal, iron and other minerals, rice and other foodstuffs, and light industrial products. Chinese officials have also studied long-range credit plans.

Any Western businessman in a position to supply the machinery and technology for China's coming revolution can make money, providing he knows: how to do business with China's FTCs; how to navigate the Chinese bureaucracy; how and with whom to negotiate in China; how to integrate a selling style into the cultural demands of a nation different from his own, and how to budget for the expenses of setting up sales in China. Providing all of these how-tos and more, this book can be your guide to a profitable venture in China—the new international business frontier.

Adam Starchild, President
Minerva Consulting Group

INTRODUCTION

China? There lies a sleeping giant. Let him sleep, for when he wakes, he will move the world.

—Napoleon Bonaparte *(1769–1821)*

Risks and Rewards

The giant is waking. The People's Republic of China has embarked on a course of expansion without parallel in history. If China reaches its goal of "comprehensive modernization by the year 2000," its achievement will exceed Japan's resurgence after World War II.

The flowering of friendship between China and the West cultivates visions of instant riches. Every businessman dreams of selling one widget to each of those billion people. There is trade, but it does not come easily. Doing business with China is different. It takes great study, investment and, above all, patience. The market is difficult to penetrate. A firm must commit considerable effort and expense before it sees black ink on the bottom line.

Politicians like talking about the "parallel interests" of China and the West. But the word "parallel" means lines that never meet. Given the red tape and uncertainty involved in the China trade, perhaps the best we can expect is an uneasy partnership. So why bother to investigate this market? Doing business with China can be profitable for single proprietorships as well as multinational corporations. Traders should decide to break into the China market when such business opportunities appear more attractive than those at home and the resources are available for carrying out such marketing. Opportunities for trade are as great as China's population.

In production terms, China is a major power. Principal imports include machinery and equipment, grain, steel, textile fibers, nonferrous metals and fertilizers. China exports foodstuffs, textiles, clothing and chemicals. It is also becoming a significant oil exporter. The major problems of China's economy are undeveloped transportation and communications, lack of skilled workers, exhaustion of agricultural land and lack of capital. China wants to solve these problems by expanding output, upgrading capacity with foreign technology and exporting goods against the tide of world recession.

China's demand for Western products remains unabated. Its wish list includes machine tools, mining equipment and aircraft parts and plants. Even when China decided to stress light rather than heavy expansion of foreign trade in 1980, imports climbed by more than twenty percent to $1.5 billion. In 1982, the total value of foreign investment in China stood at more than $2 billion, mainly in processing, compensation trade and joint venture technology.

Purpose of this Book

How to do Business with the People's Republic of China is not an academic exercise. It is a practical guide for traders who must make market selections based on a hard evaluation of the probable rate of return on investment. This book will grapple with two questions:

> Does it pay to do business with China?
> If so, how do we do business with China?

This book presents neither a cookbook nor a vague set of principles. You will answer the first question by coming to grips with China's economic system, developmental priorities and human, natural and financial resources. This will be the basis for making choices that provide the best balance between the opportunities for profit and the costs of failure. We will try to hold an honest mirror up to China. We won't fudge on risk analysis, market potential, or capital needs. We will pinpoint sources that can provide current data pertaining to your specific area of interest on a continuing basis and chart strategies for finding and doing business in the People's Republic of China. You will answer the second question by getting a sense of the cultural dimension of Sino-Western trade, an understanding of *how* the Chinese look at business and *why*. Thus, you will get some feeling for China's strategic interests and political coloration. China's ideological scene is shifting and could change radically, but it will always have needs that only external trade can fulfill. We will show how you can profit even when "the guns are at the gates." Small businessmen with Chinese operations or those who would like to expand into China will find this book of particular value, for it provides authoritative guidance on how to buy and sell in the biggest market opened to the business community in decades.

We have drawn aside the bamboo curtain, revealing the elusive reality that Chinese commerce offers. The first three chapters put China's trading patterns into a historical, programmatic, and international context. Chapters four and five show how traders can make contact and win contracts. Chapters six through eight cover administrative, legal, and financial arrangements. Chapter nine offers tips to those planning to work in the People's Republic of China. We conclude with a discussion on China's long-term prospects for Western trade, appendices, bibliography and an index. For importers and exporters, commercial, investment and international bankers, civil servants and diplomats, editors and correspondents, librarians, students, teachers and others with specialized interest in Asia, multinational executives, members of commodity firms, managers of shipping and airlines, hotel developers, tourists, indeed, anyone with a stake in Chinese trade, *How to do Business with the People's Republic of China* is required reading.

Notes and Acknowledgments

The People's Republic of China officially adopted Pinyin phonetic spelling on January 1, 1979. We accept Pinyin for names of people, but rigorous submission to Pinyin is confusing when spelling places. For example, *China* becomes *Zhonghua* and *Hong Kong* becomes the tongue-twisting *Xianggang*. Thus, in accordance with journalistic usage, some geographic names are in the old form. Addresses are in Pinyin. Some words frequently used in this book are given below in Pinyin and Wade-Giles, the system most familiar to Westerners:

Pinyin	Wade-Giles
Beijing	Peking
Guangzhou	Canton
Mao Zedong	Mao Tse-tung
Deng Xiaoping	Teng Hsiao-p'ing
Zhou Enlai	Chou En-lai

Chapter eight discusses Pinyin romanization and appendix 1 has a more complete conversion table. We wish to thank Douglas Wilkerson, a student of Chinese literature at Yale University, for providing some of these Pinyin spellings.

Appendix 2 defines abbreviations of Chinese organizations cited in this book. Appendix 3 has a metric conversion chart for readers unfamiliar with the system commonly used in the United States. We refer to remaining appendices at appropriate points in the text.

Because this is a "how to" book, we've kept opinions to a minimum. However, unrelenting detachment will scarcely serve the reader seeking discrimination. Within the context of the text, it should be plain when we render our judgment, as in the conclusion. Our opinions don't necessarily reflect the views of organizations that supplied us with information or that are affiliated with us.

A hazard in writing books of this type is that the text can become outdated as soon as it's published because of rapid economic and political change. To avoid this problem, we've cut references that would date it and stress principles that have withstood the test of time. This book is a research tool, rather than an almanac. It provides the conceptual framework to get the facts you need to make the decisions you want. In chapter four and the bibliography, we point to sources that will keep you briefed. The U.S. Congress, Commerce Department, and Central Intelligence Agency provided us with considerable information on China's trade and development. The authors are likewise indebted to leading newspapers, such as the *New York Times* and *South China Morning Post*, and a number of trade journals for short excerpts from their pages. We must also express our thanks to the American University for permission to reproduce the illustrations and Business International Asia/Pacific Ltd. for permission to copy some forms. Finally, we want to acknowledge the generous assistance of the library staffs of the National Council for U.S.-China Trade and the First National Bank of Chicago.

A cat-and-dog relationship between author and publisher is part of the mythology of publishing. However, the relationship with Reston Publishing Company has always been pleasant and professional. Special thanks are extended to Executive Editor Frederic K. Easter for providing the impetus for this project, Editor Howard Schneider for his wise suggestions, and Production Editor Jack Zibulsky for his expert work in crafting the manuscript into a useful, attractive book.

1

CHINA IN TRANSI- TION

The rise and fall of dynasties have shaped the China of today. The tensions of change and the continuity of tradition emerge out of the sweep of events. Conformity to Communist or Western ways is superficial, imposed upon the ancient cultures and customs of the Orient. An understanding of these themes is essential to anyone who wants to deal with China, for the tensions of history will persist in the China of tomorrow. Academicians will, of course, find this overview wanting. Edgar Snow, confidant to Mao and chronologist of the revolution, offers defense: "To attempt to condense China's long history into a brief chapter may be an affront to scholars but excusable as a service to readers unfamiliar with the rudiments of that history," he wrote in *The Other Side of the River*. "Kongfuzi (Confucius) thought that if he showed a man a corner of a thing, he should be able to discover the other corner for himself."[1]

As you continue to explore other corners in the mansion of China's history, make an effort to view it conceptually. Viewing history conceptually means grasping the whole rather than the immediacy. It means seeking out inner reality, recognizing that time is an organic continuum, that past is prologue. Today flows from yesterday, tomorrow from today. While it's folly to sup-

[1]Edgar Snow, *The Other Side of the River* (New York: Random House, 1961), p. 59.

1

pose that "history repeats itself," there is rippling, there is replication, there are relationships. Conceptualizing means going beyond facts to isolate causes and find meaning. "Facts" have little value in themselves. How do they fit together? Why do they fit together in certain patterns? Is the pattern you see in the facts the only one that could reasonably join them in a coherent whole? What holds the patterns together? Ask yourself these questions as you browse through the chronology in Appendix Four. Often, causality can only be made with a leap of imagination for which there is no documentation. Juxtaposition of two unrelated events can conjure insights. For example: in 1968, Soviet troops marched into Czechoslovakia; in 1969, Mao appointed Defense Minister Lin Biao as his successor and packed the Central Committee with strong army representation. Correlation isn't causality, so that relationship could be specious. A more subtle and precise analysis must include consideration of events felt and policies formulated in Boston, Berlin, Bombay. This depth of research can lead to paralyzing complexity. Thus, we must streamline our interpretation, recognizing that editing of history distorts historical reality. Despite these problems, history lets us appreciate forces that move the Chinese mind. The historical background of China is critical to understanding the present and anticipating the future. "Study the past," Kongfuzi said, "if you want to divine the future." Time spent reading history is time well spent.

Before the Revolution (1839–1948)

China's modern history began when the Great Powers secured trade concessions. Foreigners, however, were fearful of the Chinese, whose language few Europeans spoke, and whose customs fewer understood. Suspicion and greed triggered crises, culminating in the Opium War of 1839. The Chinese were concerned over the drug's effects on their youth and economy. Chinese officials resolved to stop the opium trade, which was foisted on them by British imperialists. At the conclusion of the war in 1842, the Treaty of Nanjing forced the Qing court to cede Hong Kong to Britain, open ports to trade, and recognize extraterritoriality, by which Westerners were subject only to the jurisdiction of their consular court. Western diplomats often browbeat the Chinese, and merchants meddling in Chinese affairs led to friction. Anti-Christian and anti-foreign riots, of which the Tianjing Massacre in 1870 was the most serious, erupted. Mounting peasant discontent posed a serious threat to the Qing dynasty. The most important uprising was the Taiping Rebellion. Sympathizers of the Southern Ming dynasty fought Manchu government troops from 1853–64. Chinese officials organized new armies. They defeated the Taipings, but only after well over thirty million people had been killed. A weak central regime and strong Han Chinese-led armies led to the rise of regional warlords.

Imperial China had been a civilization unto itself, living in self-imposed isolation from the rest of the world. But, in the 19th century, China entered a long decline because of mismanagement, peasant unrest, and incursions by Japan and the Western powers. War with Japan in 1894–95 forced the Chinese to recognize Japan's control over Korea. China also had to surrender Taiwan, which China had controlled since 1683. France, Germany, Great Britain, and Russia forced the crumbling empire to grant them more trading rights and territory. Humiliation at the hands of the West awakened Chinese intellectuals to the need for drastic changes, if China was to be preserved as an entity. It went through cycles of reaction and reform. For example, near the end of the Qing dynasty in 1898, the Guangxu emperor tried to copy the Meiji emperor's transformation of Japan from feudalism in the 19th century. He pictured an ideal society, in which laws would be equal in their application. Wide-ranging proposals included a nationally elected parliament under a constitutional monarchy, educational facilities at the village level, and prohibition of foot binding. In the Hundred Days from June 11 to September 21, 1898, the Manchu court initiated such reforms. The failure of these reforms was due in part to the corrupt Dowager Empress Cixi (Tz'u-hsi), who dominated the last three decades of Qing government.

The Boxer Rebellion of 1900 precipitated yet another foreign occupation, and Cixi was compelled to launch genuine reforms. The Beijing uprising was crushed by expeditionary forces of the foreign powers, and under the Boxer Protocol of 1901, the court had to consent to payment of an indemnity, stationing of foreign troops, and razing of some Chinese fortifications. Some proposed innovations, such as the introduction of a navy and legal system, remained on paper, but other important changes were made. The Qing court dropped the ancient examination system in 1905, and established a new system of public instruction, including elementary schools patterned on the Japanese model and an Imperial University in Beijing. It also sent Chinese students abroad. By 1911, there were 800 students in the United States and 400 in Europe. Most students—10,000 to 15,000 each year—went to Japan, especially after Japan defeated Russia in the Russo-Japanese War of 1905. The court also reorganized the central government and let provinces elect their own legislatures.

The Manchu reforms came too late to save the dynasty. A movement to set up a republic had been growing since Japan defeated China in 1895. In 1905, several revolutionary organizations merged to form the United League. Its leader was Sun Zhongshan (Sun Yat-sen), an anti-Manchu activist who became increasingly popular among overseas Chinese, especially those in Japan. Sun—hailed by both Beijing and Taibei as the father of modern China—launched his crusade for a republican government. He espoused a program based on nationalism, democracy, and socialism. He was fundraising in Denver when the 267-year old Manchu empire collapsed in 1911. Sun was inaugurated as the first Provisional President of the Republic of China, the first republic in Asia, on January 1, 1912. But soon he relinquished his post to Yuan Shikai, the general who led the final assault on the Manchus. Yuan had little use for Sun's ideals. He revised the constitution and became dictatorial.

In 1922, the Guomindang-warlord alliance ruptured, and Sun fled to Shanghai. The West ignored his requests for aid. In 1923, Sun turned to the young Bolshevik government. The Soviets pledged help in reorganizing and consolidating the Guomindang along the lines of the Russian Communist Party. Sun's dream of a unified republican China remained unfulfilled upon his death in 1925. Jiang Zhongzheng (Chiang Kai-shek), his successor, attacked the warlords in 1926. This drive ended with Beijing's fall in 1928 and international recognition of the Guomindang. With the nation unified and the seat of government established at Nanjing, the work of reconstruction based on Sun's teaching began in earnest. However, the Nationalist Chinese victory over the provincial warlords was never complete. Corruption and the bitter struggle with the emerging Communist Party eroded its reformist possibilities.

Another misfortune befell the republic in the form of Japanese aggression. Hungry for raw materials and pressed by a rising population, Japan initiated the seizure of Manchuria in 1931, and set up a puppet regime in 1932.

By the winter of 1927–28, the People's Liberation Army had 10,000 men. Mao Zedong's prestige rose, and, in 1931, he proclaimed the establishment of the Chinese Soviet Republic under his chairmanship in Jiangxi province. Nanjing continued to fight the revolutionaries, and, in the fifth "bandit-suppression" campaign of 1933–34, achieved encirclement of the Communists' base region in Jiangxi. In October, 1934, the Communists broke out and started their epic Long March to northwest China. A year later the forces, much reduced by rigors of the 6,000-mile long trek, reached sanctuary in the mountains of Shaanxi province. From their new base, they fought the Japanese, recruited a guerrilla army, and began land reform. Maoism, a Chinese form of Marxism-Leninism, built upon a peasant rather than a proletarian base, was tested successfully and became the Communist orthodoxy in China. Although supported by the West and far superior to the CCP in numbers, the Guomindang lacked an inspiring ideology or genuine package of reforms. Defensively entrenched in cities, it suffered from wartime inflation and corruption. After Japan's surrender in 1945, 900,000 Communist troops under Mao and Zhu De ruled a population of ninety million.

In 1946, the United States sent General George C. Marshall to China to reconcile the Nationalists and Communists. Marshall arranged a truce, signed on January 10, 1946. On January 31, a people's congress, in which

Guomindang and Communist delegations had leading roles, reached agreement for establishing a new political order. After the truce expired in June, the conflict resumed. Marshall's efforts continued until 1947, when he announced abandonment of his mediation. The U.S. State Department ordered the withdrawal of all U.S. forces from China. The civil war became more widespread. Battles raged not only for gaining territories but also for winning allegiance of populations. Within three years, the Communists forced the Guomindang to set up a truncated regime on Taiwan. In January 1949, the Communists took Beijing without a fight. Between April and November, major cities passed from Nationalist to Communist control with only token resistance. In December 1949, Jiang proclaimed Taibei, Taiwan, the temporary capital of China. In retreating, Jiang's three million troops took millions in gold. Many of China's managers, engineers, and educators fled to Taiwan.

Rehabilitation (1949–1952)

"The Chinese people has stood up."

With these words, Mao Zedong proclaimed the formation of the People's Republic of China on October 1, 1949. Shunning the traditions of China's imperial past, Communists restructured their country along Stalinist lines. Mao served as both head of state and chairman of the Communist Party. Premier Zhou Enlai directed government departments and ministries. The first years were ones of thorough reorganization. Military and economic aid from Russia helped support the new state. China faced the bleak tasks of assessment, consolidation, and reconstruction. The Communists inherited a war-torn economy and a war-weary people whose support they had yet to win. Communication lines had been wrecked, industry disrupted. Five hundred million people were poorly fed, clothed, and housed. Per capita annual income was less than $50. China's productive capacity suffered severe damage during the civil war. Moreover, after World War II, Russians had removed over 50 percent of the industrial capital in Manchuria. Even in the 1930s, industrial output accounted for only 10 percent of China's GNP, but in 1949, the absolute level of output in industry fell to only half of its prewar peak. Agriculture wasn't much better. In 1949, grain and cotton outputs were, respectively, 25 and 50 percent lower than postwar peak levels.

During this time, Communists executed political prisoners and landowners in the name of agrarian reform. Land redistribution was a bloody process. Estimates of landlords killed range from 50,000 to several million. According to documents circulated by Red Guards during the Cultural Revolution, Mao told the Politburo in April, 1956 that "two to three million counter-revolutionaries had been executed, imprisoned, or placed under control (supervised labor)." The Communists also organized production and took over enterprises that the capitalists or the Nationalist government had owned. The state budget was balanced and revenues were used for investment in the public sector. State trading companies were created to manage internal and external trade in key commodities. By 1952, the government restored price stability, increased industrial output 2.5 times and agricultural output by 50 percent, brought balance of payments under control, and more than doubled imports, with producer goods accounting for more than 90 percent of the total imports. The Communists gave women equality with men and attacked corruption and bureaucratism. They also improved sanitation and literacy. China's involvement in the Korean War in 1950–53 stimulated patriotism and strengthened the central government.

The First Five-Year Plan (1953–1957)

Spurred by ideological affinity and economic necessity provoked by the Western embargo, China signed a thirty-year pact with Russia. From 1950–55, China got $2 billion from the Soviet Union. Half of this sum was to pay for Soviet military equipment used in the Korean War or to reimburse Moscow for Soviet properties in Manchuria and the northwest that had been turned over to the Chinese. Based largely on the Soviet model, China's plan stressed armaments and heavy industry. Russia and its Eastern-bloc satellites imported 400 plants and raw materials necessary for operating. Fifteen thousand Chinese took advanced training in Russia, and 12,500 Soviet and Eastern European technicians served in China. Industrial complexes sprang up. Dams rose. Fifty million newly irrigated acres were added to China's farmland. Chinese trucks, trains, and planes found their way to foreign markets. Key sectors, such as banking and large-scale commerce, were socialized, and in 1955–56, at the same time collectivization was carried out in rural areas, most remaining industrial enterprises were brought under state control. The state determined the value of assets of each capitalist and then paid him five percent of that value each year as compensation for lost assets. Virtually the entire system of planning and control duplicated the Soviet Union's system. Trade with Communist states rose from $350 million at the decade's start to $3 billion by 1959—70 percent of China's total trade of $4.4 billion. Yet, despite high levels of industrial construction, most plants weren't finished. Growth stemmed basically from efforts to increase existing plant use. The bottom line: rapid capital growth offset by sluggish agricultural production.

The harmony of those years began to sour. Chinese leaders, gathering self-assurance, started to doubt the wisdom of depending on Russia.

The Soviet Union gave China $60 million a year, but not the kind of investment Mao needed for the utopia he envisioned. In 1954, Russia withheld grants to accelerate China's development. This forced China to collectivize, bringing dislocation in 1956, and retrenchment in 1957. In 1953, Soviet Premier Joseph Stalin died. After purges and intrigues behind Kremlin walls, Nikita Khruschev garnered enough power to denounce his former boss at the 20th Party Congress in 1956. This gave Mao the pretext to erase the last vestiges of foreign control by renegotiating the Sino-Soviet pact. To defuse dissent at home after the 1956 Hungarian uprising, Mao urged, "Let a hundred flowers blossom, let a hundred schools of thought contend." Dissent swept China. In response, Mao sent thousands to "thought reform" camps. In 1957, he went to Moscow to plead for nuclear bombs to pressure Taiwan. Failing this, Mao decided to strike out on his own. In 1958, the Great Helmsman launched the Great Leap Forward.

The Great Leap Forward (1958–1960)

The second plan continued the priorities of the first with greater stress on agriculture. Steel output was to rise from 11 to 18 million tons, coal from 270 to 380 million tons, and grain from 373 to 525 million tons. To give China an industrial base bigger than Britain, planners studied ways to convert labor surpluses into realized output. The Second Five-Year Plan never got off the ground. Its publication coincided with a surge of fervor known as the Great Leap Forward. The proponents of this movement sought to compress China's industrialization into a year or two, and thereby speed up the transition from socialism to communism. Although party leaders were generally satisfied with accomplishments of the First Five-Year Plan, Mao and his fellow radicals believed more could be achieved in the second plan if people could be aroused ideologically, and if domestic resources could be used more efficiently. The Great Leap was based on Mao's belief that willpower could overcome all obstacles. The government tried to speed development by increasing the number of workers and their hours while ignoring China's lack of capital and technology. Students formed themselves into corps and worked sixteen hours a day. Peasants left their fields to smelt low-grade pig iron in backyard furnaces. The government combined 740,000 agricultural cooperatives into 26,425 communes. The communes took control of production and operated as the sole accounting unit. Mao marshalled 100 million peasants into armies to dig canals, mine coal, work the soil. They ignored cost controls and technical constraints as restricting employment. By stressing industry, Beijing nearly wrecked China's agriculture—without accomplishing its industrial goals. The Great Leap Forward was a leap into disaster.

Although the Great Leap succeeded in involving the masses and arousing self-reliance, it brought imbalances in production and bottlenecks in communications. A spate of unreliable statistics sparked the collapse of the State Statistical Bureau. In 1959–61, China experienced economic depression, food shortages, and a decline in industrial output. The acceleration of an already over-heated economy caused damage on all fronts: industrial output, which had been pumped up nearly double by 1960, fell to 1957 levels; Soviet technicians, who had helped set up and operate factories supplied by the USSR, were withdrawn by Khrushchev in mid-1960 because of disenchantment with Beijing's policies; and agricultural output was down 20 percent because of bad weather, establishment of unwieldy supercollectives averaging 25,000 persons, and issuance of impractical instructions on farming techniques. By 1959, the country was in hunger and depression. In the 1960s, Taiwanese intelligence acquired documents describing people in parts of China agonized with malnutrition, searching desperately for roots, insects, food of any kind.

Recovery (1961–1965)

As the dimensions of the debacle became clear, Chairman Mao was sidelined—treated as a "deceased old uncle," as he was to say. The party, under the dominant influence of Liu Shaoqi, Deng Xiaoping, Chen Yun, and the like, executed corrective measures. They reorganized the commune system to give more administrative leeway to brigades and teams. The Communists arranged for emergency rations, reinstated the village as the primary decision-making unit for farming, restored the private plot, allocated a large share of industrial capacity to support agriculture, limited industrial investment to a few key industries, and turned to Japan and Western Europe for equipment and technology.

Ties between the Soviet regime and China grew weaker. Ideological disputes reflected Beijing's challenge to Moscow's leadership of world communism. For forty years, the Soviet Union was the undisputed leader of the Socialist camp. Perhaps the first challenge came after Stalin's death when, in China's view, Mao automatically became the foremost living Communist thinker—a notion the Soviets rejected. Soviet leaders still subscribe to the theory that international communism must have one center—Moscow. They will not accept a "divided Rome." The split probably had less to do with dogma than emotions—the struggle for prestige, chauvinism and fear, jealousy, greed, revenge. Subsequent Chinese territorial claims masked the basic contest for Communist primacy. Struggling to reconstruct China according to the geometry of personal principle, Mao raged against Soviet "revisionism." Among China's major criticisms of the

Soviet Union were: the betrayal of Lenin's teaching that the way to global revolution must involve violence and war, its failure to support the revolutionary movement in general and the Chinese cause in particular, and giving comfort to such "bourgeois nationalists" as Nehru and Nasser, and to the "revisionist" movement under Tito. Pro-Moscow and pro-Beijing factions split the movement. However, only Albania sided fully with China. China had criticized the Soviets as early as 1956 for their policy of "peaceful coexistence" with the West. Open Soviet attacks in 1958–59 on Mao's communes and his Great Leap widened the schism. The Sino-Soviet ideological conflict was brought out into the open on the 90th anniversary of the birth of Lenin in April, 1960. Beijing signed an 81-party Moscow Declaration of Unity, but a definitive split came later that year when the Kremlin restricted scientific information and withdrew 1,600 architects and engineers from industrial projects, leaving them unfinished.

With the Sino-Soviet break, China not only ceased to get loans or technical support from the Soviet Union, it began to pay back previous credits. Throughout the early 1960s, China exported more to the Soviet Union than it imported. By the end of 1965, the Soviet loan had been repaid. Trade with the West rose as grain imports became necessary to prevent famine. As the need for austerity decreased, China looked to Japan, West Germany, France, Italy, and Britain to supply technology. From 1963–66, China signed $200 million in contracts. The explosion of China's first nuclear device at Lop Nur on the edge of the Taklimakan Shamo in 1964 was proof of China's reasserted nationalism and commitment to military development. Lin Biao, China's defense minister, gave expression to China's militancy. In his essay "Long Live the Victory of the People's War," Lin portrayed the world countryside of underdeveloped nations surrounding and overcoming, in revolutionary struggle, the world town of industrialized North America and Western Europe.

The Cultural Revolution (1966–1969)

Beginning in 1962, Mao staged a comeback, using newspapers controlled by ideologues as his platform and teenage Red Guards as his instrument to shatter the state apparatus. Despite the return of stability by 1965, China's ruling circles debated issues that energized the Great Leap. They formed into a "red" versus "expert" dichotomy. Mao's group argued social change and mandated revolutionary measures. Broad upheaval had to jar the masses from passive, family-oriented traditions. Foreign trade was peripheral to China's life, because imports undermined the people's faith in the success of the revolution and made China vulnerable to economic "blackmail." The radicals believed reliance on foreigners rekindled the sense of inferiority caused by a century of humiliation at the hands of the West. Exposure to capitalists eroded the "revolutionary will" of the masses, creating "revisionism." Mao sought above all to restore China to greatness, and he believed this could be done only if revolutionary commitment replaced traditional practices. However, Head of State Liu Shaoqi and his followers perceived problems as basically technical ones, requiring stable, rational management. They viewed China as a weak, undeveloped country, which had to be transformed as rapidly as possible into a modern state. Modernization required imports of advanced goods. The moderates stressed the importance of economic development. They believed the radicals' policies were unrealistic and hampered China's modernization. Reliance on innovation by a small pool of experts would confine China to the ranks of second-class nations.

In November of 1965, Mao unchained his wrath to keep revolutionary ardor ablaze. Red Guards rampaged. They killed writers, historians, and scientists. The Great Proletarian Cultural Revolution was a tale of peasant crusades, pitched battles, kangaroo courts, death in high places, blood in the streets. Radicals seized control of provincial and city governments. Violence exploded as competing gangs struggled for power. Four hundred thousand people perished. Bureaucrats and managers from all levels of government and industry were sent to farms to learn egalitarianism. By mid-1968, disorder was so great that the army stepped in. As the nation turned inward, factories and schools stopped—sometimes for years. Strife badly hit industrial production. Trade slumped. The Cultural Revolution's legacy was a ramshackle economy, a politicized military, and an educational system that promoted Mao's passion for ideological purity. Although in 1967 the radical tide had started to recede, it wasn't until 1968 that Mao came to realize the uselessness of further chaos. Viewed in a larger perspective, events unfolding outside China's borders mandated the need for calm. Russia's invasion of Czechoslovakia and troop buildups along the Sino-Soviet border heightened China's perception of external threat. Hundreds of border clashes climaxed in 1969 with skirmishes in eastern Siberia. Meanwhile, Liu Shaoqi and other "revisionists" were purged. In 1969, Liu Shaoqi died in detention, but the revolution was scarcely a success. Conflict between radicals and moderates continued.

Readjustment (From 1970)

A strengthened moderate wing advocated measures to revitalize China's economy. By 1970, trade had recovered from the recession of the early 1960s. Western trade accounted for 75 percent of the total. China's policy of balanced development, with greater attention to agricultural improvement, was reflected by growing imports of fertilizers to spur farm output. Development of domestic oil resources, particularly the Taikang and Tianjian fields, virtually eliminated petroleum imports. The Arab oil embargo created a market for China's petroleum. Exports continued to be food products (rice, vegetables, processed foods), textiles, and manufactured goods. The rapid growth in trade with non-Communist countries in 1970–73 spread to both the developed countries and the Third World. Purchases of steel, machinery, and equipment from Japan and Western Europe and grain from Canada and Australia fueled imports from developed nations. The United States moved from no trade to China's third leading partner because of large agricultural purchases starting in 1972. Beijing was forced to turn to Washington when traditional suppliers were unable to meet its needs for grain, cotton, and other commodities.

In 1971, the United Nations admitted the People's Republic of China into the General Assembly and Security Council. In 1972, U.S. President Richard M. Nixon went to China to meet Mao. The two nations opened diplomatic offices in each other's country in 1973. These developments suggested that the world community no longer saw China as an outcast, and that China no longer saw itself as self-sufficient. Pragmatism was gaining momentum. This attitude was paralleled by efforts of radicals to regain their former strength. Evidently, the radical group, led by Jiang Qing, Mao's wife, no longer had Mao's unqualified support. As Mao saw it, China needed both pragmatism and revolutionary enthusiasm, each acting as a check on the other.

With banners, cymbals, fireworks, and dancing, China marked the 25th anniversary of the People's Republic in October, 1974. It was a significant date, for a revolution that survived a quarter of a century has proved its vitality. Industry continued to make progress, and foreign trade kept expanding. Typical was the 1974 purchase of two strip mines, at the cost of $382 million, from Japan and Western Germany. In 1975, the Fourth National People's Congress met under the moderate leadership of Premier Zhou. It adopted a new constitution and made provision for orderly political succession upon the passing of the Long March generation. The plan to industrialize required a radical change in priorities. Beijing began to re-examine its purchases abroad. For the first time since 1949, China went into debt. The foreign trade deficit for 1974 was $1.3 billion. In January 1975, it canceled two-thirds of its contracts for U.S. wheat. Beijing also deferred delivery of Japanese steel and fertilizer. However, it sent missions abroad to shop for items on its new list—from oil rigs to computers. China also opened diplomatic relations with the European Economic Community in September, in the hope of increasing trade. By 1975, China's GNP was 2.7 times that of 1957, the final year of the First Five-Year Plan. This works out to an annualized growth rate of 3 percent. Most growth came in industry, where output expanded at an average rate of 9 percent. Agriculture grew at the same rate as the population, 2 percent.

The more moderate Zhou tried to rectify the Cultural Revolution's damage. Prominent among those surrounding Zhou was Deng Xiaoping. The 10th CCP Congress in 1975 restored the former Secretary General of the Communist Party, who had been purged during the Cultural Revolution. In the same year, the Fourth National People's Congress named him the highest ranking of 12 vice premiers. Thus Deng was Zhou's apparent successor. Although prominent Chinese who had suffered with Deng were regaining authority, some who had profited remained. They viewed the drift toward "right deviationism" a anathema. Jiang Qing and her cohorts tried to wrest control of the party during Mao's last years. This faction gained leverage with access to Mao and the propaganda apparatus. Tension between moderates and leftists reduced Beijing's ability to deal with the issues. Policy swings caused confusion. Within the iron and steel industry, production imbalances caused shortages. The Gang of Four, however, couldn't conspire against Zhou, who alone among China's leaders approached Mao's prominence. Nor could moderates end the fundamentalist threat while Mao lived.

This stalemate ended when Zhou died in 1976. Hua Guofeng, minister of public security, was named acting premier. At the same time, posters attacking "right deviationists" appeared, alluding to Deng. Three months after Zhou's death, following rioting over the removal of wreaths in Zhou's memory from Beijing's Tian An Men (Gate of Heavenly Peace) Square, Mao stripped Deng of all posts and promoted Hua to premier. Mao died soon after. Less than a month later, moderates arrested the Gang of Four. They were charged with subverting China's culture and economy by trying to stage a coup d'etat. Hua became Party Chairman, and the Central Committee restored Deng to his former position as Vice Premier, Party Vice Chairman, and Army Chief of Staff.

Following the purge of the gangsters, China announced readiness to expand world economic ties. The Fifth Five-Year Plan (1976–80) was intended to be the launching pad for general modernization. But the first two years were disappointing. Industrial production stagnated in 1976 because of political turmoil, bad weather, and the Tangshan earthquake. Beijing had hoped recovery in 1977 would provide the basis for accelerated growth during the remainder of the plan, but shortages of raw materials and electric power left plants with unrealized potential. Worker unrest, commercial dislocation, and violations of financial regulations made these problems worse. The 1977 grain harvest remained unchanged from the 1975 level of 285 million tons. But foreign trade increased by better than twelve percent to $15 billion. Trade with non-Communist nations accounted for 83 percent of the rise in exports and nearly all the gain in imports for that year. By mid-1978, both imports and exports from non-

Communist nations increased to six times their post-Cultural Revolution level.

The year 1978 was a watershed. Changes affected every field, from education to military strategy, from agriculture to opera. In November, China signed a $500 million contract to have Intercontinental Hotels, a U.S. chain, build seven hotels in Chinese cities. All 168 of Hans Christian Anderson's tales were translated into Chinese, as were some of Mark Twain's works. Radio Beijing began broadcasting Western music. Perhaps the most significant development was the agreement between China and the United States to establish full diplomatic relations in 1979. In the last quarter of 1978, the trade balance dipped into the red. The Chinese had obligated themselves to about $600 million in down payments for plants ordered in the second half of 1978. Exports were off by 7 percent in the first quarter of 1979. Imports declined. Reacting to China's rethinking of policy, the Ministry of Finance imposed "three years of readjustment." It ordered a freeze on major contract signings, and suspended $2.5 billion in foreign credits. Three billion was in commercial loans from Western banks, $10 billion from Japan. China thus increased short-term borrowing to cover imports until it was in a position to use more economic long-term supplier credits. China reinstated all but one of the suspended contracts by the end of 1979. In 1980, China trimmed anew its extravagant modernization plans. The flawed Ten-Year Plan that was to end in 1985 was replaced by new five-year plans to take the country through the 1980s. Urban unemployment, declining spending power brought by inflation, and deficits in the state budget confirmed in 1981 that readjustment measures instituted earlier were not sufficiently stringent. The Sixth Five-Year Plan was delayed for two years while the leadership sorted priorities and set strategies to move away from the leaps, surges, and nose dives that characterized economic development under Mao. In November 1982, Premier Zhao Ziyang outlined this plan to the National People's Congress. It relied heavily on foreign trade to spur development and greatly extended the trend away from heavy industry to consumer goods and economic foundation-building. The plan was characterized by the caution and patience that have been the hallmark of Chen Yun, who was rehabilitated from disgrace in the late 1970s to take charge of China's economic planning. Its caution was reflected in the goal of an annual production growth rate of about 4 percent, substantially less than the more than 5 percent achieved in 1981–82. The plan called for an annual growth rate of 4.1 percent in consumer buying, marginally higher than the target set for industrial and agricultural production. It also expanded China's toe-in-the-water experiment with deficit financing, envisioning an annual deficit of $1.5 billion, compared with the $1.25 billion incurred in 1981.

Economic readjustment will continue into the 1990s, but it won't reduce China's need for equipment and technology. However, purchases will be selective. Top priority will be given to projects that require less foreign exchange, offer a quick return on investment, and generate potentially great export earnings. The texture of international politics will compel China to develop trading ties with nations of the Third World and Russia, its ancient enemy. Nevertheless, China will continue to look to the Western Alliance for basic imports—grain, steel products, and chemical fertilizers.

This historical overview has painted in broad brushstrokes major trends and issues that have dominated East-West relations. We have focused on China's inherited needs and problems, the evolution of Mao's revolutionary vision and alternative visions, and the role of the United States, Western Europe, Japan, and Russia in all of this. These themes continue to have relevance in contemporary China.

2

THE FOUR MODERN- IZATIONS

The year was 1928. Jiang Zhongzheng (Chiang Kai-shek) had brought China's major provinces under the Guomindang. He declared Communism a crime, and waged a pacification campaign that lasted twenty years. Beaten in the south, Mao's men retreated. Taking more than a year to complete, the 6,000 mile Long March across eighteen mountain ranges and twenty-four rivers was a series of running battles and a triumph of will. Among the survivors were several who would play key roles in China's future—Zhou Enlai, Deng Xiaoping, and Mao. From their Yan'an base, the Communists staged fifteen battles, lost 90,000 troops, and won China.

The year was 1978. In an astonishing spectacle of national ambition, China launched its New Long March. The goal of propelling China into the front ranks of industrialized nations by the year 2000 through the Four Modernizations is articulated in the constitutions of the Chinese Communist Party and the People's Republic of China. They spell out in detail purposes of key institutions and programs, which reflect the pragmatism of the post-Mao leadership. China's leaders hope the spirit that drove those marchers five decades before will prod modern Chinese to make the sacrifices and mobilize the resources to upgrade agriculture, industry, science and technology, and defense. Here is a review of China's program in terms of these four areas.

15

Agriculture

"Have you eaten?" That's the traditional greeting of people in a land shad-
owed by hunger. Prosperity brought population growth, but floods,
drought, and war brought famine. During the years 1929–32, ten million
died from starvation. We cannot exaggerate agriculture's importance.
China's economy is basically agricultural, its agriculture basically primitive. Four-fifths of its people live in rural communes. Agriculture accounts
for half of China's GNP and provides 70 percent of raw materials used in
light industry. Light industry, in turn, generates 40 percent of China's
exports. Since China must feed an ever growing urban population, heavy
industry also depends on agriculture. It affects growth of other sectors
through impact on foreign exchange. China is the world's largest producer
of rice, sweet potatoes, sorghum, millet, barley, peanuts, and tea. Cotton,
other fibers, and various oilseeds are major industrial crops. It exports rice,
fruits and vegetables, raw silk, tea and spices, seafood, and livestock products. Most goods are shipped to nearby nations. One-third goes to Hong
Kong. China imports wheat, corn, cotton, and soybeans. It may seem surprising that China, the world's largest grain producer, is also a grain importer. The reason: the internal transportation system is so overloaded, it's
economical to import wheat through the northern ports for consumption
in the north rather than ship surplus rice from the south to the north. Only
13 percent of China's land area can be cultivated, as compared with 22
percent in the United States. The area of land available for agriculture in
China is about two-thirds that of the United States, but it must support
a population four times as large. Farmers therefore have little cropland
to support themselves and the rest of the population. However, they manage to provide almost enough food for the people partly because of the
long growing season in southern China and double-cropping techniques.
While agricultural production has generally managed to increase year after
year, consumption pursues it relentlessly. Thus, in China's drive toward
modernity, agriculture has top billing. Beijing has increased agricultural
investment to guard against poor harvests that could stall this drive. In
the long run, yields may eventually approach levels of the most advanced
countries. In terms of rice yields, China is now in about the same position
that South Korea and Taiwan reached in the mid-1960s, and that which
Japan reached earlier in this century. A reorganized banking system, fea-
turing the Agricultural Bank of China, directs funds to state farms, brigades, and teams.

Grain

Despite enormous grain production, China holds famine at bay with
rationing. In an anxious race between demography and development,

China's most fundamental problem is to get a surplus of food over consumption. Consumption demands of the increasing population undermine even the best strategies for development. Difficulties in funding employment for large labor increases, while mechanizing labor will continue without relief from demographic changes. Pressures of meeting the food and clothing needs of one-quarter of mankind have made grain imports imperative. China cannot rely on grain imports to feed the future's increased population. The requirements of more than fifteen million additional people each year are too large. China increased grain output from 111 million tons in 1949 to 285 million tons in 1977. However, this increase barely kept pace with consumption. China has some way to go before it can induce peasants to accept small families and rigorous birth control. Peasants want large families because intensive cultivation needs many hands and because children are security for old age. That 65 percent of China's population was born since the Communists came to power highlights Beijing's failure to lower the nation's birth rate. This despite contraception campaigns, marriage restrictions, and pressure to limit families to two children. Even lower birth rates won't be sufficient to meet demands for higher living standards. China must therefore continue to ration and import grain. Should agriculture fail to outpace the population's consumption, China will have to allocate resources from industry to the rural sector. The exodus of refugees from China, its clashes with India and Viet Nam, and resistance of South East Asian states to Chinese "boat people" are part of a population crisis that will grow more troublesome. The decisions that must be made will be difficult and divisive.

China's grain harvest reached 295 million tons in 1978, 10 million more than the stagnant 1975–77 levels. Grain imports rose to 9.4 million tons in 1978. China reduced grain imports in 1975–76 as foreign exchange became tight. As balance of payments improved in 1977–78, grain imports rose. Beijing's willingness to incur debt will facilitate a more stable level of grain imports. China's ability to pay for foreign grain may be in question as commitments to spend in other areas accelerate. Since 1961, China has used short-term credits to ease payments. Australia and Canada have financed grain imports on 12 to 18 month terms at commercial rates. U.S. grain purchase terms are usually cash. In 1978, Congress authorized credits from the Commodity Credit Corporation for Chinese grain imports.

Irrigation

The heart of China's water problem is an unfortunate contradiction of climate and geography. Northern China has the best soil, but Southern China, with a warm climate and long growing season, has the heaviest rainfall and two-thirds of the surface water flow. Extending water resources to poorly-irrigated areas is a linchpin of policy. While chemical fertilizers, flood control, pest eradication, and multiple cropping have indeed increased agricultural output, irrigation is probably the most important factor of all. In 1949, China had only 53 million acres of irrigated land. Starting in 1956, the Chinese irrigated 100 million acres within eighteen months. One-half of China's cultivated land is irrigated, compared to 10 percent in the United States, the Soviet Union, and most European countries. Beijing authorities are stimulating crop growing by diverting the 3,200 mile-long Chang Jiang along the 1,400 year-old Grand Canal (figure 2-1). At the time the People's Republic was founded, rain was scarce and unpredictable and droughts and floods were common in the wheat region where irrigation and drainage was most needed. However, expansion of irrigation in the north required heavy investment to control rivers and dig wells. Until resources to do this became available in the 1960s, reliable irrigation in the north remained limited. Dikes and embankments needed to be repaired, restored, or built, and drainage in low-lying areas adjacent to rivers needed to be improved. Seventy percent

Figure 2-1
INLAND WATERWAYS

Source: *China: A Country Study*, Foreign Area Studies, The American University, Washington, D. C., 1981, 283.

of capital construction funds in water conservancy during the First Five-Year Plan was spent on these tasks, and only 20 percent on irrigation. By 1958, China felt these problems were basically under control, and attention turned to irrigation. The Chinese planted 69 million trees to stop flooding and soil erosion. Larger supplies of drainage and irrigation equipment will improve China's capacity to deal with drought. Beijing plans to invest heavily in land reclamation and forestry management, mainly in border regions where state farms predominate. Increases in agricultural output will depend on the slow process of putting more land under water.

Fertilizer

During the Cultural Revolution, if a farmer was asked what was the most important factor in increasing rice production, he would respond: "Mastering the thought of Chairman Mao." Now, he is more likely to say: "Chemical fertilizer." And the need for fertilizer is more clear than the need—if ever there was one—for slogans. China has ample supplies of materials for producing chemical fertilizer. However, it cannot make the quantities of ammonium sulphate and calcium superphosphate equivalents needed, and fertilization by excreta is still an important part of farming. China's agriculture has long depended on vast supplies of organic fertilizer for maintenance of yields. Since 1949, the application of both organic and chemical fertilizer has greatly increased. While the rapid expansion of production and imports of chemical fertilizer has attracted more attention, the bulk of fertilizer nutrients continues to come from organic sources. Hogs and other animals provide the major source of organic materials for fertilizer. Crops and their byproducts in turn provide fodder for livestock. Because of this interdependence, it's not surprising the Chinese have stressed livestock production, or that they have coined such slogans as "every pig is a small fertilizer factory."

The Chinese have long realized the potential for use of chemical fertilizer. After the First Five-Year Plan, chemical fertilizer production increased rapidly. They used large amounts of foreign exchange to import fertilizer and fertilizer plants. In the mid-1960s, 40 percent of China's chemical fertilizer came from local plants. During the 1970s, China introduced large-scale operations by purchasing 13 ammonia-urea complexes from Japan and the United States. By 1976, China was producing between 3 and 4 million metric tons of contained nitrogen. China is still dependent upon imports of nitrogenous fertilizer, mainly from Japan. In 1978, fertilizer imports jumped from 7.5 million tons in 1977 to 10 million tons. In 1979–82, China concluded large deals with suppliers from Canada, Mexico, the United States, Japan, and Italy. Despite sharp increases in capacity from imported plants, fertilizer imports will stay at high levels through the 1980s. China will import more potassium and phosphate fertilizers, but nitrogen fertilizer imports will level off. Imports of other agricultural chemicals and insecticides will grow.

Mechanization

The water buffalo—not the tractor—is the symbol of China's agriculture. Farming occupies the energies of 8 of every 10 people, and it's still essentially unmechanized. Most farmers use buffaloes, horses, donkeys, and mules instead of tractors. China's archaic distribution system and absence of amenities in farming hinders any substantial improvement of diet. Machinery typically replaces or enhances labor. Because China is a labor-abundant country, it benefits more from the second kind of mechanization. Mechanization will ease the peasant's labor. However, the main goal of mechanization is to free him to do other tasks, such as plant and harvest more rapidly in multiple-cropping areas.

Farms need equipment that can harvest one crop and plant another as fast as possible. The Chinese lead the world in multiple-cropping techniques. They often harvest two and sometimes three crops during the year. The Chinese start crops (usually rice) in seedbeds and then transfer them as soon as the land is ready, following the winter or an earlier harvest. They use tractors mainly for transport. Rice-transplanters are far from automated. The Chinese have successfully used American-style machinery in the northeast. Elsewhere, fields are small and terraced, so this machinery isn't of much use. Machinery investment will absorb a large share of agricultural investment, but there will be a shift in stress from buying simple machinery and tractors to more sophisticated gear. The process of distributing machinery suffered a setback in 1979 when the Chinese decided to concentrate purchases to "production bases," designated areas where work is less labor-intensive, such as forestry, fishing, and animal husbandry. Beijing's agricultural plan will suffer problems relating to machinery demand. These include poor equipment quality, lack of standardization, and scarcity of trained manpower to service and operate the machinery. Without improvement in these areas, farms will be reluctant to make major purchases.

Industry

An expanding but inadequate manufacturing sector supplies China's needs for capital and consumer goods. Backward factories provide most of China's industrial output, and the technological level and standards of industry as a whole are low. Nevertheless, China is one of the world's largest producers of a number of industrial and mineral products—including cotton cloth and antimony—and is among the most important sources of yarn, coal, and other products. China's major industries are iron and steel, coal mining, light industrial production, armaments, and textiles. China lacks complex equipment-producing plants. It needs iron and steel mills, coal mining equipment, offshore oil exploration equipment, petrochemical and synthetic fiber complexes, nonferrous metals plants, and transportation and telecommunication systems. The transportation sector has a great need for trucks and equipment used in building and repairing roads. China's development of the transportation system will also lead to producing diesel engines, oil tank cars, and ammonia carriers. China's post-Mao leadership has unleashed a massive drive to upgrade industry with Western help. Its bureaucracy is setting priorities, evaluating technologies, selecting vendors, and signing contracts.

Light industry

To lay the groundwork for achieving the Four Modernizations, China unveiled a 10-year draft economic program in February, 1978. The leadership soon recognized that the plan exceeded China's resources and capabilities. In 1978, the results of nationwide surveys of resources, projects, and manpower, as well as investigations into management practices, gave planners an appreciation of China's weaknesses. An upsurge of investment activity aggravated many existing problems, such as structural imbalances, inefficient management, and overcommitment of resources. In 1979–81, the leadership imposed a three-year period of readjustment. As part of this shift in resource allocation, agriculture and light industry gained at the expense of heavy industry. China will continue to stress light industry through joint ventures or compensation schemes to save currency. Light industry is cheap, provides consumer goods for the home market, and exports to earn foreign currency. Light industry includes textiles, footwear, ceramics, handicrafts, canned foods, consumer electronics, bicycles, sewing machines, and the like. Some of these industries were established well before 1949. While light industry needs modern technology, it poses fewer problems of management than heavy industry. Consequently, light industry is getting first dibs on materials, power, and fuel. China raised the proportion of capital investment going to light industry from 5.4 percent in 1978 to 5.8 percent in 1979. This small increase reflects constraints in expanding light industry. Since 1957, consumer goods production has grown at an annual rate of 8 percent. The process of readjustment led to a slower pace of overall industrial growth. Industrial production, which grew by 14.3 percent in 1977 and 13.5 percent in 1978, advanced at the rate of only 8.5 percent in 1979. Readjustment also caused the growth of light industry to outpace heavy industry, a significant departure from past trends. China cannot expand light industry without a steady supply of components from heavy industry—steel, machinery, electric power. Thus, China will continue to require steady investment in heavy industry. Desire for more efficient engine and tractor designs, machine tools, forges, foundries, and press lines will produce sizeable foreign contracts. For the most part, however, China will limit outside help.

Electricity

China's power shortage is serious. Rapid increases in the needs of enterprises and households, construction of towns in remote areas, and shortages of coal contribute to China's chronic shortages of electricity. In 1979, *Cheng Ming*, the well-informed Hong Kong journal, claimed Chinese industry as a whole had a 20 percent shortfall in its power requirements. Much of China's power equipment is 20 years behind the West in technology. From 1971–75, China expanded generating capacity at an annual rate of 11 percent. In the short-run, it could maintain this rate by conservation. But, in the long-run, China must maintain a growth rate for power of at least a few points ahead of industrial growth. It has shelved plans for nuclear plants, preferring to use more conventional, less costly sources of power. However, Chinese scientists are working on six-beam lasers to generate power from thermonuclear fusion. China's press has also discussed rapid development of hydroelectric generation. China has the world's greatest hydroelectric potential, and harnessing the energy of its rivers could produce up to 600 million kilowatts of annual electricity. China uses only 2 percent of its hydroelectric potential, for most of the best sites lie in areas far removed from leading industrial centers. Hydroelectric plants require years to build and demand great investment for transmission lines. China is short of generating and transmission equipment. Its 330-kilovolt lines have adequate range (300 miles) and capacity (450 megawatts), but China hasn't used them extensively. Most capacity is in the west and an extensive transmission grid would be needed to carry power to population centers. The hydroelectric industry also competes with farming for water. In the wheat-growing north China plain, wells have lowered the water table. Rainfall won't sufficiently replace the water, and irrigation without proper drainage has caused soil alkalinization.

Coal

Coal is China's largest source of energy and its second largest area of industrial development. China mines more than half a billion tons of coal each year. China's reserves of 1.5 trillion tons stand only behind Soviet and U.S. reserves. It has some of the world's largest coal bases. Ten produce more than 10 million tons annually, with Kailuan turning out more than 20 million metric tons, and three others—Datong, Fuxin, and

Fushun—producing in the range of 15 to 20 million tons (figure 2–2). Shanxi province accounts for 15 percent of annual production, 40 percent of reserves. Coal resources in the west and south are undeveloped. About half of China's coal is from the north and northeast.

Coal satisfies two-thirds of China's primary energy needs each year. It constitutes a diminishing proportion of China's energy consumption, dropping from 97 percent in 1952 to 68 percent in 1977. The switch to coal-fired power stations and the needs of industrial consumers, however, heighten demand. High rates of industrial output are essential to China's modernization and industry will need correspondingly high rates of coal-based energy. Between 1957–77, coal output grew at less than 3 percent yearly, which is inadequate for China's rate of growth. During the political chaos of 1976, strikes, slowdowns, and the Tangshan earthquake hit the industry. The earthquake killed 650,000 people and crippled the Kailuan mines, China's most important coal mining facility. However, the

Figure 2–2
COAL RESERVES AND MAJOR MINING AREAS

Source: *China: A Country Study*, Foreign Area Studies, The American University, Washington, D.C., 1981, 254.

country rallied with all large coal combines sending rescue teams, supplies, and equipment. Some mines resumed operation within two months. Kailuan's production for 1977 was 2 million tons lower than 1976 and only about half that of 1975. Overall production in 1978 was two-thirds higher than 1970's output, but production may have peaked. This slowdown could reflect China's gradual abandonment of 110,000 small, inefficient pits. They make only a limited contribution to demand because of their low-quality coal and poor access to transportation. Slowed growth will reduce coal congestion, where coal freight accounts for a large proportion of traffic. Coal must increasingly compete with farm goods for cargo space, severely straining the rail system.

China plans to increase surface mining and introduce modern equipment into existing operations. Focus will remain on opening mines and mechanizing fields. Although China has started few substantial fields since the Soviets left in the 1960s, it has tried to maintain growth by expanding mine shafts and opening rural mines. However, the Chinese cannot delay large-scale investment in modern complexes. Most of the increase in coal production will come from large mines. Although China has a few big open-pit mines, such as the Fushun West mine in Liaoning province, most of the large mines are underground shafts. Coal is generally mined by conventional blasting and hauling techniques. In 1980, the Ministry of Coal Industry said that only 6.3 percent of coal mining was comprehensively mechanized. Reversing past policies, China has invited foreign participation in coal development, and has sought bids from West Germany, Britain, and Japan. China has budgeted billions of dollars for coal equipment, and the shopping list includes hydraulic equipment, excavators, and large shovels. China wants cheap credits and compensatory trade to finance purchase of long-wall coal gear. It doesn't have much coal to spare beyond existing commitments and projected demand. Most coal exports are to Japan. It imports anthracite from North Korea. China will have difficulty finding export markets; most nations practice protectionist policies. Transportation costs also make coal uncompetitive outside the Pacific Basin.

Petroleum

The shortage of petroleum-based nitrogen fertilizer has put demand on upgrading facilities and exploring offshore reserves. Pursuant to this demand, China has negotiated with Pennzoil, Union Oil of California, Japan Petroleum Group, Japan-China Petroleum Development Company, Total Petroleum Company of France, Elf Aquitaine Societe National, Mobil Oil, Globe Physic Petroleum Company, Shell, Norwegian National Oil Company, British Petroleum, and other firms over exploration and drilling rights in eight concession areas in the Yellow and South China Seas.

Rich oil deposits also exist in the seabeds of the East China Sea. China's coast is one of the few promising unexplored offshore areas. China will postpone decisions on the scale of imports until it gets a better idea of what its reserves—and thus its borrowing power—will be.

In 1982, Beijing announced the formation of the China National Offshore Oil Corporation (CNOOC). CNOOC has responsibility for exploring, developing, and marketing offshore petroleum resources in China and monitoring offshore activities of foreign companies. It has established four subsidiaries: The Bohai Sea Oil Company, the South Yellow Sea Oil Company, the Eastern South China Sea Company, and the Western South China Sea Oil Company. The China National Oil and Gas Exploration and Development Corporation (CNOGEDC), which handled offshore operations prior to that time, has been reduced to an onshore company. Contracts signed with CNOGEDC have been transferred to CNOOC. In February 1982, China released regulations concerning the "Exploration of Offshore Petroleum Resources in Cooperation with Foreign Enterprises" (see appendix five). Although ambiguities exist, these regulations clarify many issues. Only practice will resolve remaining questions.

Based on scanty, sometimes unreliable evidence, the CIA's 1977 estimate is that onshore reserves amount to roughly 39 billion barrels. Difficulties and obstacles, however, will impede recovery and refinement of China's reserves. In 1975, 80 percent of China's oil came from Daqing, Shengli, and Dakang in the north and northeast (figure 2–3). Daqing accounted for 54 percent of output and 90 percent of crude oil exports. But most of this oil is waxy crude that needs catalytic cracking. Chinese scientists are skillfully applying rare earths as refining catalysts. Furthermore, oil reserves are large and widely dispersed. Deposits in remote areas such as the Tarim, Dzungarian, and Qaidam basins remain largely untapped. China is shifting much of its onshore development westward. However, the cost of piping oil from these areas to cities in the east could be prohibitive.

In 1976, China ranked tenth as an oil producer, with 1.8 million barrels per day (b/d). In 1978, it produced 2.08 million b/d, 11 percent higher than 1977. Generally, China needs all the oil it can produce. Domestic oil consumption has grown at an average rate of 15 percent since 1970—an excessive rate since it has eaten into export surpluses. In 1979, petroleum supplied over 20 percent of China's energy needs, up 7 percent from 1978. This shift toward greater use of oil will continue, despite efforts to spur coal production. Because of increasing domestic consumption and the importance of crude oil exports in foreign trade planning, China's oil industry will absorb a large share of state investment and foreign capital. China will have little surplus except for sale to Japan. Japanese refiners have been reluctant to import large volumes of Chinese crude because of the oil's low gravity and pour point. Crude exports totaled $760 million

Figure 2-3
MAJOR OIL BASINS AND OIL FIELDS

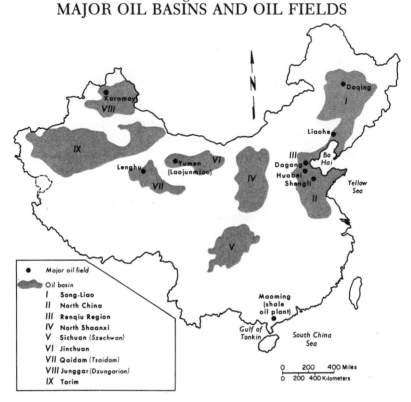

Source: *China: A Country Study*, Foreign Area Studies, The American University, Washington, D.C., 1981, 257.

in 1975, and $665 million in 1976. These shipments provided 10.6 and 9.2 percent of China's export earnings. In 1977, China earned $1 billion from oil, 13 percent of export earnings. China's net oil exports for 1978 amounted to 380,000 b/d compared with 280,000 b/d in 1975. With crude oil output rising at an average rate of 11 percent since 1974 and future demand likely to exceed 16 percent annually, China has had to move quickly to start talks with Western firms about cooperative development of oil resources. In 1976–79, China spent $500 million on Western technology—survey vessels, drilling rigs, helicopters—to develop gas and oil. Yet, the Chinese are wavering between a policy of rapid development to earn more foreign exchange and a more conservative program of balanced oil, gas, coal, and power development.

Petroleum-based chemical production is a pivotal Chinese industry. Plants producing fibers, plastics, and resins provide both materials for manufacturing and substitutes for fibers and fertilizers, freeing land for food production. Since 1972, petrochemicals dominated plant import programs. Petrochemical and metal industries accounted for 90 percent of the major contracts in 1977–78. In 1978, China signed about $3 billion in contracts covering four ethylene plants and three hydrocracking units.

Oil developments are occurring rapidly. Recommended journals reporting on China's oil industry include Hong Kong's *Petroleum News Southeast Asia* and Japan's *Japan Petroleum*. They provide solid running accounts and trade data on facilities and marketing arrangements.

Iron and steel

The iron and steel industry outstrips all other sectors in potential foreign exchange expenditures. Bethlehem Steel has helped develop an iron mine at Hubei (figure 2–4). Projects to develop downstream facilities, such

Figure 2–4
MAJOR IRON AND STEEL FACILITIES, 1980

Source: *China: A Country Study*, Foreign Area Studies, The American University, Washington, D.C. 1981, 243.

as concentrators and fabrication plants, are also under discussion. These projects could cost up to $20 billion. Because of high costs and China's limited experience in constructing integrated plants, steel modernization will stretch into the 1990s. Large iron mines are reasonably efficient, whereas small ones are crude. Benefication practices have been improved and high-grade concentrates are often produced, even from low-grade magnetite and hematite ores. Considering its age, the Anshan steel complex is performing well. Anshan, in northeast China, is one of the world's largest steelworks, producing 7 million tons of steel in 1978. Employment stands at more than 200,000—more than the entire British Steel Corporation. Yet, Anshan suffers from all the weaknesses that have made steel a primary burden on China's economy. These include lack of investment in benefication, lack of capacity for alloy steels, and poor quality of iron ore. Open hearths are common and fabrication facilities are archaic. Since Anshan represents more than a fifth of China's steel making capacity, modernization of the complex's 54 mills and workshops is vital if the industry is to meet China's steel targets. With general plant under-utilization, China is reluctant to launch bold, new projects. Bottlenecks remain in producing finished rolled steel—an important product in an industralized country—and high quality alloys. Furthermore, an attempt to increase the variety and quality of metal products will require the development of purification and benefication facilities for enhancing the quality of raw materials, iron ore and coal.

Nonferrous metals

China is one of the world's richest mineral areas, fully capable of supporting a first-rank economy. Nevertheless it's deficient in nonferrous metals production and has become more reliant on imports to meet growth requirements. Chinese planners picture nonferrous metals as a primary source of income. They are interested in making compensation trade arrangements with foreign firms.

China's natural wealth includes tin, mercury, titanium, antimony, tungsten, manganese, molybdenum, zinc, copper, nickel, uranium, bismuth, gallium, and lead. China's tin reserves are large, totaling at least 500,000 tons. Estimated mercury reserves of about 400,000 76-pound flasks place China among world leaders. Half of the world reserves of antimony ore—two million tons—are in China. It could easily satisfy its own demand and export. However, in relative terms, the 10,000 to 13,000 tons China produces annually do not amount to much money. China's tungsten reserves—one million tons—are the world's largest. Tungsten is being mined at an annual rate of 15,000 to 20,000 tons of concentrates each year. Domestic consumption has steadily risen, because of the expanded use of drill bits and machine tools. The Chinese produce an entire line of tungsten products, including synthetic sheelite, paratungstate, powder, wire, and carbide. China's molybdenum reserves of 8 to 10 million tons (0.33–0.39%) are among the world's largest.

Chinese deposits of rare earths are large. Since 1960, China has emerged as an important producer and consumer of barium, zirconium, and beryllium. The *London Mining Journal* reported in its 1976 annual review that:

> China has developed by its efforts a fairly comprehensive and expanding, high-quality metals industry, basic to electronics, semi-conductors, and special instruments and detectors. Surpluses of many metals are available for export. Tellurium, arsenic, cadmium, and gallium are produced at 99.9999 percent quality. Many more are produced at 99.999 percent quality, including copper, lead, zinc, tin, bismuth, cadmium, antimony, gallium, nickel, phosphorus, sulphur, boron, arsenic, and tellurium. Lithium for atomic energy and advanced-technology use is produced at 99.99 percent grade.

China has made important mineral discoveries. These include uranium, copper, lead, and zinc in Sichuan, bauxite in Pingguo in Guangxi province, silver in Henan province, reserves of 8 million tons of copper in Jiangxi, and lead and zinc in Yunnan province. Many of China's nonferrous reserves lie in remote regions of the south and southwest. The terrain is rugged, and transportation is undeveloped. China is negotiating with foreign firms on how best to exploit these deposits. For example, Fluor of the United States has conducted an engineering study for an open-pit copper complex in Jiangxi province.

Tin, tungsten, and antimony dominate China's exports. They accounted for 93 percent of nonferrous sales in 1976. China also exports molybdenum, fluorspar, and talc. Markets for all these metals are weak. Changes in sales or pricing policies could affect markets heavily. China's main competitors for other metals are Third World nations. It doesn't want to offend developing countries by adopting an aggressive export policy. Production of traditional export metals—mercury, tin, tungsten, and antimony—hasn't grown enough to let China market greater quantities abroad; the Chinese have failed to exploit their reserves to the extent necessary to become a major exporter. China has supplemented lagging domestic metals production with imports, chiefly aluminum, copper, nickel, and lead. China's nonferrous metals industry made little progress in the 1970s. Indeed, output of tungsten, tin, mercury, and antimony was still below the level of the late 1950s. Aluminum was the only metal that grew sharply in the last decade. As new capacity became operational, production doubled, reaching 375,000 tons in 1976. The copper industry had almost no growth. Production, totaling 290,000 tons in 1970, advanced to 300,000 tons in 1976. China's production of manganese has been sufficient for domestic needs.

Beijing has stressed agriculture, petroleum, transportation, and fertilizer industries, leaving limited resources to metals. As a result, the industry has failed to develop new sources of raw materials. It remains dependent on outdated technology and needs new refining capacity to boost output. A lead and zinc plant and a few aluminum refineries were the only major nonferrous facilities to come online in the 1970s. High development costs have also retarded production. Nonferrous mines are generally small and wasteful, often unearthing low-grade ores. China has scheduled expansion of output of aluminum, copper, nickel, platinum, titanium, tungsten, and zinc, and has approached both Japan and Italy for facilities to process aluminum and copper. Expansion of power generation and transmission facilities has greatly increased demand for aluminum and copper. China is definitely in take-off stage in aluminum consumption. Lack of cheap power, high-grade resources, capital, and technology are factors in holding back development. China will import plants as well as mining and drilling equipment to increase nonferrous minerals productivity.

Transportation

Throughout China's history, distribution has always been a fundamental economic problem. The country's size—2,486 miles from north to south, 2,983 miles from east to west—is one handicap. Recognizing that the creation of an effective transportation system is the key to China's economic development, planners have made transportation one of the most important elements in successive five-year plans. The development of transportation is linked to the development of China's economy, consolidation of defense, and strengthening of unification. The shift of population centers from coastal to inland areas has also stimulated demand for transportation. Main rivers run from west to east, acting as a barrier between urban centers. The Grand Canal, the only major waterway running from north to south, is important in the national distribution of coal and foodstuffs along its 1,105 mile route and links the most densely populated areas of China. Water transport is traditional and works well. Steamers can navigate about a quarter of China's 105,000 miles of inland waterways. Since the Chinese have used rivers and canals for thousands of years, there won't be much expansion.

Growing trade has strained China's port and shipping system. Ships still experience long delays because of poor dockside equipment. A major effort is underway to upgrade a number of Chinese ports, including Shanghai, Qingdao, Qinguangdao, Tianjin, and Hungpu. (Foreign contractors should stay abreast of the port situation. Port delays continue to constitute a serious problem. All timetables, schedules, and references to time in contracts should factor in port delays.) Officials are trying to alleviate the problem. Authorities in both Shanghai and Guandong are pushing shippers and cargo handlers to move goods more quickly to decongest harbors. Officials are levying fines against shippers who can't move their goods through port cities within stipulated times, and Shanghai and Guangzhou are both equipped with mobile pneumatic unloaders, grab-type portal cranes, and shipboard cranes. Ten ports are involved in the grain trade. They can unload 17 million tons of grain a year. Chinese ports cannot accommodate vessels over 100,000 GRT. Most harbors have a draught limitation of 35 feet. Since 1973, containerization has made headway in Tianjin, Huangpu, and other ports. Most container traffic is transshipped via Hong Kong or Japan. China has a merchant fleet operating around the world. In 1977, the ocean-going merchant fleet consisted of 450 vessels with a total DWT of 6.8 million tons. Most vessels are in the 25–35,000 ton class. China usually buys vessels second-hand on the international ship market. Shipyards produce a small number of 25–35,000 tonners each year. Apart from these vessels, China owns ships flying Somali and Hong Kong flags of convenience, operated through shipping firms on Hong Kong and Macao.

Two-thirds of China's freight goes by rail (figure 2–5). Railways also provide the army with most of its strategic mobility and logistic support. Capacity on stretches of railway has reached saturation. As part of the modernization plan, China wants to adopt heavy-duty rails, automatically controlled crossings, and computer tracking.

In 1979, China had one car per 100,000 people, or 100,000 cars for the whole nation. It has 435,000 miles of highway, 2 percent of which is paved. Apart from a few truck routes like the road to Tibet, surfaced roads exist only in urban areas. Truck production is low. In its drive to conserve oil, Beijing won't expand motor transport.

Since the 1920s, airplanes, including various military aircraft, have been made in China. However, China buys most civil airliners abroad. In 1980, its civil fleet included Soviet and British aircraft and recently acquired Boeing 707 and 747 jets. Service to China's cities continues to expand. The Civil Aviation Administration of China (CAAC) operates flights that link over 70 cities within the country. China has signed air service agreements with Bangladesh, Canada, the Federal Republic of Germany, Greece, Iraq, Italy, Japan, Laos, Nepal, the Netherlands, the Philippines, Spain, Sweden, Thailand, the United Kingdom, and the United States. Foreign flag carriers operating between China and international capitals include Air France, Aeroflot, the Civil Aviation Administration of Korea, Ethiopian Airlines, Iran Air, Japan Airlines, Swiss Air, and Tarom of Romania. The CAAC has weekly flights between Shanghai and Hong Kong. Hong Kong's Cathay Pacific Airways has also been allowed to run charter flights from Hong Kong's Kai Tak international airport to Guangzhou. In 1964, expanded international airports were

Figure 2-5
RAILROADS AND MAJOR PORTS

Source: *China A Country Study*, Foreign Area Studies, The American University, Washington, D.C., 1981, 280.

completed at Shanghai and Guangzhou. Airport construction has greatly increased since Beijing's airport was built in 1958.

In nearly all aspects, China must look to the West for transportation technology. Its shopping list includes diesel locomotives, jet transports, centralized traffic control systems, and shipyard facilities.

Science and Technology

The Chinese were the first masters of science. Until the 15th century, China led the world in developments—often by hundreds of years. The Chinese invented gunpowder, paper, printing, porcelain, canal locks, the wheelbarrow, the compass, and the clock. They were the first to cast iron, build iron suspension bridges, and develop deep-well drilling. After 1949, the

Communists began training large numbers of scientists and engineers in the hope of catching up with the West. In 1958, Chinese scientists synthesized insulin at the Biochemical Institute of Shanghai. By 1964, China had exploded an atomic bomb. In 1970, China launched its first satellite. But one of the areas the Cultural Revolution hit hardest was science. Red Guards stormed classrooms, wrecked equipment, subjected China's finest minds to public harangue and pig farming. Scientific development came virtually to a standstill. A debased educational framework gave rise to a lost generation of 2 million restless, semi-literate youth. China is desperately short of teachers, managers, technicians, and workers who can master and diffuse high technology. The underlying framework of knowledge and understanding that provides support for scientific endeavors is unsound, managerial skills are sparse, and manufacturing know-how is in short supply. These factors restrict China's ability to absorb foreign technology. Extensive purchases of industrial technology and efforts to upgrade power, transportation, and communications won't guarantee economic growth. The critical factor is China's ability to adapt these products and processes to its own needs and allow indigenous innovation and development.

The post-Mao leadership is aware of the importance of education, science, and technology in modernization. They've restored many research organizations the Cultural Revolution abolished. Professionals now have a greater voice in deliberation and are paying more attention to basic research. In 1977–78, two major planning conferences were held, one for natural science, the other for more general technical matters. These efforts culminated in the National Science Conference, held in March, 1978. Amid much fanfare, the 6,000 attending scientists drafted a master plan. At the conference, Fang Yi, vice president of the Academy of Sciences and minister of the State Science and Technology Commission, said the plan will shape China's endeavors for the next generation. It called for the establishment of a nationwide research system with a number of modernized bases for scientific experimentation. Scientific resources will flow to eight research areas: agriculture, energy, raw materials, computers, lasers, space, high energy physics, and genetic engineering. Touching on oil, coal, and electric power, Fang also mentioned the need to develop other sources of energy, including geothermal, solar, nuclear, and wave. In materials research, Fang cited metallurgy. He held up the needs of the steel industry as an area of priority, especially in the benefication of hematite. Fang went on to discuss a number of nonferrous industries where research is needed. He also reported a timetable for launching space probes and laboratories.

China sees progress in science as the key modernization. After years of lagging behind the West, the Chinese now aspire to global scientific leadership. The government has systematically upgraded China's scientific establishment. Eagerness to get modern technology is reflected by the number of foreign firms invited to give technical seminars, the number of Chinese visitors to foreign firms and institutes, and China's insatiable appetite for scientific journals and technical documents. China's interest in buying specific technology is another promising sign. In earlier import periods, purchases of technology were linked to the purchase of complete plants. To conserve foreign exchange, Chinese units tend to buy only technology that cannot be produced in China. Despite threats of a Maoist anti-intellectual backlash, Chinese are more confident of progress in this area than in any other of the Four Modernizations. China's need for foreign science and technology is clear. What is not clear is how much will be bought, in what sectors, and in what form. Certainly, China won't make itself dependent on outside help as it did in the 1950s. Foreign participation will be that of an advisor, although the distinction between advice and control could be blurred. Despite heavy spending on science and technology, shortages of personnel will persist. Therefore, China will concentrate resources on a limited number of projects having a reasonable possibility of quick payoff. It wants to buy a variety of foreign measuring instruments, analytical devices, and control mechanisms used in monitoring production quality and quantity, especially in energy-related industries. China is also interested in Western communication technologies, from laser devices to manufacturing facilities for television sets. It plans to develop a wide range of telecommunications and electronic production systems and products, including a domestic communication satellite.

Education

"Serious sabotage by the Gang of Four wrought havoc with China's science and education," Fang Yi said in 1977. "Various fields of work are keenly feeling the shortage of successors for scientific and technological endeavors." But learning is respectable again, especially into what the Chinese (who have a fetish for numbers) call the Five Golden Blossoms: atomic science, semiconductors, computers, lasers, and automation. Under the Five Ones Program, primary school children read one science book, tell one science story, do one experiment, explain one natural phenomenon, and predict one scientific advance.

China's intellectual system is still weak. During the Cultural Revolution, education was in a turmoil of radical reformation. By 1978, three out of every four children were in school. Officials claim a literacy rate of more than 90 percent. China's educational system stresses scientific and technical training to give students the skills needed to modernize China's economy. In repairing the damage wrought by the Cultural Revolution, authorities discovered urban teenagers are being over-educated for the country's needs while schoolchildren in rural areas are dropping out of school or graduating partly or wholly illiterate. In 1979, 1.02 million students attended 633 universities and institutes of higher education. The supply of qualified teachers and scientists, however, to staff colleges and research institutes is limited. Libraries and laboratories are scarce and poorly equipped. Considerable investment will be needed to develop the laboratory equipment industry. In the face of these problems, the Chinese have adopted a policy of giving higher priority in allocating resources to a select number of key schools throughout the country. Beijing is restoring its educational system by reinstating ranks for professors and rehabilitating scientists who were shunted to other work. As part of the Cultural Revolution's egalitarianism, schools dropped national exams in 1966. Students were admitted to higher education on the basis of class background and political orientation. Schools have not only reinstated exams, they have made them rigorous and uniform. Beijing is also letting thousands of China's top students attend Western institutions. In 1979, 1,300 foreign students from 77 nations studied in China. China had 2,700 students studying in 41 nations. China's willingness to let students live abroad—despite the risk of ideological contamination or defection—underscores its determination to mine Western ideas and technology. Beijing is encouraging overseas Chinese and foreigners to teach in China, and has manifested interest in Western methods of instruction, including those used by the better business schools. Although these reforms foster inequality, they are popular among a people who have long valued the mind.

Computers and telecommunications

U.S. sources rate as technically adequate the Chinese line of DJS-18 and Model 111 large-scale computers, dating from the early 1970s. ALGOL-60 is the most popular computer language in China, as well as in Eastern Europe and the Soviet Union. The major weakness in Chinese computer manufacture, common to many latecomers in this industry, is the lack of viable peripherals and other input-output devices. Most input data is prepared either on paper or magnetic tape rather than cards. Important users of computers, such as the Daqing Oil Field, the Academy of Social Science, and the Ministry of Railways, are developing their own hardware and software. Large-scale computers, such as the DJS-18 that was displayed in Guangzhou in 1974, use libraries of existing software. The AUGUST 1, China's first computer, made its debut in 1958. It was modelled after the Soviet URAL-1. In 1964, China constructed the first large, fully transistorized computer. In 1974, the Chinese completed the first integrated circuit computer. The DJS-11 was designed with a 130K memory to operate at one million operations per second. This relatively large storage consisted of four core memory units of 32K words, each equipped with independent controls. In addition to Soviet machines imported during the 1950s, China has computer imports from the United States, Britain, France, West Germany, Italy, and even Hungary and East Germany.

Japan will probably be the greatest beneficiary in this area of trade. It is second only to the U.S. in numbers of computers installed. Firms such as Hitachi Ltd., Toshiba, Fujitsu Ltd., Oki Electric, and Mitsubishi have moved aggressively to market office computers, minicomputers, calculators, peripheral and terminal equipment, and related products. Japan's computer industry is strong on the manufacturing side, but weak in service and support of its exports. China on the other hand is an ideal customer, since it neither requires nor desires the normal computer sale support beyond the initial training of technicians. The United States not only faces Japanese competition, but political obstacles. For example, Control Data Corporation's (CDC) sale of a Cyber 172 computer to China threatened to become a major issue during the 1976 presidential election campaign. While the Chinese said the system would be used for oil exploration, some experts said the safeguards preventing military use would be difficult to enforce. The Ford administration finally consented to the sale. CDC had to maintain a resident expert in China to watch over the machine. China's production managers admit they are years behind the West in computer design and manufacturing techniques. The quality of integrated circuits is patchy and Chinese engineers want to move to large scale integration as developed in Japan and the United States. Managers from Shanghai's Radio Factory Number Three have discussed partnership possibilities with a number of foreign firms. Honeywell, IBM, Prime Computer, and NCR have negotiated a variety of trade arrangements. Most imports have been large turnkey systems incorporating software for such applications as geological exploration, scientific computation, and input/output economic analysis. In 1980, China had an installed base of 1,500 computers. It will produce most small systems and minicomputers and import most large systems. The general unreliability of China's telephone network, however, makes it questionable whether network systems can be effective.

In China, a large, cheap labor force is available. An "abacus army" has long performed routine calculations. And although computers can expedite these and other tasks more efficiently and with fewer errors, there is little incentive to replace people with machines. Nevertheless we believe the Chinese market for computers is promising. The size and complexity of Chinese structures, their training of computer personnel, the Chinese propensity for creative imagination in science and commerce, and the indispensability of systems in managing a modern society lead us to project a dramatic expansion of data processing in China over the next two decades. There is a correlation between the number of computers in a country and its gross domestic product. The ratio of the two gives some measure of a nation's prosperity relative to other countries. Whether an increase in the number of computers stimulates or results from a growing economy is debatable. It's probably a reciprocal relationship. The conclusion for developing nations is that you cannot have one without the other. China is an undeveloped country, and, as such, has special needs, problems, and possibilities. In China, demand for computer technology will be strong in these areas:

- Advanced accounting and other commercial applications.
- Immigration control, police data, national security.
- Medical administration.
- Student instruction.
- Industrial control.
- Utility monitoring.
- Traffic control.
- Civil engineering.
- Weather forecasting and seismic analysis.

Obviously, this isn't a definitive list.

If Sino-Western relations continue on their present course, vast markets will shape up for all types of information processing products. Although the future is bright for an expansion of computer use in Third World countries such as China, certain political controversies will emerge. Indeed, the fact that the computer industry is poised to become one of the largest economic sectors will widen the gulf between the rich and poor nations. Third World leaders also see the control of 85 percent of the world's supply of computers in the hands of ten Western firms and large amounts of crucial data on Third World nations stored in Western databanks as a threat to sovereignty. If the West can ease these concerns, the Computer Revolution could dwarf all previous advances in science and technology in China. The Computer Revolution could be to China of the 1980s what the Green Revolution was to India of the 1960s. Computers are indeed revolutionary—a term not to be used lightly in context with China—because they allow poor countries to jump stages of development the West had to pass through over the course of centuries. These countries may not have to build a scientific base, but may in fact speed up the creation of this type of infrastructure. For example, satellites may make it unnecessary for poor countries to build an expensive, redundant ground telecommunications system that was required in the past.

Development of telecommunications has been uneven since 1949. Growth in this sector has been rapid during times of industrial expansion, but stagnant when growth in the rest of the industrial sector slowed. The reasons for this pattern are that greater communication is needed during times of rapid industrial growth and telecommunications depends on other industrial sectors for equipment and service. China's leaders acknowledge that their system is inadequate and are planning to overhaul it over the next decade. Considerable resources have been spent on improvements for international and domestic communication facilities. However, microwave and coaxial cable networks have yet to cover the country. The demand for radios and television receivers is much larger than current production can fulfill. Sales of light industrial consumer goods such as radios, cameras, and watches give planners a way of reducing outstanding purchasing power and the risk of inflation, important since many necessities such as clothes, housing, and certain foods are rationed at low prices. Communication devices appeal to the Chinese. Of course, these facilities are necessary for the function of every complex economic and political system. When analyzing China's need for telecommunications, we must recognize it employs a wide range of communication techniques that don't need modern equipment. Nearly all Chinese are organized by occupation, residential area, age, and sex into one or more mass organizations—Labor Unions, Women's Associations, Poor and Lower Middle Peasant Associations—that transmit information from leaders to the people and vice versa. Regular study sessions, mutual criticism meetings, and discussion of plans allow Chinese leaders to communicate through face to face contacts. China is divided into 29 provinces. The average province has 30 million people. Although they share much of the same political and cultural tradition, provinces differ significantly among themselves in language and geography. Each provincial capital is the center of a telecommunications network that includes newspapers, radios, and television stations. An important function of the system is to relay national news and editorials. However, each province has sufficient political, cultural, and economic identity to necessitate independent programming.

Although only about 15 percent of China's population lives in urban areas, the potential demand for telecommunications equipment for collective use is still large in relation to China's present capabilities. By conservative estimates, there are 50,000 medium and large-scale industrial enterprises, two million residential-based social organizations, and many social and administrative units, such as hospitals and public security offices. Many of these organizations lack telephones and televisions. Although China's telecommunications sector has made strides toward self-reliance, it won't be able to satisfy all domestic requirements for economic and technical reasons. The domestic telecommunications sector will continue to expand, but the relative unimportance of consumer demand for telecommunications and China's highly developed methods of communicating using unsophisticated equipment will dampen trade opportunities. Market potential appears brightest for sales of individual pieces of advanced equipment that the Chinese aren't able to produce in large quantities. The bulk of China's imports of telecommunications and cinematic equipment has come from Japan, the United States, the United Kingdom, France, and West Germany. Many of the world's leading producers of telecommunications equipment have been suppliers to China for many years. Siemens of West Germany has sold telex and telegraph equipment to China. Northern Electric Company of Canada has sold multiplexing equipment, and Nippon Electric Company of Japan has sold equipment for satellite communications.

The Chinese are pushing semiconductor research and development. The semiconductor chip—a thin slice of crystal silicon in which are embedded minute circuits—is the essential ingredient of virtually all modern electronic products. China is set on building its own semiconductor manufacturing base to reduce imports and eventually compete in export markets. China's consumer electronics industry is growing at an astonishing rate. Television production, for instance, reached 4.8 million units in 1981, a 93 percent increase over the previous year. Much of this increase, as well as the growth in production of electronic watches and other electronic consumer goods, was made possible only by importing semi-conductors and other components in large quantities from Hong Kong and Japan for assembly into complete products in China. In 1981, Japan alone exported more than $250 million worth of semiconductors to China.

There are risks associated with providing technology and technical assistance to China, including increased military competition. While control of dual-purpose technologies is necessary and legitimate, it is clear that China will develop with or without the superintendence of another state, such as France, or organization, such as the Consultative Group Coordinating Committee Alliance, a confederation of 15 nations acting jointly to restrict exports of strategic technologies to Communist nations. It is in the interest of the West to provide for technology transfer and build a relationship between China and ourselves. Failure to encourage the acquisition of technology would reaffirm the position of those in China who were reluctant to turn outward and would accelerate the demise of leaders and policies that best serve our own interests. We will discuss this important issue more fully in the next section.

Defense

Of defense, Sunzi, the 6th century B.C. Chinese military theorist, said it best: "What enables the wise sovereign and the good general to strike and conquer, and achieve things beyond the reach of ordinary men, is foreknowledge." The same must be said for the shrewd executive. Foreknowledge lets us negotiate from a position of power, because information is power. The right information can mean the difference between a contract withheld and a contract proffered. But secrecy cloaks China's defenses. "All warfare is based on deception," Sunzi wrote. "China conceals its secrets best of all," Alexander Solzhenitsyn agrees. China's plans are unrevealing, and its industrial budget camouflages defense spending. Nevertheless, we can respond to patterns in China's defense.

Intentions

The purpose of this section is to understand what motivates China's defense. This subject is relevant to everyone who wants to deal with China, for its military is at the heart of what China is and where it is going.

For several reasons, China is going to approach arms deals with caution. First, it's difficult, if not impossible, to get arms internationally without political entanglements. The technical expertise it needs to make the best choice of equipment is lacking. Pressures to "keep up with the Joneses" are difficult to resist. Finally, donors or sellers could impose controls, which add further complications. It's too much to expect arms trade will build a Chinese military machine that cannot work without parts from London or Los Angeles. China won't depend on others as it did on the Soviet Union.

Without question, deals contributing to China's arsenal entail risks, for China is given to bouts of political instability (the Great Leap, the Cultural Revolution, the Gang of Four) and military adventurism (Korea, India, Viet Nam). To paraphrase Lenin, capitalists aren't eager to be hanged by the rope they've sold. Long-term weapons can be sold to short-term friends. The Chinese could also serve as middlemen between Western merchants and the likes of Pol Pot. However, withholding war material from marketing channels could be an error. The problem of peace lies not in reducing stockpiles, but in reducing tensions. In this context, the psychological dimension—personalities, perceptions, and projections—takes precedence over the hard facts of military capability—air strikes, landing craft, missile batteries. A nation can never be too pessimistic about enemy intentions, for intentions can change instantly, capabilities cannot. Thus, prudence requires that rivals demand parity or seek superiority with each other. That these perceptions accelerate the velocity of the arms race is an unfortunate inevitability. The history of warfare has been a catchup game between weapons of offense and the countervailing weapons of defense. No sooner is a new weapon devised than the means to combat it comes into existence. Capability deficit means a power imbalance. This can trigger hysteria, self-delusion, and miscalculation on either side—inviting it to "cry havoc, and let slip the dogs of war." If a nation perceives a capability gap vis-à-vis its rival, that nation will fill the gap from any available source. If the United States cannot satisfy China's defense needs, it will find dealers in Britain and Germany and the international black market. There was a day when people thought the same about trafficking in slaves: "If we don't sell, someone else will." On analysis, the analogy breaks down. It wasn't moral outcry in Parliament and Congress that ended the slave trade. It was the enforcing might of the British navy and Federal army, embryonic movements toward nationalism in the colonies, and the decreasing demand for slavery as an "economic necessity." Can a condominium of Great Powers stop arms trade, particularly with poor, unstable countries? We admit to pessimism. Force is a reality in the international system, and the only way to limit arms trade is to reduce the demand for weapons. That is unlikely in view of the economics of the business, paranoia of competing systems, and prestige developing states see in owning sophisticated arms.

China's Politburo has given defense lowest priority relative to agriculture, industry, and science and technology. But defense could be the most important beneficiary of Western trade. And the Soviet Union is inclined to give the Fourth Modernization a rank akin to the Fourth Horseman of the Apocalypse. China is still hammering out priorities. Foreign arms deals—as they materialize—will suggest where its true priorities lie.

China views containing Soviet expansionism as the central issue of diplomacy. To that end, it has normalized relations with the United States, signed a Treaty of Friendship with Japan, and reached a commercial understanding with Europe's Economic Community. War in Europe implies world-wide conflict. The world's two largest alliance systems—NATO and the Warsaw Pact—stand eye to eye on the continent, forming a dense concentration of forces and arms in a confined area. China's contact with NATO led Supreme Allied Commander Alexander Haig to speak of China as the 16th NATO power. China has condemned America's failure to stand up to the Russians in the Persian Gulf, and has championed Pakistan, possibly to the point of letting it join the nuclear club. The Kremlin's profound dread of China complicates matters. ("Kremlin" means fortress—an accurate reflection of Russia's mentality.) Upheaval in Eastern Europe and China are Russia's strategic obsessions. Many sophisticated Soviets believe war with their largest and most unfriendly neighbor is inevitable. Fear of China was a major incentive behind Brezhnev's policy of detente with the West. He didn't want to wage cold wars—with the threat of hot ones—on two fronts. Soviet strategy has three objectives: 1. To make the Soviet bloc, as represented by the Warsaw Pact Organization, impregnable to attack; 2. To support wars of liberation everywhere; 3. To reduce the power of capitalist enclaves—the Western alliance—and socialist renegades, including the Chinese camp.

The roots of conflict between China and Russia predate Communism. Since Tartar Mongols in the Medieval age overran Russia, Russians have feared marauding orientals. In 1206, Genghis Khan, a Mongolian tribal leader, united the tribes and undertook conquests marked by cruelty. With 150,000 horsemen, he created the Mongol Empire, stretching from the Pacific to Russia. After subjugating northern China by 1217, he went on to conquer Turkestan, Afghanistan, and Persia. By the 1400s, Mongol rule over central and southern Russia was weakening. In 1491, Ivan the Great crushed the remnants of the Golden Horde. The Muscovite Empire was firmly in power when Ivan the Great died in 1505, but the Mongols had put a permanent mark upon the Russian character and institutions. Czarist imperialism in the 17th, 18th, and 19th centuries extended control over Siberia and Chinese border areas, which had traditionally been client states or buffer zones of the old Chinese and Mongol dynasties. A goal of China's policy is to bring under its control all territory it deems Chinese. According to Chinese officials, Mongolia, much of Central Asia, and large tracts of Manchuria were "annexed by Russian thieves" under "unequal treaties" of the 19th century. In all, they claim, Chinese territory in Russian hands adds up to more than 400,000 square miles, a region as large as Western Europe. Today, Soviet leaders reinforce collective paranoia by salting the wounds of World War II. There are shrines to war dead in most Russian cities, a war that reaped economic ruin and 20 million Soviet deaths before Marshal Georgi Konstantinovich Zhukov's Red Army crushed the Fascist *Wehrmacht*. While paranoid in motivation, Soviet policy is predatory in practice. Persistent Soviet efforts to expand at China's expense mark Sino-Soviet relations. Of the countries that have a common frontier with China, only Russia is capable of invading and fighting on Chinese territory. China believes the Soviets want to split the Chinese nation and occupy border regions, or, more realistically, Finlandize areas inhabited by minorities. China's minorities total 60 million, 6 percent of the population, but they occupy half of China's land.

In March, 1969, blood stained the snow of what the Russians call Damanskiy Island and the Chinese call Zhenbao. This island is in the Ussuri River, which flows between the northeastern province of Heilongjiang in Manchuria and the Maritime Territory of the Soviet Far East. In three all-out battles, the Soviets called in armor and field artillery to pound the Chinese. Tensions rose to the point where Soviets hinted they might strike against China's nuclear installations unless Beijing agreed to negotiations aimed at settling the conflict. Though the crisis has subsided, both nations anticipate war. The Soviet Union has built massive bases in Outer Mongolia for a strike force, with networks of barracks, rocket pads, ammunition caches, and underground communication centers. China has similar systems in frontier regions. China's obsession: the 46 highly-mobile, missile-equipped Soviet divisions emplaced along the 4,500-mile Sino-Soviet border. This strength is supported by a larger air force, the Soviet Pacific Fleet of 140 warships, and a nuclear arsenal. In 1981, China had 1.6 million men on the Soviet border—a force that Beijing may augment if Moscow raises combat readiness of its own one million frontier troops. China asserts relations among nations must be conducted on grounds of "mutual respect for sovereignty and territorial integrity, mutual nonaggression, noninterference in each other's internal affairs, equality and mutual benefit, and peaceful coexistence." It maintains the border question can be resolved through negotiations, free of threat. Toward this end, China and the U.S.S.R. have tried to ease tensions. China wants to patch differences so it can devote some of its border troops to modernizing. Six months after the Ussuri River clash, talks started. The countries have held subsequent meetings intermittently. In March, 1979, a ten-man Chinese delegation started wide-ranging talks in Moscow. The Chinese team left Russia when Soviets invaded Afghanistan in December, 1979. (Afghanistan borders China and oil-rich Iran, and this represents a new strategic dimension to U.S.-China relations.) China supports the Afghan rebels and requires Russia's evacuation of Afghanistan as a precondition for detente. In light of recent history, the possibility of real detente seems slight. However, only the willfully stupid will assume Sino-Soviet conflict will last forever. China and Russia could one day forge an ideological relationship reminiscent of the 1939 Hitler-Stalin pact. Conversely, if tensions escalate, the Soviet Union could stage a preemptive attack. If they do attack, they will opt for an overland *blitzkrieg*. Some non-Communist Chinese observers believe the Soviet army could hack through Beijing's best forces garrisoned in the northwest and overrun the underpopulated western province of Xinjiang in six weeks. If this happens, China will follow established guerrilla tactics: surrendering cities, drawing the enemy into the countryside, and awaiting opportunities to encircle, counterattack, annihilate. It counts on enmeshing Soviet forces in China's vast areas just as Japanese forces became bogged down in the late 1930s. As China develops a more integrated industrial and communications system, wise passivity and peasant cunning won't be enough to defeat Russian aggression.

Proxy warfare replaced rhetoric as Viet Nam launched a Christmas offensive into Democratic Kampuchea (Cambodia) in 1978. China supported Pol Pot's regime as a buffer against Soviet-backed expansionist Viet Nam. This policy alienated world opinion. The Khmer Rouge's genocide of three million people has ample documentation. China responded to Pol Pot's defeat and a number of border clashes by invading Viet Nam in February, 1979. The ethnic antagonism between the Chinese and the Vietnamese dates back to the 2nd century B.C. The Chinese grabbed control of Viet Nam for a thousand years, labeled the area Annam (pacified south), and exacted tributes of pearls, precious stones, elephant tusks, and valuable woods for the emperor. When the Chinese withdrew in 939, Annamese armies terrorized neighboring Cambodia and Laos. That China backed Viet Nam during wars with France and America did little to lessen this hatred. Since 1978, Viet Nam has driven 250,000 Chinese overland into China. Thousands more fled by sea. Viet Nam views the Chinese as a fifth column in any future conflict, a view shared by most non-Chinese Asian countries. China described its first war in 17 years as a limited counterattack. The People's Liberation Army (PLA) officially sustained 20,000 casualties.

The Chinese react whenever they feel their sovereignty threatened. According to article 19 of the 1978 constitution: "The fundamental task of the armed forces of the People's Republic of China is to safeguard the socialist revolution and socialist construction, to defend the sovereignty, territorial integrity, and security of the state, and to guard against subversion and aggression by social-imperialism, imperialists, and their lackeys."[1] They fought U.N. troops in Korea when they thought these forces might cross the Yalu River and enter China. They battled with India over their Himalayan border. They have come into armed conflict with the Soviet Union over the ill-defined border along the Heilong Jiang. China will fight "the Cuba of the East" again when its prestige or security is threatened, even though war undermines its economy and revives anti-Chinese feeling in Southeast Asia. Britain's lease on 90 percent of Hong Kong expires on July 1, 1997. If sovereignty talks with Whitehall over Hong Kong's future collapse, China could try to take the New Territories by force. In view of the economic importance of the British colony to the mainland, that is unlikely, unless the two nations cannot break the diplomatic impasse with face-saving concessions.

During Deng Xiaoping's visit to the United States in 1979, he agreed to respect "the realities" of Taiwan without formally ruling out force to annex the island. What are the realities? Taiwan's well trained, highly motivated military is capable of rugged defense. In 1980, it had 539,000 troops and 316 combat jets. The Republic of China has a host of gifted scientists and an accelerated nuclear defense program. If China launches an assault that appears to doom Taiwan, a desperate Taibei won't hesitate to atomize Fuzhou. Except for skirmishes over the coastal islands of Quemoy and Matsu in 1955 and 1958, Beijing has refrained from direct action. Despite its numerical advantage, China's military is in such poor shape it would have difficulty defeating Taiwan. The military of the People's Republic is hampered by outdated tactics and equipment so primitive that much of its artillery has to be hauled by horses and oxen. China's lack of submarines, surface escorts, and tactical aircraft to support even a small amphibious assault on the 13,948 square-mile island 90 miles from its shore renders such an operation presently unfeasible.

[1]The People's Republic of China, *The Constitution of the People's Republic of China* (Beijing: Foreign Language Press, 1978).

Capabilities

"Weapons are an important factor in war, but not a decisive factor," Mao said. "It's people—not things—that are decisive." And, with 4.5 million troops, Beijing has the world's largest standing army. The People's Liberation Army is a tough, disciplined corps whose armaments are aging but whose combat capability can never be doubted. There are also a million security police and a militia of seven million, most of them armed with makeshift weapons. China could defend itself in any home-based war, but military deficiencies allow it little ability to range beyond its borders. China lacks the industrial base to support lengthy lines of communication. China's armed forces have held enormous political power. Besides its military duties, the PLA helps execute party policies and programs. Excessive political involvement emasculated the army. As radicalism of the Cultural Revolution threatened the party's inner ring, Mao asked Defense Minister Lin Biao to impose order. The army shielded defense scientists in their compounds from the mobs. In 1969, Mao wrote Lin into the constitution as his successor. Two years later, sensing Lin had grown too strong, Mao purged him. The party is now replacing the army in China's power structures. "Our principle is that the party commands the gun," Mao wrote in 1938. "The gun must never be allowed to command the party." At the height of the army's power, PLA commanders held leading posts in 21 of 29 provinces. This number dropped to 13 when Mao died in 1976 and by 1978 was down to seven. Beijing is also appointing more civilians to the party commissar's job in the local military. In 1980, China replaced 11 regional commanders and hundreds of senior officers as part of an effort to streamline its war machine.

In the early 1970s, China cut defense spending. It saw no point in continuing to crank out obsolete weapons, and America's disengagement from Viet Nam enhanced its sense of security. At the 1979 National People's Congress, Finance Minister Zhang Zhingfu said defense allocations would rise from $9.3 to $12.8 billion (17.8 percent of the total budget), because of China's Viet Nam incursion. In 1980, the military budget was ¥19.7 billion, about 8 percent of China's GNP. Renewed stress on defense sparked debate on foreign imports and the relationship between defense investment and industrial and scientific development. The military is the most politically powerful group that supports the leadership's economic plans. Modernization of China's military is linked with modernization of China's economy—especially development of its technical and scientific capabilities, achievement of greater productivity and quality control, and expansion of leading sectors such as metals, machine building, chemicals, fuels, and space. While the economic objectives of the military and state coincide, problems will arise over questions of resource allocation, that is, whether output should be used to increase the supply of producer goods or allocated to the military as an unproductive end user. This debate ended with a consensus to hold military spending at a level that allows for most essential aspects of defense modernization, curtails large-scale military construction projects, and integrates military and civilian enterprises to make better use of civilian capacity in military plants.

China's massive population is one facet of its military complex. In 1980, China had 10,000 medium T-34 tanks. The 100 mm T-59, its mainstay, is based on the Soviet design of the late 1950s. China's airforce is second-rate. In 1980, it consisted of 5,200 front-line aircraft serviced by 490,000 men. Most of China's 2,200 jets are obsolete compared with Soviet combat aircraft. China's most potent bombers are 100 antiquated, medium-range TU-16 Badgers of Soviet design. It also has several TR-4 Bulls (a copy of the U.S. World War II B-29), some Soviet IL-28 Beagles, and 100 museum-piece TU-2 short-range piston bombers. Other aircraft include: 200 MiG-15s, 1,500 17s, 2,000 19s, 100 21s, and some Chinese-built short-range F-6s and F-9s. Unlike the U.S. airforce, the Chinese airforce has the entire strategic air defense mission. Employing a variety of radar-slewed and optically-guided tube-fired gun systems, the Chinese have several thousand antiaircraft batteries. These systems are useful only for low altitude over limited portions of air space. Several hundred CSA-1 surface-to-air missile batteries provide some high altitude coverage. China has 400 operational airfields, of which 200 are jet-capable.

In 1890, Admiral Alfred Thayer Mahan published his geopolitical conception that posits naval power as the key to world domination. His perception that the seas of the world connected landmasses rather than separated them influenced a generation of U.S., British, Russian, Japanese, and Chinese strategists. Although China's navy is the world's largest in terms of manpower (350,000), it's negligible by great power standards. In 1981, China's naval strength comprised 2 nuclear powered subs, 11 destroyers, 16 frigates, 12 patrol escorts, 170 missile boats, 350 gunboats, 470 landing craft, 900 coast and river defense craft, and other oilers, minesweepers, and torpedo boats. China has a steady construction program for all classes of warships in modernized naval yards. Chinese naval strength is an important element in the balance of power east of the Suez.

China's nuclear capabilities are having an ever greater bearing on Asia's power structure. China has had a thermonuclear deterrent force since 1964. In 1955, it contracted with the Soviet Union for nuclear power and research reactors to build its first atomic pile and cyclotron. China also looked to Russia to provide the industrial underpinnings for its nuclear venture. If the Soviets were to pick the one assistance program they regret most, it would be this agreement. At the time, the Soviets referred to it as "a splendid expression of the Soviet Union's foreign policy of peace." A large slice of China's expenditures continues to go into intermediate and intercontinental missiles. In 1978, 6,200 engineers and 3,500 scientists were working on atomic hardware. Their testing program is generating nuclear devices for missiles and bombers, stored in silos and hardened caves near the northern border. By 1980, China had several hundred nuclear warheads, both fission and fusion, 20 kilotons to 5 megatons yield. It had 55 medium-range ballistic missiles with a range of 600 miles, and 59 intermediate-range missiles with a range of 1,500 miles. China also has a missile strong enough to launch a satellite with a range of 4,000 miles. China has successfully tested its first long-range intercontinental ballistic missile, capable of carrying nuclear warheads any place in the Soviet Union or to the west coast of the United States. The liquid-propelled CSS-X-4—China's surface-to-surface experimental No. 4—showed that China intends to allocate resources to hold its own in what it calls "a world in great turmoil." In 1982, China exploded a tactical nuclear weapon in a wide-ranging military exercise against a simulated Soviet invasion. This suggests a shift to an active defense strategy to replace the "people's war" concept of letting invading enemy troops in and then harassing and engulfing them. From the standpoint of protecting non-critical urban workers, China's civil defense system is superior to the Soviet's. This broad defense effort places civilian populations in a state of constant vigilance, reducing vulnerability to sudden attack. Intricate systems of air-raid tunnels are designed to channel people out of Beijing into the countryside when the enemy strikes.

Needs

China's Viet Nam invasion dispelled Maoist illusions that sheer manpower can compensate for inferior technology. Troops are well-trained and adequately armed with light weapons, but lack field transportation, maintenance, service, communications, and medical support. Even if China hopes to maintain only a conventional force, it would require the production of the most modern aircraft, ships, and weaponry. Any attempt to develop even a limited missile system with nuclear capabilities would entail great capital, skilled labor, and research expenditures. China needs armored personnel carriers, trucks, and helicopters, jet engines, radar components, satellite reconnaissance systems, underwater submarine detection and night vision equipment, radio and tropospheric communications equipment, and electronic and optical counter-measure devices. It's also interested in antiaircraft weapons, tank and tractor redesigns, marine diesel engines, antitank missiles, and military equipment production facilities.

To modernize China's ill-equipped armed forces, Chinese teams have browsed in Germany, Sweden, Britain, and Italy. They have showed interest in France's Mirage 2000, the Holographic One-Tube and Milan antitank missiles and antiaircraft missiles. French Prime Minister M.

Raymond Barre signed an understanding worth $350 million before the readjustment. In 1979, British Prime Minister James Callagan said his government will sell Harrier jump-jet fighters to China as part of a $2 billion trade deal. Because of its limited range, Britain regarded it as a defensive weapon.

From 1972–78, U.S. trade with China and the Soviet Union was on equal standing. After Russia's invasion of Afghanistan in 1979, President Jimmy Carter put China in a different category from the Soviet Union so that "dual use" technology could be made available to Beijing as a rule, rather than as a case-by-case exception. In 1980, U.S. Defense Minister Harold Brown said the United States will sell China a satellite ground station, which had potential military intelligence applications. Following Secretary Brown's visit to China, the State Department's Office of Munitions released a list of product categories for which the U.S. will consider license applications for export to China. Dual use civilian technologies, such as computers with metal-refining and petrochemical applications and security communications gear, may now be exported. However, the U.S. won't permit the sale of lethal military technologies. Commerce Department licensing guidelines state in part that "licenses will no longer be disapproved merely because the end-user is military or the end-user is engaged in military activity, if the proposed export is otherwise appropriate for a stated and accepted end-use. Licenses may be approved even if the equipment or data could be used in the design, development, or manufacture of tactical military items."[2]

Summary

The Four Modernizations represent trading areas with tremendous potential for profit. China's leaders are looking westward to bring the world's oldest continuous civilization into the 21st century on schedule. They acknowledge that these themes will remain constants throughout the next generation and will guide in the development of foreign trade.

Agriculture

Agricultural development commands top priority. Not only must the countryside feed the nation, it must provide savings to fuel future growth and be able to consume goods produced by its developing industries. To

---

[2]U.S. Department of Commerce, *Doing Business in China* (Washington, D.C.: GPO, November, 1980), p. 28.

do this, China will try to cap population growth and locate labor-intensive machinery in rural areas to use productively the vast armies of unemployed.

Industry

China will increase exports, expand foreign trade, and encourage foreign investment. The quickest route to First World capital, technology, and marketing is often through the local branch of a multinational corporation. China no longer views multinationals as the handmaiden of neo-colonial exploitation, because it recognizes that external trade contacts can be beneficial to the Chinese. As a rule, the poorest countries have the fewest external contacts and the richest have the most extensive foreign trade. The People's Republic reaps substantial gains from comparative advantage. It exports products that have a high labor and natural resource content and imports products that it could produce only with great expenditure of scarce high-technology resources. It exports products, such as specialty foods, silks, and handicrafts, that command a high price abroad but are of little use at home. With these earnings, it imports wheat, steel-mill products, and electronics that win a comparatively low price in world markets, but are needed to run China's economic machinery.

China will accelerate the growth of light and textile industries by exporting consumer goods. The implications of this are twofold. First, China will increasingly shun prestige projects. Instead of constructing stadiums, airports, and conference halls, China will channel resources into bottleneck-breaking programs—irrigation systems, electrical grids, and communication and transportation infrastructures that spur efficient agricultural and industrial output. Secondly, China increasingly will encourage entrepreneurs. The ideological commitment for an equitable distribution of income will pale as the state turns to the dynamic of self-initiative to promote economic development. Modern industry requires self-reliance and risk-taking, a belief in progress, and the need for a fluid, interdependent meritocracy. Profit-seeking will supplant featherbedding; capitalistic pragmatism will diminish socialist romanticism.

Science and technology

China will expand education. It will reform the school curriculum, stress vocational training, and dispatch scholars abroad. Political purity will take a backseat to technical expertise and scientific curiosity.

China will seek to increase energy production. Although investment in heavy industry will be low on China's list of priorities, China is determined to reduce tension in the supply of fuel and power by increasing petrochemical, coal, and electrical productivity. This will require breakthroughs in applied science and industrial innovation, and the use of foreign knowledge, equipment, and financing.

Defense

Because of apprehension of Soviet designs in Asia, pressures to increase defense spending will mount. However, analysis of defense spending patterns of the late 1970s and early 1980s lends credence to the thesis that defense will have the lowest priority. Classical Marxism predicts that the country with the strongest economy will inevitably have the edge over its opponent, ideological justification for resisting a change in policy that could have dislocating consequences for China's economy. China's defense modernization program will be successful only if China enjoys prolonged political stability, retains access to foreign capital and technology, avoids military campaigns, and moves to modernize agriculture, industry, and science and technology.

3

TRADING BLOCKS

The thrust of China's trade policy is toward Japan, Western Europe, and the United States. Japan is well ahead of the field because of proximity and other special links. Of European countries, West Germany will maintain its lead. The United States, however, will enjoy the most growth, because traders will exploit tariff changes.

Sino-Japanese Relations

Following the split with the Soviet Union in the early 1960s after the failure of the Great Leap, China turned toward Japan to expand trade. By the mid-1960s, Japan had become China's leading trade partner, accounting for 14.9 percent in 1966. Between 1960–72, Japan's trade value and volume grew 10 percent each year, twice China's overall trade growth. Why has Japan achieved trade primacy with China? Price. Quality. Customer relations. Ability to bargain effectively. Technological leadership in many industries. Japan is China's most natural partner. Japan is closer to China than any other industrial country and has the best transportation links to it. The Japanese economy is advanced in areas where China is weakest, especially in technology and industry. China is well endowed with resources Japan lacks, notably coal and oil. China does three times more trade with Japan than any other country. The value of

Sino-Japanese trade has regularly exceeded $3 billion each year. In 1980, F.O.B. exports from Japan were $5.1 billion. C.I.F. imports came to $4.3 billion. Japan's share of China's total two-way trade was 25.2 percent, far more than any other country. An idea of the size of China's growing trade may be gained by considering the Japan-China Long-Term Trade Agreement (appendix six). In February 1978, Tokyo and Beijing signed a $20 billion two-way trade agreement. Seven months later, Japan proposed the amount be doubled. China granted Japan exclusive rights to extract oil from Bohai Wan. The Chinese will trade crude oil for Japanese steel and factories. Basically, the agreement is a form of barter, but Japanese exports of plants and technology will be made on a deferred basis. A $4 billion plant in Shanghai will be the largest project of this kind. Japanese firms and Foreign Trade Corporations will execute actual transactions under separate contracts. The largest part of Japanese exports will be iron and steel. This agreement is the first in Sino-Japanese history to commit Japan to a long-term target for buying Chinese oil or coal. Purchasing had been conducted semi-annually or annually. The Japanese will drill in shallow water. For deep-water sites off the continental shelf, China wants the most advanced technological help possible. This will mean U.S. corporate involvement. Japan gets 90 percent of its oil from the Middle East through U.S. multinationals. America's control of oil flow is a potent tool of leverage. Accordingly, Japan is seeking ways to diversify suppliers. The Japan National Oil Company negotiates with China and refines Chinese oil in Japanese-owned refineries.

Beside oil, China exports food, raw materials, and agriculturally-based manufactured goods to Japan. Excluding mineral fuels, 84 percent of China's exports were related to agriculture in 1978. China and Japan have exchanged large numbers of delegations concerned with steel, transportation, and communications. Although Japan's dominance of China's foreign trade should continue, China will diversify foreign ties to avoid dependence on any single country or group of countries. This may lead to a leveling off of trade with Japan. Furthermore, Japan has trade ties with Taiwan, the U.S., OPEC, and Western Europe. These ties form a web of limitations affecting Sino-Japanese relations. China hopes capital and technology from firms such as Asahi Glass, Nippon Steel, and Komatsu meshed with Chinese labor will force economic take-off. However, it doesn't want to become Japan's coal bin or a dumping ground for cheap products. Sino-Japanese relations are good, but fears arising from history, anthropology, and politics could strain that relationship.

Sino-Western European Relations

"A specter is haunting Europe—the specter of communism." Karl Marx's opening words to the *Communist Manifesto* take on ironic meaning as

Chinese Communists roam Europe cutting capitalist deals. For 4,000 years, China has regarded the rest of the globe with contempt. Two hundred years have come and gone since Western Europe pioneered the Industrial Revolution and the socialism on which China's Communism is based. It says much for its historic disdain of the outside world that a Chinese head of state has tarried until the final quarter of the 20th century to visit this quarter of the world. Chairman Hua Guofeng's 1979 European tour reflects the Politburo's wish to carve diplomatic beachheads throughout the West. China wants to assure that all is not quiet on the Western front, making it impossible for Moscow to relax deployment in Warsaw Pact regions or send more troops to the Sino-Soviet border. Thus, China has tacitly supported the Atlantic Alliance, the Common Market, and the striking Poles at the Lenin Shipyard in Gdansk. In 1975, China opened diplomatic relations with the European Economic Community (EEC). In 1978, China signed a nonpreferential (MFN) trade agreement with the EEC, which established a joint trade commission that meets yearly, alternately in Beijing and Brussels. The EEC will liberalize import quotas and restrictions that pertain to Chinese goods, and China will "give favorable consideration" to imports from the EEC. Both sides will try to balance trade. China will be able to expand imports from the EEC since high technology can match China's needs. The EEC will find it hard to increase Chinese imports because the market for such traditional goods as silk, furs, and porcelain is shallow. Raw materials, particularly tungsten, tin, and antimony, will compensate the difference (appendix six).

Even before Mao died, China courted countries on Russia's southern flank. The Federal Republic of Germany, in particular, was second only to Japan in supplying industrial goods to China during the early 1970s. But the post-Mao leadership has moved further to promote a tougher policy toward Russia, and to offer the People's Republic as a willing trade partner and a good market for arms. Accordingly, China has shopped widely for goods. Carrying buttons-to-bombs shopping lists, China has concluded deals with nearly all West European countries. Beijing conspicuously favors the European right and Communist heretics, Yugoslavia, and Rumania. Yugoslavia's Marshal Josip Tito made his first China trip in 1977, paving the way for full normalization. Rumania's President Nicolae Ceasescu, who traveled to Beijing in 1978, has special standing with the Chinese, because he refused to side with Moscow during the Sino-Soviet quarrel. China's exploitation of Europe's fear of Kremlin duplicity is paying off. In 1978, Bonn hosted Soviet President Leonid Brezhnev, but little came from four days of talks over issues such as Berlin and Central European forces. The Soviet Union's deployment of SS–20 missiles has irked West Germany. Carrying three nuclear warheads, they could raze every European capital. China is capitalizing on the division between the Soviet west and European east.

The Europeans were among the first to export industrial goods to

China. In 1970, 67 percent of Western European exports to China consisted of manufactured products, of which iron and steel, nonferrous metals, and machinery and equipment were the most important. Western European purchases from China included crude materials—such as oilseeds, nuts and kernels, textile fibers, hides, skins and minerals—which accounted for 44 percent of total 1970 imports. In 1975, Western Europe accounted for 19 percent of China's foreign trade, the majority of which consisted of industrial imports. Since then, the Chinese have gone to the Swedes for help in mining, railroads, and telecommunications, the British for coal-mining equipment, and the Danes for help in improving shipping. In 1978, France concluded a $14 billion agreement, but readjustment forced Beijing to cancel Parisian contracts for two 900-megawatt nuclear reactor plants worth $2 billion. At Liaoyang, 30 miles south of Shenyang in northwest China, 40,000 Chinese and 130 foreigners (mostly French) are finishing one of China's largest petrochemical complexes. In 1973, China placed this contract with a group of French firms led by Technip and Speichim. The Liaoyang contract was part of a wave of orders for petrochemical, synthetic fiber, and fertilization plants between 1972–79. F. Uhde of Germany built a high-density polyethylene plant, and Snam Progetti of Italy built a polypropylene plant. With equipment from Japan and West Germany, China built fiber plants at Shanghai and Tianjin. Pullman Kellogg's Dutch subsidiary got a contract for handling eight urea fertilizer plants. British firms won contracts for oxo-alcohol and aeronautics plants. The Hawker Siddeley contract for Tridents and Rolls Royce engines was valued in excess of $300 million. In 1979, China and the United Kingdom signed a Long-Term Trade Agreement (LTTA) calling for bilateral trade totaling $14 billion over 1979–85. Before signing the LTTA, China and Britain had already reached a major agreement for the joint development of nonferrous mineral resources. In 1978, Lurgi signed an agreement to develop nonferrous metals and build two aromatic complexes at Shanghai and Nanjing. The Lurgi contracts are on a cash basis, financed through compensation trade. Lurgi's parent company, Metallgeschaft, one of the world's largest metal trading firms, will ship ore concentrates from China. In 1978, China placed an order worth $1 billion for mining equipment alone. Of this, West Germany got $500 million and Britain $200 million. Much of the German equipment is for mining in Jilin province. German exports also include chemicals, helicopters, and oil equipment.

Sino-United States Relations

During 30 years of hostility, including three years of combat in Korea, China typically denounced the United States as "a haven for imperialistic crooks." America responded in kind. In 1963, for example, President John F. Kennedy spoke of China as a regime itching for war and a menace to the United States. Such feeling was in the mainstream of thought. Tensions in Berlin and Cuba, terrorism in Burma and Malaya, and the invasion of South Korea aroused Western leaders. They looked at the face of Communism and saw a form of totalitarianism that retained the core of the method and spirit of fascism. Today, pragmatism is shaping both nations into a coalition of shared purposes. Perhaps this can transcend— or outlast—ideological differences.

A short history

The cycle of hostility and hospitality between the U.S. and China started when the first Yankee clipper sailed for Guangzhou in 1784. When the *Empress of China* returned to the United States laden with silks and spices, the captain turned a profit of 35 percent. The American fantasy— that the U.S. could be China's protector—began about the turn of this century. On one hand, there was the zeal, mostly idealistic, of missionaries in China. Every year following World War I, a thousand missionaries were on furlough from China. They brought to their parishes tales of disease, poverty, and ignorance. Americans contributed money not only for the salvation of souls but for healing the body and improving the mind. "Hardly a town in our land was without its society to collect funds and clothing for Chinese missions," Secretary of State Dean Acheson writes. "Thus was nourished the love portion of our love-hate relationship that was to infuse so much emotion into our later China policy." America's treatment of its Chinese population represented the converse of this relationship. In the 19th century, Chinese "coolies" were recruited and sometimes shanghaied to work on the railroads. The American reaction to them was often discriminatory, even hysterical, although the Chinese were usually hardworking and thrifty. Racist agitation brought congressional exclusion acts and quotas in 1917 and 1921.

Following the establishment of the People's Republic in 1949, U.S. diplomats stayed to see what China's attitude would be toward the United States. It showed no interest in an official American presence, so the U.S. withdrew diplomatic representation in 1950. In 1951, the United States recognized Taiwan as China's true government, "even though the territory under its control is severely restricted. The Beijing regime," Dean Rusk said at the time, "is not the government of China. It does not pass the first test. It is not Chinese." The Korean War further polarized perceptions of each nation's goals. Typically, China thought the United States was trying to achieve world hegemony, strengthen neo-colonial, dependent economies, and uphold the structures of imperialistic power. Typically, the United States thought China was trying to forge a new, militant Red bloc with Beijing as its leader, become the dominant force in Asia by sapping the Free World's power and prestige, and prove that wars of liberation can be fought victoriously anywhere. The fall of Nationalist China came as a shock to the U.S. public, with its feeling of friendship toward the Chinese. The revolution's success became political ammunition against the Democratic Party. Although ensuing congressional investigations of the State Department didn't substantiate the theory that Communist infiltration was responsible for the Communist's victory, the inquisitional atmosphere, fanned by excesses of the McCarthy era, did irreparable damage. China specialists were fired or transferred, and frank assessments from those best qualified were not always forthcoming because of reluctance to express views that might be labeled "communistic." In 1955, bilateral contacts were made at the ambassadorial level in Geneva and Warsaw. There China and the United States agreed to repatriate nationals. While these talks didn't produce substantial changes, they gave both governments a better understanding of each other's views, thus reducing the risk of war by miscalculation. America's need for direct dialogue became clear as Sino-Soviet relations cooled. This could not be done easily, for the two countries had been bitter antagonists since the Korean War. President Harry S Truman had ordered the U.S. Seventh Fleet into the Taiwan Straits, thereby depriving Beijing of the chance to complete the revolution by "liberating" Taiwan. Moreover, the ring of American bases surrounding China's perimeter and its "police action" in Viet Nam were threats to China's security. U.S. steps to normalize relations included ending restrictions on passports for travel to China and allowing trade to China on the same basis as most other Communist nations. Buoyed by domestic accomplishment and by a more favorable outlook in the United Nations, the Chinese, while at international table-tennis matches in Japan, invited the American table-tennis team to China—the first official invitation to Americans to the mainland since the Communists took power. Then, in one of the boldest actions of his life, Mao invited President Richard M. Nixon for an eight-day visit to China in February 1972, opening the way for strategic cooperation between the world's strongest nation and the most populous nation. Nixon called this trip an historic beginning in building a "bridge across 16,000 miles and twenty-two years of hostility" that had divided the United States and the People's Republic. In Shanghai, Nixon and Prime Minister Zhou issued a communique outlining principles that won accord. Both sides agreed to expand contacts in science, technology, culture, sports, and journalism, to facilitate trade, and to maintain official channels (appendix seven).

Because of this shift in orientation, Sino-American trade jumped dramatically in 1971–72. Much of this trade was in grain. By 1973, America was China's second largest trading partner, a position maintained in 1974 when trade surpassed $1 billion. The most significant political event in the post-Mao era was the normalization of relations between China and the

United States in 1979. In the year prior to normalization, Japan had signed a $20 billion trade agreement with China, France had negotiated a $14 billion trade agreement, and Britain managed a $1.2 billion deal for exports and credits. President Jimmy Carter decided it was time to accept "simple reality" and recognize the People's Republic of China. With the full normalization of diplomatic and commercial relations, the United States became China's second greatest supplier of imports and third largest partner in overall trade. In 1979, the U.S. was the leading supplier of agricultural products to China. In March 1979, the two nations elevated liaison offices to embassy status. A year later, they put into effect a most favored nation agreement signed in July 1979. The MFN clause means tariffs on Beijing's goods will be reduced to the lowest rates levied on imports from other U.S. trading partners. It guarantees that concessions granted to each other by either of the two contracting parties shall be extended to all other nations having similar treaties with either of the two contracting parties. High tariffs on nations not having MFN status inhibit sales. For more than 50 years, the United States has generally followed an unconditional MFN policy in its trading relations. However, under provisions of the Trade Agreement Extension Act of 1951, Congress withdrew MFN status from all nations "under the control of international communism." The Trade Expansion Act of 1962 expanded this definition to include "all Communist countries." The Chinese attach great importance to MFN; it shows the nations have a relationship consistent with "conditions of equality and mutual benefit." A second-class relationship would compel China to seek deals elsewhere. The trade agreement also provides for protection of patents, copyrights, and trademarks, arbitration procedures, and safeguards against market disruption.

Since the 1972 Shanghai *Communique*, U.S. trade has grown from a few million dollars to $5.5 billion in 1981, an increase of 14.3 percent over 1980. The level of trade between 1972–82 fluctuated substantially because of changes in China's purchase of agricultural goods. Wheat continues to be America's prime export commodity to China. Sales in 1981 amounted to $1.3 billion, a 22 percent increase over 1980. China's buying plans, influenced by harvest yields, industrialization plans, political disruption, hard currency shortages, and other considerations, has demonstrated China's ability to change quickly. From a balance of trade of negative $800 million in 1974 for total Chinese trade, China reduced imports and expanded exports to the point of achieving over $1 billion in trade surpluses in 1976. The U.S.-China trade position reflected this change, going from U.S. surpluses of $675 million in 1973 to a deficit of $32 million in 1977. In most years, the United States has enjoyed an export surplus. In 1980, exports to China ($3.7 billion) exceeded imports by $2.7 billion. America's share of the Chinese market has been small, but is expanding. In 1977, the U.S. share was 2.5 percent. In 1981, it came to 13 percent. In the same period, Japan's share rose marginally 0.4 percent to 24.3 percent. In 1978, Deng Xiaoping, China's senior vice premier, remarked that "as far as volume of trade between China and the U.S. is concerned, surely it will not be less than our trade with Japan." February 28th, 1982 marked the tenth anniversary of the Shanghai *Communique,* in which both sides agreed to "facilitate the progressive development of trade between the two countries." In those 10 years, trade has grown rapidly, to a total of $16.9 billion. Three-quarters of that trade occurred since the United States established diplomatic relations on January 1, 1979. Such growth is clear indication that expanding economic relations are partly a function of healthy diplomatic relations.

The Taiwan question

Having heard stories of the chaos of the regime's final years on the mainland, visitors to the Republic of China on Taiwan depart amazed. The island's cities are filled with active, nourished, adequately clothed people. Taiwan is one of the best run and least corrupt nations in Asia. An effective land-reform program eliminated rural destitution and absentee landlords. A Taiwanese—and this is no small matter compared with the fate of the Chinese—can choose his schools, occupation, and religion. If he has the money and time, he can travel to foreign lands. However, the national press is censored, and foreign newspapers that present an unfavorable image are forbidden. Jiang Zhongzheng (Chiang Kai-shek), who died in 1975, wielded absolute power. Martial law is still in full force "to combat the Communist menace." Military justice deals with any hint of political opposition. Even so, Taiwan's standard of living is superior to that of China. But Taiwan's modernity is due in no small measure to 30 years of financial help from the West. Between 1950–53, for example, the United States gave more than $1.25 billion of economic aid to the Nationalist government. This figure doesn't include the $2 billion charged in the same period to military aid.

Taiwan, like Israel, has made great strides since 1949, feels besieged by its neighbors, and has the support of strong U.S. lobbies. Saul Bellow's comments about the Israelis apply well to the Taiwanese: "No people has to work so hard on so many levels as this one," he writes in *To Jerusalem and Back.* "In less than thirty years, [they] have produced a modern country—doorknobs and hinges, plumbing fixtures, electrical supplies, chamber music, airplanes, teacups. It is both a garrison state and a cultivated society, both Spartan and Athenian. It tries to do everything, to understand everything, to make provision for everything. All resources, all facilities are strained." China still regards Taiwan as an errant province and has no choice but to woo Taibei with concessions and overtures of friendship. In 1981, Taiwan rejected the most specific proposal for reunification made by China since 1949. Ye Jianying, China's equivalent of a chief of state, suggested representatives meet for "an exhaustive exchange of views." "After the country is unified, Taiwan can enjoy a high degree of autonomy," he said. "It can retain its armed forces. The central government will not interfere with local affairs on Taiwan." The chance for peaceful union seems slim. Nevertheless, unofficial trade between China and Taiwan has flourished, amounting to $240 million in 1980. Taiwan supplied electronic and other technical products in exchange for food, herbal medicines, and traditional goods.

In the first of several major crises over Quemoy and Matsu following the Korean War, the United States incorporated the Republic of China into its Pacific defense system. A mutual defense treaty signed in 1954 pledged the United States to the defense of Taiwan. In 1978, Washington acknowledged a view shared by Nationalists: "There is one China and Taiwan is part of China." Except for fifty years as a colony of Japan, Taiwan has been part of China for three centuries. The *Communique on the Establishment of Diplomatic Relations* said the United States recognized Beijing as "the sole legal government of China." Then it affirmed: "Within this context, the people of the United States will maintain cultural, commercial, and other unofficial relations with the people of Taiwan" (appendix seven). On January 1, 1979, however, the United States formally recognized the People's Republic of China and severed diplomatic relations with Taiwan. It also terminated the Mutual Defense Treaty. Nevertheless, the United States will continue to sell "selective defensive weapons" to a government whose legitimacy the U.S. no longer accepts. The administration of President Ronald Reagan hinted at stronger U.S. support for Taiwan. However, a major objective of Reagan's Asian policy is to build up an anti-Soviet coalition involving the PRC. In 1982, the Reagan administration, in an effort to cultivate this strategic relationship, released an ambiguously worded communique announcing that the U.S. would reduce, and possibly halt, arms shipments to Taiwan. China meanwhile affirmed as policy its quest for "peaceful reunification" of Taiwan with China. Washington's insistence upon linking the reduction in arms sales to Taiwan with the Chinese pledge for peaceful reunification stalemated negotiations. The document said the U.S. government "does not seek to carry out a long-term policy of arms sales to Taiwan, that its arms sales to Taiwan will not exceed either in qualitative or in quantitative terms the level of those supplied in recent years since the establishment of diplomatic relations between the United States and China, and that it intends to gradually reduce its sales of arms to Taiwan, leading over a period of time to final resolution." The Chinese interpret the qualitative and quantitative stipulation to mean that current U.S. sales of weapons are the bench-mark for future sales. Administration officials say this language allows for more advanced weapons to be sold to Taiwan if China upgrades its own armaments. Similarly, while the Chinese insist "final resolution" means the U.S. will eventually cease arms shipments to Taiwan, the administration says this phrase refers to an overall solution to the reunification issue. U.S.-China "normalization" is a patchwork of communiques, declarations, and private understandings, with no end of nuance and much left unsaid and undone. Beijing has yet to reach a peaceful accommodation with Taibei, and, until that happens, the United States will provide for Taiwan's defense. To underscore this point, Reagan authorized the sale of sixty F-5E fighters, worth $240 million, to Taiwan two days after he issued the communique.

What, finally, are the implications of the Taiwan question? Since the 1950s, the crucial obstacle to improved relations from China's viewpoint was U.S. support of Taiwan. Taiwan remains a sensitive issue to U.S. investors, who have invested $500 million in Taiwan's enterprises. The U.S. Export-Import Bank has its third largest interest in Taiwan (following Brazil and Mexico), totaling $1.8 billion. Taiwan's annual trade of $24 billion ranks it among the world's top 20 trading nations. Its trade with the U.S. was $7.4 billion in 1978 and $9.6 billion in 1979. It exceeded $11 billion in 1980, up 29 percent over the previous year. Turnover between the People's Republic and the United States came to $4.8 billion in 1980, although mainland China's population is 65 times larger than Taiwan's. These are reasons why the U.S. cannot condone China's conversion of Taiwan into another Tibet. We can agree that there is only one China, and its capital is Beijing. Nevertheless, the trading community's interest will be best served by a relationship that doesn't threaten Taiwan's economic system.

Organizations in the private sector will find that a "two nation" policy will fail. Given the political situation and the prevailing suspicions on both sides of the straits, the notion that you can deal with both the People's Republic of China and Taiwan "equitably" is delusion. The decision is clear: either you must choose to work with one side or the other. You will make that decision within the context of your corporate values and goals.

Trading opportunities

In striving for modernization, China must import a wide range of capital equipment and technology. China has turned to the United States for some of these supplies. In areas such as offshore exploration and development, computers, and aircraft, U.S. firms have a competitive, technical advantage. The United States and China complement each other economically. China's rich resources of coal, oil, minerals, and hydraulic power need exploration and development, and the United States has advanced technology in these areas. Chinese construction and management is below world standards. American architects, engineers, contractors, and consultants could play a major role. Petrochemical technology, fertilizer processing, aircraft, machine tools, computers, and telecommunications equipment are categories in which U.S.-China trade has flourished. Crude petroleum has been the top U.S. import from China, accounting for over 15 percent in 1981. Gasoline and naphtha are also important imports, as are textile goods, chemicals, and handicrafts. As plans develop for modernization of oil and petrochemical industries, oil field exploration, drilling, and refinery know-how will be priority Chinese imports. The most successful area of U.S. sales to China in the early 1980s has been in petroleum exploration, drilling, and production equipment. In 1972–82, U.S. sales in this area totaled more than $150 million, and involved such firms as Dresser Industries, the National Supply Division of Aramco Steel Company, Baker Tool Company, Caterpiller Tractor, and many smaller firms. Steel plant technology, construction equipment, pulp and paper equipment, mining equipment, and advanced medical and scientific instrumentation are all promising areas for export of U.S. goods. Polyester staple and aluminum are U.S. commodities with notable export success in the past and strong prospects for the future.

America is particularly competitive in agribusiness. Chinese agriculture is relatively backward, and U.S. agricultural techniques are among the most advanced in the world. China imports grain and cotton, while the U.S. has a surplus of agricultural products. China is interested in buying seeds, fertilizer, and machinery. It has approached firms such as John Deere & Co. and International Harvester because their products will enhance agricultural productivity. Pullman's Kellogg unit, which builds large fertilizer processing plants, had people in China before the U.S. Liaison Office did. The Chinese have even consulted McDonald's about applying fast-food techniques for use in China. Agricultural products have consistently dominated U.S. exports and will continue to represent a major portion of U.S. sales for the foreseeable future. China operates on a thin cushion of domestic foodstuffs and the variability of its harvests will continue to make the United States a sporadic supplier of wheat, corn, cotton, and soybeans.

U.S. deals have burgeoned in recent years. China has issued invitations to a broad range of American firms—Exxon, U.S. Steel, the Continental Group, and hundreds of smaller companies. These firms have signed significant design and engineering contracts for iron mines, oil technology, raw materials, forestry products, agricultural machinery, and advanced machine tools. The Chinese are particularly interested in U.S. manufactured components, peripherals, small systems, seismic survey technology, specialized equipment, and quality controls and instrumentation. Highest on their shopping list is machinery to increase productivity without disrupting the labor-intensive balance of China's economy. They are also interested in products and services that can give a quick boost to their foreign currency income, such as tourism. For many U.S. firms, the Chinese market isn't a good one. Beijing won't import what Americans would most like to sell—consumer goods. China wants to buy the machine that makes the pencils, not the pencils themselves.

Goods from China that enter the U.S. market are subject to the same rules that apply to imports from other countries. Chinese products must meet all standards set by U.S. regulations—safety, pollution, labeling, and food and drug standards. Chinese foreign trade corporations have become more receptive to meeting these requirements.

Visiting scholars, diplomats, and businessmen agree: the Chinese like Americans. The reasons are historical. These are people whom Americans befriended in trade, missionary, and educational relations, and as allies in a great war. Of course, Americans aren't the only foreigners wooing the Chinese, but they do seem to enjoy a special relationship. Although British, French, or Japanese gear is sometimes cheaper, American firms have the edge. The reasons are practical; products marked 'Made in the U.S.A.' command a reputation for quality, style, and state-of-the-art sophistication. The Chinese assume American products must be the best since the United States is the leader in innovation. If the new protocol favors Americans, it also places them on the top rung of the price ladder. Americans with apartments in China pay double and sometimes triple the rent charged to, say, Mexicans. The reasons, finally, are political. China deems it important to trilateralize tensions among the superpowers. This balance checks any aggressive ambitions by any one of the three superpowers and it guards against any two of them combining against the third. However, our friendship and trade relations with China should not be a device to needle the Soviets. "There has been the temptation to deal with China on a purely tactical level—to tighten our bonds when we are annoyed at the Soviets and slacken them again when things calm down," former Secretary of State Henry A. Kissinger explained.

> "We need a long-term strategy that does not fluctuate with the ups and downs of our Moscow policy. We have a fundamental interest in the independence and territorial integrity of China. As China gets stronger, it may treat us with greater reserve; we should not delude ourselves about that. But in the next decade or so, there will be a considerable parallelism of interest, which we should conduct soberly and really almost independently of the Soviet Union."[1]

To the Chinese, political considerations eclipse all other considerations. Prior to normalization, China was reluctant to buy from the United States, unless the product was markedly superior. As a result, sales of American industrial goods were never large. In 1977, for example, the U.S. share in China's imports of manufactured goods from the industrialized West was

[1]Henry Kissinger, "Kissinger: What Next for the U.S." *TIME* (interview), May 12, 1980, p. 24.

only 2.9 percent in contrast to 15.8 percent for West Germany and 61.5 percent for Japan. Now that Sino-American diplomatic relations have been established, China won't discriminate against U.S. products for political reasons alone. If relations between Washington and Beijing deteriorate, however, U.S. trade will suffer. Historical sentiment and technical superiority are only two legs of the tripod. American recognition of China's strategic significance in international relations will sustain Sino-American ties and complete the tripod.

4

Appraising the Market

The feasibility study

In 1978, the *Beijing Review* published Mao's "Ten Principles of Military Operations."[1] Rotarian platitudes aside, we would do well to adapt his rules to commercial operations:

MAKING
CONTACT

1. Attack weak points of enemy forces first, then stronger ones.

2. Start small. Start rural.

3. Be forces oriented.

4. Concentrate and achieve local superiority. Annihilate the enemy.

5. Thoroughly plan and prepare.

6. Make a total commitment.

7. Stay mobile, but attack enemy positions.

8. Attack weak points of cities first, then stronger ones.

9. The enemy is our source of supplies.

10. Rest between exertions, but allow no respite.

Principle five suggests the need to prepare a feasibility study. A feasibility report is a predictive tool to gauge the likelihood of profitability of the China market. It gives

[1]"The Ten Major Principles of Military Operations," *Beijing Review*, March 24, 1978, p. 8.

you a charter for redirecting corporate strategy and a structure for judging the situation on its merits rather than on your preconceptions. The aims of the study are as follows:

1.   To estimate the probable market for your product or service.

2.   To clarify goals of your venture.

3.   To define a sales strategy.

4.   To calculate the cash flow projections and funds repayment capacity.

A market-oriented firm will constantly try to know its customers and their requirements better. This knowledge will reduce the chance that market changes will take that firm by surprise. In making a marketing forecast, the minimum approach entails contacting customers, suppliers, competitors, local export groups, banks, and service organizations who can give advice. A second approach requires spending more money than the minimum approach, but the cost of a mistake could well exceed the cost of your research. Your firm must generate a systematic picture of its relevant opportunities by first considering: growth opportunities within its present product-market scope, i.e., market penetration, market development, and product development; opportunities within its core marketing system, such as backward, forward, and horizontal integration; and finally opportunities outside its core marketing system, such as concentric, horizontal, and conglomerate diversification. Market segmentation, market positioning, market entry strategy, marketing-mix strategy, and timing strategy are elements in ascertaining overall feasibility. The grand design must be translated into discrete, concrete tactical plans that specify sales targets, budgets, and work assignments. The feasibility report, therefore, should cover these areas:

1.   The current market situation.

2.   Problems, opportunities, objectives.

3.   Strategies to meet problems and objectives.

4.   Marketing tactics.

All questions can be reduced to one question: Does it pay? Or, more precisely, will entry into the China market reap a justifiable return on investment? The return on investment is the benefit the investor receives over his original investment. However, we must take the broad view. ROI should also imply return on ideas, return on innovation, return on improvement, return on individuals—worthy considerations in embarking on any enterprise. Your objective is to deliberate a choice that will optimize outcome. Deliberation consists of your capacity to define the criteria of successful action, evaluate the consequences of each alternative course of action, compare the consequences of each course of action with the criteria, and identify the course of action that conforms most closely with the criteria. To make a decision, you need hard, unshakable facts, real facts, not assumed facts. Experts and surveys can provide this information. The actual choice will involve a trade-off between accuracy and expenditures of time and money. You must weigh the anticipated benefits of uncertainty reduction against the estimated cost of information, judging the quality of that information by its validity and reliability. Validity indicates whether an investigation measures what it intends to measure. Reliability, a subset of validity, indicates the extent of random variation. It guarantees only that the results of duplications of the study will be consistent. It doesn't insure the results are correct. In deliberating whether to act, you will use statistical methods, such as correlation, cycle, end-use, and input-output analysis. However, only the most simple decisions lend themselves to pure quantification. Computer-spun gaming presents only an illusion of precision. But computer programs cannot represent certain fundamental realities, such as the psychology of consumers in different cultures. High-level deliberation depends more on hunches, gossip, and gut instinct than on the disciplined analysis needed to solve Euclid's *Pons Asinorum*. Thus, you will turn to non-numerical forms of thinking (the delphi method, executive consensus, historical analogy, scenario creation, and mature judgment) to obtain final resolution.

Successful importing and exporting is really no more than matching products to markets. Exporters should determine the potential market for their goods and services in China. Importers should ascertain China's ability to produce the commodities they desire. These questions, difficult enough in any country, are more complex in the Chinese context. China releases little information about its economy and even less about its trading plans. The purpose of this book isn't to provide specific answers to your marketing questions, but to show where you can find them. The following sources of information will suggest the shape of China's market. They will be the basis for drafting the feasibility plan and proposal.

The National Council for U.S.-China Trade

The Washington-based National Council for U.S.-China Trade is the starting point for U.S. firms judging the China market. Financed by membership dues from 500 firms, this private, non-profit organization can smooth the way for making contact with China. It was established in 1973 with encouragement from both governments to promote bilateral trade. The council has close ties at all levels of the Chinese government. It maintains excellent working relations with the State Economic Commission, the Bank of China, the Ministry of Foreign Economic Relations, the China Council for the Promotion of International Trade, and many industrial ministries and bureaus of the State Council. Recognizing that the size of firm doesn't exclude it from success in Chinese markets, the council offers an affiliate status to companies with sales or gross revenues of less than $10 million. The council hosts bilateral trade delegations, sponsors conferences on topics of trade interest, and represents firms wanting to deal with China to both Chinese and American authorities. It allows access to files of resumés of China specialists seeking private sector employment. The council issues timely market alerts, including purchasing interests of Chinese corporations and factories and invitations to bid on equipment. It also publishes a confidential newsletter, organization charts, and industrial maps. The council's most important publication, *China Business Review*, is an authoritative source on developments in China's trade. The *Review* contains interviews with officials, reprints speeches on trade-related matters, analyzes certain developments, and provides coverage of the Guangzhou Trade Fair. The journal is free to members, available to others on a subscription basis. Even if you choose not to become a member of the council, we recommend you subscribe. (Prentice-Hall International distributes National Council publications outside the United States.) Export Industrial Committees (EICs) are under the council's aegis. They promote trade, communications, and technical exchange between U.S. and Chinese firms. They also help in sending delegations to China, developing position papers and staff briefings, and maintaining a good relationship with China's Washington embassy. These committees provide member firms newly attracted to the China market with opportunities to make initial contact. More established firms use EICs to monitor developments and keep their presence before Chinese eyes. The council's Washington, D.C. library houses the most complete and up-to-date collection of materials on China's trade economy in the United States. It has over a quarter of a million articles, compilations of U.S. and Chinese laws, statistics on China's foreign trade and economy, information on Chinese organizations, and specialized, bilingual technical directories. A research staff will respond to telephone and letter requests for information from members. The council's Beijing office is staffed with bilingual personnel. Because of daily contact, the council can get timely information from the Chinese on trade policy, personnel changes, business negotiations, and market opportunities. This information is wired to the United States, where it's disseminated to interested firms the same day. The office can also indicate whether your proposal is still under discussion. Representatives visiting Beijing can use its services, which include temporary secretarial, confidential message, mail, telex, and cable receipt services, photocopying, and meeting space.

Main office:
    1050 17th Street, Suite 350
    Washington, DC 20036
    Phone: (202) 429–0340
    Cable: USCHINTRAD
    Telex: 64517

China office:
    Beijing Hotel, Suite 1136
    Beijing
    Phone: 55.1361
    Cable: USCHINTRAD
    Telex: 22637

Research centers

Outside the United States, major collections of current information on China include the following:

Canada:
    Federal Government Department of Industry, Trade, and Commerce
    Asia Division, China Desk
    240 Queen Street
    Ottawa, Ontario K1A OH4

    Canada-China Trade Council
    199 Bay Street, Suite 900
    Toronto, Ontario M5J 1L4

Hong Kong:
    Office of the Commission for Canada
    Asian House, 14/15 Floor
    1 Hennessey Road
    P.O. Box 20264
    Phone: 5–282422

    Chinese Chamber of Commerce
    24 Connaught Road
    Central
    Phone: 5–234191

    American Chamber of Commerce
    322 Edinburgh House
    Phone: 5–234380

    United States Consulate
    Commercial/Economic Section
    26 Garden Road
    Phone: 5–239011

Japan:
    The Japan External Trade Organization
    2 Akasaka Aoi Cho
    Minato-ku, Tokyo

United Kingdom:
    The Sino-British Trade Council
    25 Queen Anne's Gate
    London, SW1

Banks

Chinese banks or banks with China ties are sources of information about currency restrictions, credit terms, and the political and economic situation. The Bank of China, the foreign exchange arm of China's banking system, carries out international financial transactions. It monitors foreign exchange receipts and expenditures, issues letters of credit and guarantee, and arranges foreign currency loans to finance expensive import items. U.S.-based banks can offer a number of services, including working capital loans, short-term advances against shipping and collection documents, direct loans to foreign importers, handling of letters of credit and drafts, and assistance in locating Chinese markets.

Chinese banks:

Bank of China
Beijing Branch
17 Xi Jiao Ming Xiang
Phone: 330887
Cable: HOCHUNGHUO BEIJING

Bank of China
Guangzhou Branch
137 Chang Ti
Cable: CHUNGKUO GUANGZHOU
Telex: 44074 BKCA CN
          44075 BKCA CN

Bank of China
Hong Kong Branch
BOC-2A,
Des Voeux Road
Phone: 5-234191

Bank of China
Luxembourg Branch
9-11 Grand Rue
Phone: 21791 (all departments)
          26934 (foreign exchange)
Cable: CHUNGKUO LUXEMBOURG
Telex: 3546

The Hong Kong and Shanghai Banking Corp.
1 Queen's Road
Central,
P.O. Box 64
Hong Kong
Phone: 5-222011
Cable: HONGBANK HONGKONG
Telex: 73205 HSBC HX

The Hong Kong and Shanghai Banking Corp.
Shanghai Branch
P.O. Box 151
185 Yuan Ming Yuan Road
Phone: 218283
Cable: HONGBANK
Telex: 33058 HSBC CN

The Hong Kong and Shanghai Banking Corp.
New York Branch
5 World Trade Center
New York, NY   10048
Phone: (212) 839-5000

In the United States, the Hong Kong and Shanghai Banking Corporation has offices and agencies in Chicago, Seattle, San Francisco, and Los Angeles. It also has offices in a number of other countries, including France, Germany, the Netherlands, Switzerland, the United Kingdom, Canada, Australia, New Zealand, and Japan.

The Chartered Bank
P.O. Box 21
4-4A Des Voeux Road
Central, Hong Kong
Phone: 5-224011
Telex: 73230 CHABK HX

U.S. banks:
Bank of America
International Banking Office
315 Mongomery Street
San Francisco, CA   94104
Phone: (415) 622-3456

Bank of America
Hong Kong Branch
Fowwah Centre
210 Castle Teak Road
Phone: 12-434241

The Chase-Manhattan Bank, N.A.
1 Chase Manhattan Plaza
New York, NY   10015
Phone: (212) 555-2222

The Chase-Manhattan Bank publishes the biweekly *East-West Market*. This report covers developments in trade with Communist countries. More information is available from Chase World Information Corporation, One World Trade Center, New York, NY   10048.

The First National Bank of Chicago
Worldwide Banking Department, China Group
One First National Plaza
Chicago, IL   60670
Phone: (312) 732-4000

The First National Bank of Chicago
Beijing Branch
c/o Beijing Hotel, Room 7022
Beijing, Peoples Republic of China
Mailing Address:
FNBC
P.O. Box 9031
Beijing, Peoples Republic of China
Suite 0375
Phone: 55–2232, 55–6531, 55–8331, 55–7266

Service and trade organizations

The following organizations can also give you data and tips on China's competitive possibilities. They can often provide more useful advice in a few minutes than a firm could get by having someone spend days scanning publications.

Agribusiness Council
299 Park Avenue
New York, NY   10017

American Apparel Manufacturers Association
1611 North Kent Street
Arlington, VA   22209

American Iron & Steel Institute
150 East 42nd Street
New York, NY   10017

American Textiles Manufacturers Institute
1501 Johnson Building
Charlotte, NC   28281

Chamber of Commerce of the United States
International Division
Washington, DC   20062

Electronic Industries Association
2001 "I" Street, N.W.
Washington, DC   20006

Far East-America Council of Commerce and Industry
1270 Avenue of the Americas
New York, NY   10020

International Executives Association, Inc.
One World Trade Center, Suite 1207
New York, NY   10048

Motor and Equipment Manufacturers Association
P.O. Box 439
Teaneck, NJ   07666

National Association of Manufacturers
1776 F Street, N.W.
Washington, DC   20006

National Foreign Trade Council
10 Rockefeller Plaza
New York, NY   10020

National Machine Tool Builders Association
7901 Westpark Drive
McLean, VA   22101

Other organizations

Depending on your requirements, you may also want to check these organizations:

- University libraries
- State development agencies
- Transportation companies, freight forwarders, and custom house brokers, especially in Hong Kong
- International organizations (The United Nations, for example, publishes national trade and production statistics in its *UN Statistical Yearbook*, *Monthly Bulletin of Statistics*, and *Commodity Trade Statistics, Series D*. However, to identify appropriate data from these publications, you must first know what the commodity classification numbers are for your product. The United Nations' *Standard International Trade Classification* is a guide to the Standard International Trade Classification System, used by 80 percent of UN member countries.)

Online databases

To remain competitive, you must have access to new facts and ideas. But, because of the explosion of knowledge and the constraints of time, you face information overload. Most university libraries have online databases. Using certain keywords, you can search through thousands of book, magazine, and journal summaries to get information you need. Some packages will print one-paragraph abstracts. Using this online system allows the computer to screen unnecessary information and pinpoint subjects of specific interest, such as Chinese bauxite mining in 1982. Stipulating pertinent nouns and time-frames, you may search for specific titles. You can also search the databank retrospectively for specific topics or establish a personalized menu that selects articles of interest as they are added to the databank each month. Databases save time and present a broader perspective than you would otherwise glean through normal reading. ABI/Inform, the largest and oldest management and business information database, covered 550 journals worldwide in 1982. No single person could possibly read 550 journals. Since the state of the art is relatively new and better products are coming out every year, it would be a disservice to recommend particular packages. Instead, we suggest you consult CGS's annual *Directory of Online Information Resources*. Each listing includes a description of the database, who produces and sells it, and where those firms or persons are located:

> CSG Press
> 11301 Rockville Pike
> Kensington, MD   20895

Research guides

The manual equivalent of online databases are research guides, available in most libraries:

> *Facts on File.* An index and summary of current events, year by year, updated weekly.
>
> *Reader's Guide to Periodical Literature.* An index to widely-circulated magazine articles.
>
> *The Business Periodicals Index.* A cumulative index to business periodicals.
>
> *Technical Book Review Index.* Digests of book reviews of scientific, technical, and business books.
>
> *F & S Index International.* An index to international business news.
>
> *The New York Times Index.* An index of articles appearing in *The New York Times.*
>
> *Far Eastern Economic Review Index.* A quarterly index of articles appearing in the *Far Eastern Economic Review.*

Newspapers

Newspapers are always good sources of data and analysis. *The New York Times*, Britain's *Financial Times*, and Hong Kong's *South China Morning Post* cover China's trade extensively. China's first English-language newspaper began publication on June 1, 1981. The *China Daily* is published five days a week:

China Daily
Circulation Department
2 Jintai Xilu
Chao Yang District
Beijing
Cable: 2492

Books and periodicals

Since the days of Marco Polo, Westerners have found Chinese commerce enigmatic and exasperating. Publishers have risen to the challenge. Today, thousands of books on China line our shelves. It is futile, therefore, to offer an exhaustive bibliography. However, we can recommend a few volumes. The books listed in the bibliography have helped enhance our understanding of China and can help you close gaps of information in this book with a wealth of information and insight.

The editorial staff of appropriate trade magazines can provide further perspective. *Ulrich's International Periodical Directory* (R.R. Bowker Co., New York) can help isolate names of publications that deal with your specific interest. The following magazines are useful sources of information on China, both in terms of editorial and advertising content:

Asian Affairs: An American Review
(Bimonthly)
The American-Asian Education Exchange
88 Morningside Drive
New York, NY   10027

Asian Affairs: Journal of the Royal Society for Asian Affairs
(Triannual)
The Royal Society for Asian Affairs
42 Devonshire Street
London, W1N 1LN
United Kingdom

Asia Letter
(Weekly)
Asia Letter Ltd.
P.O. Box 3477
Sheungwan Post Office
Hong Kong

Asia Quarterly
(Quarterly)
Centre d'Etude du Sud-Est Asiatique et de l'Extreme Orient
Avenue Jeanne 44
B-1050
Brussels, Belgium

Asian Studies Indexed Journal Reference Guide
(Annual)
UCIS Publications
G-6 Mervis Hall
University of Pittsburgh
Pittsburgh, PA   15260

Asian Survey
(Monthly)
University of California Press
Berkeley, CA   94720

The Asian Wall Street Journal
(Weekly)
22 Cortlandt Street
New York, NY   10007

The Broadsheet
(Monthly)
China Policy Study Group
62 Parliament Hill
London,   NW3 2JT
United Kingdom

Business China
(Monthly)
Business International Asia/Pacific Ltd.
Asia House
One Hennessey Road
P.O. Box 385
Hong Kong

China Aktuell
(Monthly)
Institut für Asienkunde
Rothenbaumchaussee 32
2000 Hamburg 13
Federal Republic of Germany

China Business News
(Weekly)
China Business News, Inc.
475 Fifth Avenue, Suite 1210
New York, NY   ·10017

China Business Report
(Monthly)
Institute for International Research, Ltd.
70 Warren Street
London
United Kingdom

China Business Review
(Bimonthly)
National Council for U.S.-China Trade
1050 17th Street, N.W., Suite 350
Washington, DC   20036

China Council Report
(Quarterly)
China Council, Asia Society
133 East 58th Street
New York, NY   10022

China Economic News
(Weekly)
Economic Information & Consultancy Co.
342 Hennessey Road, 12th Floor
Hong Kong

China Exchange Newsletter
(Six times yearly)
Committee for Scholarly Communication with
the People's Republic of China
National Academy of Science
2101 Constitution Avenue, N.W.
Washington, DC   20418

China Newsletter
(Bimonthly)
Japan External Trade Organization
2–5, Toranomon 2-chome
Minato-ku
Tokyo 107
Japan

China Sources
(Monthly)
China Media Ltd.
P.O. Box 4436
Kowloon, Central
Hong Kong

Far Eastern Economic Review
(Weekly)
P.O. Box 160
Hong Kong

Quarterly Economic Review: China
(Quarterly)
Economist Intelligence Unit
Spencer House
27 St. James Place
London, SW1A 1NT
United Kingdom

China publishes a number of journals in Chinese with English tables of contents, including *Chemistry Bulletin, Architecture Journal,* and *Science Bulletin.* Guozi Shudian, China's exporter of books and periodicals, distributes trade literature. China's weekly *Beijing Review,* monthly *China Reconstructs,* and monthly *China's Foreign Trade* have useful articles. However, its reports aren't necessarily more focused than Western analyses. In 1979, when China's State Statistical Bureau released economic figures for the first time in 24 years, Chinese officials privately admitted some numbers came from declassified CIA reports:

> Guozi Shudian
> P.O. Box 399
> Beijing
> Cable: GUOZI BEIJING
> Phone: 891178

> Peace Book Company
> Chung Shang Building 7/F
> 9–10 Queen Victoria Street
> Hong Kong
> Cable: PEACEBOOK HONG KONG

U.S. government organizations

In 1981, the United States amassed a balance of trade deficit of $39.7 billion, the highest to date. The deficit with Japan alone was nearly $16 billion. These figures explain why the U.S. government is eager to help you develop foreign markets. The departments of the Treasury, Agriculture, and Energy can provide a range of specialized services. The Department of State and the U.S. Customs Service can be particularly useful:

> Department of State
> 2201 "C" Street, N.W.
> Washington, DC   20520
> Phone: (202) 655–4000

> U.S. Customs Service
> 1301 Constitution Avenue, N.W.
> Washington, DC   20229
> Phone: (202) 566–8195

The U.S. Government Printing Office publishes many illuminating reports describing China's business climate and trade. For a catalog of listings, write to:

> United States Government Printing Office
> Superintendent of Documents
> Washington, DC   20402
> Phone: (202) 783–3238

U.S. government publications include Congressional Committee reports, studies by agencies of the Executive branch, and papers from the Congressional Research Service, the research arm of the U.S. Library of Congress. The Congressional Information Service (CIS), a commercial firm, has indexed and abstracted the great bulk of these studies. *The CIS Index to Congressional Publications and Laws* is published in monthly supplements for quick access and then cumulated annually for efficient backlog research:

Congressional Information Service
7101 Wisconsin Avenue, N.W.
Washington, DC   20014

The Department of Commerce can assist in both market analyses and products selection. It offers traders the world's best array of trade information services. It has published market studies and has an ongoing effort to develop further market information. The People's Republic of China Division in the International Trade Administration of the Department of Commerce keeps abreast of Chinese foreign trade policies, organizations, and projects. This division also prepares an annual report on *China's Economy and Foreign Trade:*

The United States Department of Commerce
International Trade Administration
PRC Affairs Division, Room 4044
Washington, DC   20230
Phone: (202) 377–3583/4681

Specialists in the Trade Development and Assistance Division follow developments in important economic sectors such as petroleum equipment, construction equipment, and telecommunications technology in China and other centrally-planned economies. They track Chinese market conditions and advise on the appropriate Chinese organization to contact:

Office of East-West Trade Development
Trade Development and Assistance Division, Room 4816
Washington, DC   20230
Phone: (202) 377–2835

The Trade Promotion Division is responsible for the Commerce department's activities in sponsoring trade exhibitions in China and for organizing delegations to China:

Office of East-West Trade Development
Trade Promotion Division, Room 4823
Washington, DC   20230
Phone: (202) 377–4161

The Central Intelligence Agency's National Foreign Assessment Center issues timely analyses on China's trade dynamics, such as *China: International Trade Quarterly Review.* To get subscriptions to CIA publications, contact:

Document Expediting (DOCEX) Project
Exchange and Gift Division
Library of Congress
Washington, DC   20540

or:

National Technical Information Service
5285 Port Royal Road
Springfield, VA   22161
Phone: (703) 557-4650

You may buy specific publications in paper form or microfilm. Direct questions concerning these reports to:

The Director of Public Affairs
Central Intelligence Agency
Washington, DC   20505
Phone: (703) 351-7676

The corporate intelligence agency

The stakes and resources of many firms doing international business justify the establishment of a Corporate Intelligence Agency. Anyone considering doing business with China, where downside risk is great, should form such a group. For most firms, this formation will mean reorganization rather than the creation of a new department. Personnel from marketing, operations, finance, and planning are candidates for consolidation. The power of this group should correlate with the development of the overall organization. As trade expands, the structure will evolve from an import/export shop to an international department and finally to a multinational division with areawide markets and operating strategies. The purpose of a corporate intelligence system is to spot, analyze, and deal with social, political, and economic trends that bear on the execution of the corporate mission. It's a centralized, systematic means of focusing attention on political risks. That a corporation should get involved in political intelligence is a new concept, although such firms as Mitsubishi Electric Corporation and Royal Dutch/"Shell" have long had stellar groups. This might explain why Japanese and European firms have done well in global markets compared to U.S. firms. Traditionally, companies based overseas investment decisions almost exclusively on such economic factors as per capita income, wage levels, tax rates. They felt political risk was the bailiwick of the State Department and the Central Intelligence Agency. But no longer can you plunge into foreign ventures merely by relying on the strength of Washington's judgment. Government officials have their axes to grind—the reduction of the balance of payments deficit, and the expansion of political influence through market penetration. The job of the corporate intelligence agency isn't to duplicate existing analyses, but to confirm and expand on them. A strong secretariat will anticipate problems before they reach the critical stage. It will recognize when company foreign policy needs an overhaul. Such an organization must be staffed by professionals. First-hand experience in lands and languages abroad is desirable, but they must all share a contempt for dogma, provincialism, and bureaucracy. Building a flexible, creative second-level team that will not shy from dissent will require the support of senior management. In fact, the agency's head should have voting representation at all top-level deliberations.

As worldwide economic and political conditions continue to churn, some managers prefer to solicit assessments from outside the firm. They hire consultants to analyze market and political risk, weave those assessments into corporate strategy, and offer custom-tailored advice on how to minimize risks and maximize benefits.[2] Recommended analysts:

> Probe International
> 1492 High Ridge Road
> Stamford, CT   06903
> Phone: (203) 329-9595

> Frost & Sullivan
> World Political Risk Forecasts
> 106 Fulton Street
> New York, NY   10038
> Phone: (212) 233-1080

Outside advice can provide fresh insight and counteract group thought. However, you would be better off forming your own internal section. A permanent staff would have a clearer idea of the business than an outside team. Their assessments, therefore, would be more applicable to the demands of your firm.

Intelligence agencies are typically divided into three divisions: foreign intelligence, operations, and counterintelligence.

The quality of a firm's strategy rests in large measure upon the soundness of its intelligence—information that has been collected, analyzed, integrated, and interpreted. Useful intelligence must be adequate, timely, accurate, well-coordinated, quickly and properly distributed, and considered by decision-makers within a careful context of values and objectives. Firms that wish to develop commercial intelligence can take these steps:[3]

1. Keep permanent files on all competitors. Monitor information about their size, financial standing, credit policies, management, product lines, prices, services, locations, and distribution channels. Continually buy their products and tear them down. Evaluate their operations and leadership in the context of their goals and results. Buy a small number of shares in a publicly-owned firm that will bring annual and earnings reports and press releases. Subscribe to a clipping service that scans news-

[2]Louis Kraar, "The Multinationals Get Smarter About Political Risks," *Fortune*, March 24, 1980, pp. 86–88.

[3]Robert Hershey, "Commercial Intelligence on a Shoestring," *Harvard Business Review*, Sept.-Oct., 1980, pp. 22–28.

papers and journals for news about designated competitors. Collect information on patents filed, research activities, acquisition or divestiture announcements, lawsuits, and changes in top personnel. Firms entering a new market are particularly interested in learning what the marketing budget to sales ratio is for their competitor. (Some of this information is confidential and not easy to get. In the U.S., firms should make vigorous use of the Freedom of Information Act of 1966 to find what the competition and government are doing.)

2. Require that field sales personnel provide feedback on the interests and activities of customers, suppliers, distributors, competitors. (Exxon, for example, gets sophisticated appraisals through its regional divisions. Esso Eastern in Houston sometimes provides its managers in Asia with an "alert reporting list" of events that can affect business. If Exxon detects signs of radical change in government policy, it may add 1 to 5 percent to its required return on investment.)

3. Assign key officers to spend several days a year overseas talking with customers and administrators. (Of course, a few days in Beijing won't turn a CEO into an "old China hand." However, field exposure will give top managers a better understanding of the concerns of their underlings.) After the visit, the officer should file a brief report of his perceptions—the economic and political climate, business progress, contacts with government and diplomatic officials. These memos will seem unimportant at the time, but when collated with other perceptions, they frequently denote the start of a trend.

4. Relate the information to your company's mission. Most firms don't suffer from a shortage of information. They have too much. A firm must establish a logical structure for dealing with its unique problems within the context of China's economic development. One way to do this is to require that your intelligence people answer a list of questions on a regular basis, the answers of which will affect the firm's strategy and performance. Answers will give you the substance for the feasibility study and a framework for reviewing the progress of the project. Responses must be short and clear. A response more than a paragraph long for each question should be returned for condensation. Often, one word or phrase will do. If management needs more information, analysts can prepare subsidiary reports. These questions may seem simple, but crisp answers will demand considerable reflection and analysis.

    A.   Marketing Questions:

        1.   What is the market for our product?

        2.   How can we best meet this market?

        3.   Who are our customers?

        4.   Who are our competitors?

5.   What needs to be done to assure success of the plan?

B.   Political Questions:

1.   What political developments will affect our firm's interests?

2.   What impact will political leaders have on decisions that affect the firm?

3.   How is the political leadership reacting to demands placed on the political system?

4.   Are the present forms of political alignment likely to continue?

5.   What is the impact of key political changes on our firm's operations?

Determining China's wants and needs is difficult and frustrating. China generally doesn't issue requests for trade, nor does it publish much detailed information about its future economic and foreign trade plans. China rarely releases information about the existence, addresses, and responsibilities of important economic units. This situation is improving, however. China has disclosed some aggregate information about its economy. Chinese organizations interested in foreign trade are publicizing their existence and areas of responsibility more aggressively than in the past. Chinese leaders are also more forthcoming about national priorities and goals of their own organizations. The key to grasping China's situation is to have a spongelike ability to absorb boundless bits of information. You get that information by talking to officers of firms that do business with China and by combing government reports. Data published by trading partners remains the greatest source of hard information on the Chinese economy. Refugees have continued to furnish nitty-gritty details of life in China, but the importance of this information has diminished as information from other sources has grown. Sometimes, press releases containing charges of ideologues and modernizers have helped explain problems in the administration of communes and plants that use foreign machinery and equipment, and the distribution of consumer products. These reports must be weighed carefully because they surfaced for political rather than informational purposes. In addition to official releases, reports of tourists, businessmen, technicians, and diplomats have continued as a leading source of information on China's economy. This source must also be used with caution since China admits only visitors who are sympathetic to the regime and it controls the movement of guests. As the kinds and numbers of visitors increase, and as second and third visits are made, efforts to screen what authorities would prefer not to be seen or heard becomes less effective.

We don't recommend a return to the heady days of gunboat diplomacy and banana republics, when companies like United Fruit and Jersey Standard intervened in the internal politics of other countries. We live in an amoral world that routinely engages in paradoxical behavior. Nevertheless, a firm's interference in the affairs of a host nation can only backfire; the tribulations of Lockheed in Japan and ITT in Chile are but two examples. Efforts to change policy should only be done through legitimate channels, if at all. There are more salutory ways of using commercial intelligence, including changing pricing strategy, distribution methods, sales techniques, and marketing strategy.

Counterintelligence is intelligence cubed. Suspicion rules. Anything can be viewed as its opposite because the greater the apparent veracity, the greater the potential deception. Industrial espionage is hardly a new phenomenon. The ancient Chinese were so eager to preserve the secrets of silkmaking, they prescribed death by a thousand cuts for revealing it to outsiders. The quickest way to get key information is to steal it, buy it from someone who has stolen it, or hire people who have the information away from competitors, pump them for information, and then cut them loose. Sometimes, the mere prospect of a job is enough to get the information from another firm's employee. Although some firms continue to make elaborate illegal efforts to learn about competitors' plans, they cannot engage in such industrial espionage without risking legal action and moral condemnation. The FBI's arrest of Japanese employees of Hitachi Ltd. and Mitsubishi Electric Corp. in 1982 for stealing IBM design secrets is instructive. That Japanese were snared didn't surprise some counterintelligence officers, who say the Japanese are almost as active as the Soviets, particularly in high-technology centers in California and Massachusetts. While Chinese intelligence casts a smaller net than the Japanese, the mesh is just as fine. Because China's patent law is sketchy, firms must continue to monitor use of their products to forestall infringements on their patents.

Information can leak out of any part of a company as it moves through the company. It originates as policy in the boardroom, is written up on word processors, sorted and distributed through the mailroom, rests on desks and workbenches until the policy is initiated, and finally is ejected as trash out the loading dock. An intruder can tap into that flow anywhere, buying it on a floppy disc from typists, rerouting it out of the mailroom, and even going through the trash. The motive for some spies is money, for others revenge. The most likely sources of spying are at the bottom of the corporate hierarchy. Top management usually has a vested interest in the firm's welfare. Janitors, typists, clerks—possibly underpaid and mistreated—have the most to gain and the least to lose. A number of systems can detect intelligence violations. But no matter how good the hardward is, when the system fails, it's a people failure. The best way to solve that problem is by striving to keep employees loyal, treating them fairly, and warning them about the importance of corporate security.

A good analyst should be prized above all employees and rewarded accordingly. He must have a glutton's appetite for paper—newspapers and journals, production statistics, lists of names at official ceremonies, maps, charts of radio traffic flow, the text of toasts at banquets, railroad timetables, photographs of switching yards, and shipping figures. Because an analyst must work with fragmentary information about China, he must get many of his insights by interpreting what official reports do not say. He is devoted to patterns, and, in the absence of hard evidence, he must trust his ability to extrapolate. He must know how to analyze problems with no solutions, seek relevance in the seemingly irrelevant, and isolate the crucial issue within the cluster of facts, opinions, and feelings that can obscure questions of policy. He must separate passion from argument and rationalization from reason, generate and evaluate ideas, test hypotheses, infer consequences, marshal evidence, forecast outcomes, abandon untenable pursuits, make probabilistic decisions, and prevail in didactic and dialectic exchange. He must have respect for facts, laws, logic, evidence, principles, abstraction, imagination, and discrimination. He must think clearly and creatively and have an insatiable desire for knowledge. He must be strong, able, and motivated. However, he also needs one other quality. From Mark Twain's *Innocents Abroad* to Graham Greene's *Quiet Americans*, the theme of innocence abroad has been a literary staple. What the writers had in mind was not innocence in the sense of guiltlessness, but rather innocence in the sense of naivete. The consequences of bringing this unworldliness to bear upon the world have been absurd or disastrous. In studying the situation in China, therefore, the analyst's attitude—indeed, our attitude—must be one of realism and humility. We can read stacks of books on China—history, biography, exposition, expostulation, argumentation, harangue, theory, threat. When we step in Guangzhou, we may truly believe we know something of China. However, what we start to discover is the vastness of our ignorance.

Entering the Market

Developing business with China can be productive once you understand its hierarchy and customs. There is no best way to enter the market. Initial contact, product introduction, and preliminary negotiations are usually done by mail. However, contact with Chinese delegations and diplomatic officials in your country can be effective. If you get a response from Beijing, it's usually a positive one. Trade organizations won't respond if they aren't interested. They may ask for more information or express an interest in holding talks. Firms seeking to import should ask for information about the availability and specifications of commodities they seek to buy from Foreign Trade Corporations (FTCs). FTCs prefer to meet with prospective importers before starting detailed negotiations. Thus, importers should solicit invitations to China to get acquainted with units and their product lines. The Chinese Export Commodities Fair in Guangzhou is still the most important place for a first meeting. However, invitations to attend minifairs for specialized products in Beijing, Shanghai, or other cities are common. In many cases, attendance at the fair won't produce substantive technical or commercial discussions; FTCs don't normally send top officials to the fair to discuss the sale of plants and complex equipment. Although invitations are relatively easy to obtain, they are still necessary to enter fair grounds. Invitations may be secured through fair officials or Chinese diplomatic offices.

The proposal

Initial contact between China and the trader should be a proposal. The proposal is a formal solicitation for business with Chinese units. A senior officer from your firm should sign a cover letter explaining the essence of the proposal. It should concentrate on just one product or product line. China's bureaucracy will be unable to react effectively if the scope of the proposal is too diffuse. Develop a package along these lines:

• Past Activity

Include a brief history of the firm, profit-loss statements for the last three years, and short résumés of principal managers and owners.

• Present Status

Include the most recent annual report, bank references, Dun & Bradstreet ratings, and a summary of operations, product lines, market position, sources and uses of funds, and distribution channels.

• Future Expectations

Relevant to China, what does your firm plan to do for the next five years? How, where, why, and when do you plan to do this? Make a realistic cash flow and profit and loss projection for at least one year. Include brochures, manuals, and catalogs. Annotated attachments can present product specifications, methods of construction, and evidence of quality. Present your case crisply, meticulously, and in the best possible light. If you must include promotional material, distinguish it from the business proposal. The Chinese are hungry for technical data. They are not hungry for emotional Madison Avenue hyperbole. Advertising that adopts a hard-sell approach is unlikely to yield results, for it plays an informative rather than a persuasive role. Chinese will want to debate a widget's every specification. They won't buy until they are completely informed, whatever the terms. Note that the Chinese are generally unaware of foreign firms and industries. They want to assure themselves that they are getting the best and that they are dealing with people whom they can trust.

Keep the language barrier in mind. The cover letter should be sent in two versions: one in English and one in Chinese. Regardless of your first language, using English in correspondence with the Chinese is prudent. China has more interpreters of English, and business and technical people who understand English than any single other non-Chinese language. Make both versions identical in content. If possible, translate some of the product literature. The language written and spoken in China today is basically the same used by Chinese all over the world. However, time and Communism have brought changes in expression and terminology. If you use a professional translating service, make sure it's familiar with simplified Chinese characters. Proposals will require technical as well as linguistic competency. These organizations will print or translate technical, legal, and financial documents:

> China Consultants International, Ltd.
> 801 Kam Chung Building
> 54 Jaffe Road
> Wanchai, Hong Kong
> Phone: 5-270639
> Cable: ENTRECHIN HONGKONG
> Telex: 75368 AMRHK
>
> China Translating and Publishing Company
> 4 Taiping Qiao Street, 5th Floor
> Beijing
> Phone: 664446
> Cable: TRANSPUB BEIJING
>
> ITA International, Inc.
> 4010 Washington
> Kansas City, MO   64111
> Phone: (816) 561-3955
>
> National Council for U.S.-China Trade
> P.O. Box 57023
> Washington, DC   20037
> Phone: (202) 429-0340

When the proposal is ready, make sure you know to whom to send it. A trade bureaucracy has sprung up in China, and letters sent to the wrong agency are seldom forwarded. The Chinese will ignore requests that are impossible to satisfy, such as unacceptable visa applications. In your initial approach, contact the China Council for the Promotion of International Trade and the Chinese embassy. Request they introduce you to the appropriate FTC or industrial ministry. Embassy officials generally aren't involved in negotiations, but they will offer advice on preparing proposals. They may also transmit proposals to appropriate organizations:

> The China Council for the Promotion of International Trade
> Liason Department
> 4 Taiping Qiao Street
> Beijing
> Cable: COMTRADE BEIJING
> Telex: 668981, 662835, 660436

For all addresses, specify China by its full name: "The People's Republic of China." "Mainland China," "Communist China," "Red China," and "The Republic of China" are unacceptable forms.

Australia
> Embassy of the People's Republic of China
> 247 Federal Highway
> Watson, Canberra
> ACT 2602

Belgium
> Embassy of the People's Republic of China
> Boulevard General Jacques, #19
> 1050 Brussels

Canada
> Embassy of the People's Republic of China
> 415 St. Andrew's Street
> Ottawa
> KIN 5H3

Denmark
> Embassy of the People's Republic of China
> Oregaardsalle #25
> DK 2900 Hellerup
> Copenhagen

Federal Republic of Germany
> Embassy of the People's Republic of China
> 5307 Wachtbergniederbachen
> Konrad-Adenauer Str., 104
> Bonn

France
> Embassy of the People's Republic of China
> 11 Avenue George V,
> Paris 8E

Italy
>   Embassy of the People's Republic of China
>   Via Giovanne, Paiseillo 39
>   Roma 00198

Japan
>   Embassy of the People's Republic of China
>   5–30 Minami Azabu, 4-chome
>   Minato-ku, Tokyo

The Netherlands
>   Embassy of the People's Republic of China
>   Adriaan Goehooplaan 7
>   Den Haag 070–55.15.15

Norway
>   Embassy of the People's Republic of China
>   11 Inkognitojaten
>   Oslo 12

Sweden
>   Embassy of the People's Republic of China
>   Bragevagen #4
>   Stockholm

Switzerland
>   Embassy of the People's Republic of China
>   Kalcheggweg 10
>   Bern

United Kingdom
>   Embassy of the People's Republic of China
>   31 Portland Place
>   London, W.1

United States
>   Embassy of the People's Republic of China
>   2300 Connecticut Avenue, N.W.
>   Washington, DC   20008

>   Consulate General of the People's Republic of China
>   1450 Laguna Street
>   San Francisco, CA   94115
>   Jurisdiction: Arizona, California, Hawaii, Nevada, New Mexico, Orgeon
>   Washington

>   Consulate General of the People's Republic of China
>   520 12th Avenue
>   New York, NY   10036
>   Jurisdiction: Connecticut, Maine, Massachusetts, New Hampshire, New
>   Jersey, New York, Ohio, Pennsylvania, Rhode Island, Vermont

>   Consulate General of the People's Republic of China
>   3417 Montrose Blvd.
>   Houston, TX   77006
>   Jurisdiction: Louisiana, Texas

Dispatch multiple copies of the proposal. The Chinese will distribute them throughout the trading apparatus and duplicating machines are rare. It's useful to send information to appropriate end-users, such as hospitals, schools, and research institutes. Needless to say, the task of compiling a comprehensive list of production units is time consuming.

It can take at least a year before the first nibble and serious contract negotiations. China's bureaucracy works slowly and even its most efficient offices have overworked English-language staffs. For this reason, letters should be concise and in Chinese. One firm wrote the Chinese for three years without receiving one letter of acknowledgment. Suddenly, a cable arrived inviting the president to visit China the following week. A deal was reached. If three months pass without a word, send supplementary information followed by telexes or cables. If a favorable response doesn't seem to be forthcoming, get advice from FTC agents in Hong Kong. They are authorized to contract for the sale or purchase of foreign merchandise:

> The China Resources Company
> Bank of China Building, 12th Floor
> Hong Kong
> Phone: 5–235011
> Chemicals, machinery, metal and minerals, textiles.

> Hua Yuan Company
> 37 Connaught Road
> Central, Hong Kong
> Phone: 5–445061
> Light industrial products.

> Ng Fung Hong
> Bank of China Building, 3rd Floor
> Hong Kong
> Phone: 5–222218
> Cereals, oils, foodstuffs.

> Tech Soon Hong, Ltd.
> Connaught Road
> West, Hong Kong
> Phone: 5–456041
> Native produce, animal byproducts.

Also, contact the National Council in Beijing or your embassy or consulate in China. For U.S. firms:

> Embassy of the United States
> 17 Guanghua Road
> Beijing
> Phone: 522–033

> Consulate General of the United States
> 1496 Huaihai Road
> Shanghai
> Phone: 373–103 × 215, 216

Consulate General of the United States
Dongfang Binguan, 11th Floor
Guangzhou
Phone: 69–900 × 1000

Consultants

The odds are against a small company that wants to go it alone. Experienced consultants can better help them gauge the feasibility of a China venture and even influence decisionmakers who may not be reached through regular channels. Chinese officials state they want to deal directly with the firm responsible for selling or buying. Nevertheless, because of the lack of accurate information about China, the difficulty in delivering business proposals to the correct organization, and the high cost of maintaining offices in China, employment of consultants will continue. Chinese have also used consultants to increase their own foreign contacts. The following consultants can help you establish trade links with China:

A.M.C. Import & Export Ltd.
Loong San Building, Room 702
1040–142 Connaught Road
Central, Hong Kong
Telex: SPEAK HX 83301

Herbert B. Azif
1500 N.W. 103 Lane
Coral Springs, FL   33065
Phone: (305) 752–6274

Balfour-H.H. Trading Ltd.
111 Connaught Road
Hong Kong
Telex: 66442 BMOL HX

Balfour, Maclaine International
Wall Street Plaza
New York, NY   10005
Phone: (212) 425–2100
Telex: ITT 420059 RCA 232072

China Promotion Ltd.
9–15 Yee Wo Street
Causeway Bay, Hong Kong
Cable: HKCHONGCHI HONGKONG
Telex: 76270 CHOCH HX

Jardine, Matheson & Co., Ltd.
Connaught Centre
Hong Kong
Telex: 73255 JMGHO

May Lee International
11 Broadway, Suite 1617
New York, NY   10004
Phone: (212) 425–4349

Minerva Consulting Group, Inc.
200 Park Avenue
New York, NY   10017
Phone: (212) 972–1020
Cable: MINERVACO

Noble Trading Company
809 Cameron Street
Alexandria, VA   22314
Phone: (703) 549-5966

Pickands Mather & Company
1100 Superior Avenue
Cleveland, OH   44114
Phone: (216) 694–5700

Textile Fibers, Inc.
280 Madison Avenue
New York, NY   10017
Cable: TEXTIBER

After the Chinese invite you to attend a fair or hold a seminar, promptly return the enclosed card signifying acceptance to reserve housing. You will have about three months to prepare for the trip. Sometimes, you will go as part of a trade mission, managed by organizations such as the Conference Service Bureau and Expoconsul:

The Conference Service Bureau
17 Battery Park Plaza
New York, NY   10004
Phone: (212) 747–1755

Expoconsul
Division of Clapp & Poliak, Inc.
Princeton-Windsor Office Park
P.O. Box 277
Princeton Junction, NJ   08550
Phone: (609) 448–3200

Visa formalities

Visitors to China must undergo passport, health, customs, and currency formalities. Once the invitation has been received, you must apply for an entry visa at the embassy or consulate where the invited firm is located. For the fair, standard visas are valid for 35 days. They are not renewable, but may be extended. Some representatives have been able to procure visas valid for up to a year. In some cases, the Chinese have granted multiple entry visas and certificates designating long-term residency. Only firms that have a large contract and long-term relationship will get such treatment. Submit visa forms in duplicate with your passport, four passport photographs, the processing fee, the original invitation, and a letter from your firm certifying your status. State the purpose, date, duration, and ports of entry and exit on the form. In the case of rail travelers from Hong Kong, the correct port is Shenzhen. The form also requires you to indicate information about your former employment, place of birth, languages you know, religion, and political party. Passports mailed to the Washington D.C. embassy are usually returned in one week. In some cases, the embassy won't grant the visa until the last moment. Those planning another trip in the interim should get another passport. China rarely issues visas to citizens of South Africa, Israel, or South Korea. Don't submit a passport having stamps from these countries or from Taiwan province. If you have such a passport, get a second one from the State Department. Leave the first one at home to avoid a possible incident. The visa form will ask you to list cities you wish to visit, route of travel in China, and means of transportation. You may not have a definite itinerary. When in doubt, add towns to the list. Once a visa is granted and you are in China, it's hard to add other cities, but easy to drop them. It's easier for businessmen to go on tourist visas than commercial visas. Sometimes, tourists have secured appointments in Beijing with FTCs and other commercial organizations. However, such appointments are hard to arrange and at best provide only a chance for an introductory call. Firms cannot expect to have worthwhile discussions in China unless they are invited by the China Council for Promotion of International Trade (CCPIT), an FTC, a local entity, or a ministry.

Travelers should have smallpox vaccination and innoculation against cholera and yellow fever, if they come from places where those diseases are found. Typhoid innoculation and gamma globulin are recommended for Hong Kong travelers. Check specific requirements at time of application.

Customs

Customs may refuse to admit a person with more than one still camera, movie camera, radio, cassette recorder, television, typewriter, or watch. You may bring in a maximum of 24 rolls of film for still camera and 3,300 feet of eight mm movie film. Bring your own office equipment. Visitors may bring a typewriter, tape recorder, film projector, copying machine, and kindred items for conducting business. Much of this equipment is scarce in China. Business machines imported for temporary use are exempt from duty. Precious metals, jewelry, business machines, cigarettes (up to three cartons), and liquor (up to four bottles) must be itemized and cleared to prevent black markets. Antiques more than 150 years old won't be sold in China, and, if acquired, may not be exported. Visitors who bring in Chinese antiques should notify customs to avoid complications. (Prices on Chinese antiques are high. The cost of old vases, jade, and paintings is double or triple what it is in Hong Kong, Taiwan, or Singapore.) Prohibited imports include arms and ammunition, explosives, wireless receivers and transmitters (other than a personal radio), Chinese currency, Chinese drafts and bills, stocks and bonds, animals or birds, opium, morphia, poisons, lottery tickets, and printed material detrimental to China's politics, economy, culture, or ethics. Items that may not be taken from China include Chinese money, gold, platinum, silver, and other precious metals, books, photographs, or tapes pertaining to Chinese national secrets, or items of artistic value relating to the Chinese revolution, history, and culture. Prospective residents without diplomatic privilege should declare the number of cases of belongings imported within the following six months to exercise exemption from duty. Remember to make allowances for importing goods from abroad found in short supply in China. The China Travel Service in Hong Kong, or the inbound airlines, provide forms for declaring personal effects:

The China Travel Service
    Yu To Sang Building
    77 Queen's Road
    Central, Hong Kong
    Phone: 5-259121
    Cable: TRAVELBANK

    27 Nathan Road, 1st Floor
    Kowloon, Hong Kong
    Phone: 3-664127

    Hung Ho Station
    Kowloon, Hong Kong
    Phone: 3-330660

    35-33 Rua Vis. Paco de Arcos,
    Macao
    Phone: 3770

Transportation

China may be reached by international air service to Beijing or Shanghai, by train, airplane, or hovercraft from Hong Kong to Guangzhou. In 1979, the first direct commercial flight in many years between the United States and China touched down in Shanghai, and Pan American World Airlines unloaded a charter planeload of tourists. In 1980, the two countries agreed to allow regularly scheduled flights. The most convenient way to enter China is via major European cities: Paris via Air

France, Zurich via Swiss Air, Frankfurt via Lufthansa; or Tokyo via Japan Airlines or the Civil Air Administration of China. The direct flight time from Tokyo to Beijing is about four hours. Baggage collection and customs will take half an hour, and the drive to your hotel will usually take another half hour. These airlines provide regular service to China:

Aeroflot Soviet Airlines
545 Fifth Avenue
New York, NY   10017
Via the USSR to points in China.

Air France
1350 Avenue of the Americas
New York, NY   10019
From Anchorage, Boston, Chicago, Houston, Los Angeles, and Washington D.C., via Paris to Beijing.

Ethiopian Airlines
405 Lexington Avenue
New York, NY   10174
Via Addis Ababa to Shanghai.

Japan Airlines
655 Fifth Avenue
New York, NY   10022
From New York, Anchorage, Honolulu, Los Angeles, and San Francisco to Beijing and Shanghai.

Pakistan International Airlines
545 Fifth Avenue
New York, NY   10022
From New York, via Karachi to Beijing.

Swiss Air
608 Fifth Avenue
New York, NY   10020
From New York, Boston, and Chicago, via Zurich and Geneva, to Beijing.

Hong Kong remains the most common departure point for visitors to Guangzhou, via train, jet, boat, or hovercraft. From Guangzhou, you can make same day connections to Beijing, a three hour flight. The Guangzhou to Beijing express takes 37 hours to travel its 1,442 miles. The China Travel Service of Hong Kong is the sole agent for handling train reservations for trips into China. Passengers get off the Hong Kong train at Lowu, and walk across a covered bridge to customs. Lunch is served before completing the two hour ride to Guangzhou. The train trip will reveal much about China and will constantly remind you of its population. Once you've arrived in China, the China International Travel Service (CITS) will handle your travel arrangements, including transfers, guide services, and hotel bookings. Make sure you confirm reservations with CITS well in advance of your departure from China:

China International Travel Service
6, Dong Chang An Avenue
Beijing
Cable: LUXINGSHE BEIJING
Phone: 557558, 557496, 551379

CITS also has branch or sub-branch offices in Shanghai, Tianjin, Guang-zhou, Hangzhou, Nanjing, Suzhou, Wuxi, Jian, Nanchang, Zhenshou, Xian, Shijiazhuang, Shenyang, Anshan, Dalian, Changchun, and Jilin.

5

NEGO-TIATING THE CONTRACT

Chinese organizations are more inclined to invite firms that offer to hold technical seminars in China than firms that want merely to deliver a sales pitch. They exploit enthusiasm aroused by foreign companies to get free consultancy services. However, seminars give businessmen a good opportunity to sell the merits of their technology to agents of end-users. Seminars may be narrow or broad, but all should stress your firm's most advanced technologies. The Technical Exchange Department of the China Council for the Promotion of International Trade is the usual host for such seminars, but industrial ministries and scientific and technical association have also sponsored specialized seminars. The Chinese will expect you to send your most technically-oriented spokesman. The Chinese lack of technical capability is offset by their keen business sense, and their technicians will want to know everything worth knowing about your product. China's industry tends to be vertically integrated. Therefore, you must be able to answer questions relating to all levels of production. Never go to China alone, as the Chinese will ask more questions than anyone can answer. A fair-sized delegation has six members, consisting of a top executive, an engineer, sales representatives, and sometimes a translator. A high-level officer should make the first personal contact with the Chinese party. This will show your commitment to establish a long-term relationship. In actual negotiations, technicians—those most knowledgeable about the design and performance of your company's products—will make the best impression on the Chinese. Of course, someone must have authority to negotiate and sign a contract. For time-conscious businessmen, the pace of Chinese negotiators is frustrating. The Chinese are patient and attentive to detail. It will be to your advantage to be equally patient and attentive to detail. Plan to stay for as long as the negotiations continue. Don't underestimate the time lost in translation. Post-seminar negotiations can last for as little as 15 minutes or as long as three years, although five days to two weeks is typical. Most transactions at the fair in Guangzhou are conducted within ten days.

The complexity of the subject will determine the schedule of the seminar. Usually, the session opens at 9 a.m. with a pot of tea. The seminar is split into a three hour morning session followed by a two hour break and another three hour afternoon meeting. The setting varies with the size of the audience, which ranges from 5 to 50. For a small group, armchairs may line the perimeter of the room. For a larger audience, the Chinese will provide an auditorium. They can also supply a screen or blackboard. For visual effect, your best bet is overhead projection. It's cheap, versatile, and can be easily updated. Flip charts and chalkboards look amateurish and are hard to read. Movie projectors are available, but slide projectors (especially carousel models) are scarce. The Businessman's Center at the U.S. Embassy in Beijing will supply such equipment to American teams. Japan Airlines' Executive Service will print English and Chinese business cards. Forget company trinkets. The concept of the individual is at odds with the official views of a state-controlled economy. To the Chinese, you are representing your industry and your nation, not just your firm. As a token of friendship, you may present a small gift to another organization. The first day of the seminar will be devoted to getting-to-know-you chit-chat. Shortly, the Chinese will start probing after your presentation. They are prepared for these sessions, having analyzed materials sent in advance of the seminar. Because of this, some businessmen skip the text and go directly into discussions. However, you should present at least a summary of the topic to assure that the Chinese haven't missed major points. Technical seminars lead to contract negotiations in relatively few cases—perhaps 25 percent. Don't be discouraged. The main purpose of the seminar is to start a long-term relationship. According to one British trader, over 80 percent of those who present seminars eventually get deals. Invitations from some Chinese organizations make it clear they intend to move into commercial negotiations immediately.

The Chinese distinguish technical and commercial negotiations. In format, commercial negotiations resemble the technical seminar. The Chinese reach decisions privately and collectively. Three or four negotiators may be present, some of whom may abruptly leave or wander in.

It's important not to ignore any member of the Chinese team as titles do not readily clarify the authority of particular officials. The seemingly most uninterested person could be calling the shots. The Chinese periodically break from negotiations for discussions among themselves or request one day recesses to take you on scenic tours. These delays give Chinese time to reassess strategy and pass findings to other members in the trading bureaucracy. Outings allow the opportunity for expressing suggestions or comments that wouldn't be made in a more formal setting.

In negotiations and seminars, we must consider a number of factors. Westerners have thought China existed in a world of its own, cut off from life beyond its borders. Two symbols of China are its Great Wall and Forbidden City. China's isolation isn't simply an adage. It's an important factor for those who seek trade. But closer acquaintance reveals what seems to be a Great Wall of mutual ignorance is more like a one-way mirror, excluding foreign scrutiny while giving China a clear view of the outside. Foreigners have found their hosts to be well-informed, and current with technical developments. Chinese negotiators represent a variety of organizations—universities, research facilities, end-users, and trade bureaus. They are universally recognized as hard, patient bargainers.

> Chinese diplomats, at least in their encounters with us, proved meticulously reliable," Kissinger writes. "They never stooped to petty maneuvers; they did not haggle; they reached their bottom line quickly, explained it reasonably, and defended it tenaciously. They stuck to the meaning as well as the spirit of their undertakings. As Zhou was fond of saying, 'Our word counts.' I soon found that the best way to deal with him was to present a reasonable position, explain it meticulously, and then stick to it. I sometimes went so far as to let him see the internal studies that supported our conclusions. Zhou acted the same way.[1]

Because of the pressure on Chinese officials to get modern technology, they will try to get as much information as a firm is willing to give away. But they realize firms cannot disclose proprietary information. As in other potentially contentious areas, you should state your policy clearly and they will accept it. Chinese negotiators are under great pressure, so allowances must be made when problems arise. Also make allowances for yourself. Because of jet lag, you should never negotiate on your day of arrival. A shift in a person's circadian timing system can cause mental fatigue, psychological disorientation, vision impairment, and other physical strains. All of China, including Hong Kong, is on Beijing time, thirteen hours ahead of Eastern Standard Time in the United States.

How relationships develop during the negotiating process governs Chinese attitudes on how they will conduct business. They put unusual stress on getting to know their partners and maintaining relationships with

[1]Henry Kissinger, "The China Connection," *TIME*, October 1, 1979, pp. 53–54. [From Kissinger's *White House Years*, Boston: Little, Brown and Company, 1979.]

"old friends." In Imperial China, trade with the West was carried on in the guise of tribute. Foreigners were obliged to follow elaborate rituals, like those imposed on envoys from China's tributory states. China's emphasis on buying the most modern technology reflects a wariness of getting cheated. (In the 1950s, they bought Soviet equipment they now believe was second-rate.) The Chinese view foreigners as a source of suffering inflicted on them over the last century, beginning with the Opium Wars and enduring through trade embargoes after World War II. Two themes run through China's trade policy: "self reliance" and trading on the basis of "equality and mutual benefit." The first principle suggests China will avoid foreign trade and a foreign presence to preserve its independence. If there is trade, negotiations and transactions are to be conducted as between equals. The relationship must be neither exploitive nor patronizing. Culture predisposes the Chinese to rely on personal and long-term relationships as contrasted to the Western preference of impersonal, formal legal mechanisms. A congenial atmosphere and a context in which discussions are taking place are immensely important. In Western society, a legal contract is context free. All meaning is in the words of the contract. In high-context cultures like China, the entire circumstance is more meaningful. Negotiations will therefore take longer in China because the Chinese will need time to get to know you. (The organization of this book reflects this contextual mentality somewhat. Before getting into the "how tos"— how to negotiate the best possible deal with a Chinese corporation, how to identify who is likely to be your most advantageous partner in China, how to arrange creative financing that addresses China's foreign exchange constraints—we developed a context in which to present these issues. We did this in the first three chapters by trying to answer three questions: What forces have shaped China's present needs? What does it need? What are China's relations with major trading partners?)

Foreign firms that have been the most successful in China are those that have maintained the most continuous and closest relations. While a long-term relationship is necessary, it's hardly sufficient. The Chinese have many "old friends." As proof of their friendship, they expect their friends to offer attractive terms and prices. The Chinese are honest and, once a bargain is struck, they will more than hold up their end of it. They expect the same of Western businessmen. If mountains must be moved to get a shipment of goods to the Chinese party on the date agreed and at the price specified, the Westerner who arranged the deal had best be prepared to move those mountains. As long as you remain true to your word, you have little fear of competitive replacement.

Company negotiators must be temperamentally as well as technically qualified. Developing countries have characterized world executives as arrogant, impersonal, heavy-handed, rigid, impatient, tense, pampered, racist, aloof, and parochial. Doing business in China demands more sensitivity than businessmen are accustomed to demonstrating in Chicago, for example. Warmth, friendliness, a ready smile, an interest in people, and the ability to earn the regard and respect of others from different backgrounds are essential. Flexibility—the ability to adapt—and energy—the ability to work long hours and endure stress—are also important, as responsibilities tend to be broader and less defined in China. Bear in mind that your representatives may have to stay in Beijing for weeks. The opportunity cost of sending talented specialists to China may therefore be considerable. Those not cheerful about foreign travel, extended absences, long stays in austere hotels, and the absence of night life may find themselves distinctly unhappy in Beijing. Try to send people with experience working in developing countries, particularly those nations of Southeast Asia where Chinese culture and customs remain strong.

The Chinese consider venting frustrations with abusive language a sign of defeat. If you hit the ball hard into their court, sooner or later they will hit the ball hard back into your court. Pounding the table is especially bad form. Traders given to rage for whatever reason should recall the stark advice from that poet of the British empire, Rudyard Kipling:

It is not good for the Christian health,
To hustle the Asian brown;
For the Christian riles, and the Asian smiles,
And he weareth the Christian down.
And the end of the fight is a tombstone white,
With the name of the late deceased;
And the epitaph drear: "A fool lies here,
Who tried to hustle the East."

If you use strong emotion, you will lose their confidence and contract. In human relations, the Chinese prize poise, reason, self-control, self-confidence. In Taoism, the symbol of strength is the graceful bamboo that yields to the wind, while the strong oak snaps. Water submits to all it touches, yet it cuts through rock. This spirit is exemplified in Mao's poem of sixteen characters:

Enemy advances,
We retreat.
Enemy halts,
We harass.
Enemy tires,
We strike.
Enemy retreats,
We pursue.

In negotiations, understatement is better than bluster, the willingness to backstep can bring accord. The forceful bending of another person's will is a transient victory. The only way another person will accept your view is for him to grasp it from within. Your task is not to get the Chinese negotiator to agree with you, but to get him to reach out for your ideas. You do this by building self-esteem. Everyone likes to feel important, ideological sentiments to the contrary. You feed his sense of importance by treating him with decency and generosity. Courteous, even elegant, manners show that you think he is important. As you build his sense of importance, he will be more inclined to respect and believe you. Questions, expressions of doubt, and arguments indicate willingness to receive your ideas. When you observe these signs of reaching out, you know that the time is ripe to implant your ideas. You will tailor your pitch to the specific needs of the Chinese. To the Chinese, economic success means getting only the technology they can absorb, and at the best price, quality, and terms. Before you make your sale, you will inquire about the problems China faces relevant to the functions of your firm and suggest how these problems can be lessened by your product. You will also raise and answer objections to buying your product before the Chinese express them.

Ageless with wisdom, a Chinese proverb urges: "He who treads softly goes far." And executives who frame a deal in a climate of mutuality are likely to score again. But firmness in the face of an apparent breakdown of discussions can snatch victory from defeat. The Chinese have been known to test their opponent's position only to introduce a more favorable offer at the eleventh hour. Last-minute negotiations on the way to the airport and terminal contract signings are part of the folklore of the China trade—and they still occur. But a strategy of intractability must be a logical decision, not an emotional one. If you know your opponent has established a fall-back position, you must force the issue since failure to do so means your exploitation. You must avoid boxing the Chinese side with an ultimatum, even though you are prepared to back up the ultimatum or they think you are prepared to back it up. If you box them in, they will resist and make counter-demands. Knowledge of what the Chinese side can or will do presupposes that your intelligence is accurate. But you must not let the absence—or abundance—of data impede you. Perfect information is only possible in games like chess, which are circumscribed by a framework of ironclad, artificial rules. In the negotiating game, there are no clear rules, no time-outs, no replays. In successful negotiations, either both sides win or no one loses. If you feel you've lost, the relationship will be unstable, because you will work for a change. But a contract in itself won't determine a winner. Some winners will be those who look carefully at the market and then walk away. A failure of strategy is seldom a failure of intelligence, but of evaluation and judgment. You won't know all the details, but if you're clever enough to observe what is going on, you will know the basics. The difficulty is in applying the information you have. Since all risks cannot be calculated, the business strategist must resort to force of will, hunch, and bluff to optimize gain.

Negotiating is the process by which two parties attempt to resolve differences. At the start, there will be a great disparity between the expectations of the two teams. Your mission is to close the gap. You do that by conducting negotiations in such a way that your opposites disclose themselves and their assumptions to you. You do this by watching mannerisms, asking questions, and by allowing for emotional stresses and cultural differences. By reading your opposites, you will learn what their real needs and priorities are. You will also be able to detect disagreements and coalitions within their team and know when to take a hard or soft line. A barrage of words will often mask true needs. Your task is to distinguish what they really want from what they profess. Explain what you want and see whether there are alternatives outside the fixed positions, or accommodations that could satisfy both sides. Developing alternatives to fall back on allows you to negotiate with the strength of detachment. There is always power in knowing you can walk away. That should never cease to be an alternative. In combat, the willingness to die is paradoxically a deterrence to death. Likewise, the willingness to abandon the talks can save the talks.

A knowledge of human behavior is essential to the negotiator. An individual's existence is a constant struggle to satisfy a hierarchy of needs. Behavior is the reaction of the person to reduce pressure on those needs. People must negotiate to meet needs. The Chinese are master negotiators, because they are masters of psychology. They have a gift of absorbing clues from the environment, judging people at both analytical and intuitive levels. For example, Chinese jade dealers watch a buyer's eyes to see if he will pay a high price for a specimen. Confirming this sly practice, psychologists have determined the pupils of a person's eyes widen when he is looking at something that pleases him. The Chinese interpret these interactions on a second-to-second basis. By watching the pupils and other indices of physical changes, they can respond rapidly to mood changes. They notice if a person pauses too much in speaking, if his voice changes, if an otherwise placid person becomes tense. As they observe these nonverbal attitudes, the subconscious interrogates the conscious: Can he be trusted? What does he want? How do I feel about him? Why do I feel this way? As this stream of inquiry flows over the subconscious, the wheels of hard analysis start to turn. Only at the most superficial mathematical level is there a distinction between the analytical and intuitive. It is as futile to find this line of demarcation as it is to quantify all thought processes. It's also a mistake to ignore body language and simply rely on words and numbers to define meaning. The mind is more subtle and powerful in most respects than the most sophisticated computer, and you must use all the mind's facilities to deal in the negotiating environment.

We have no illusions about the difficulty of negotiating with the Chinese. Their negotiating style is a blend of the Byzantine and evangel-

ical. Communists can be stiff in negotiations, padding talks with long re-
citations of history and dogma. They are well aware of the ploys used by
other negotiators in the mating dance of *quid pro quo*. The Chinese are
tough-minded, well-prepared, and willing to use a variety of tactics to get
the best deal. They are masters at pitting competitors against one another
to attain the best deal. Chinese units try to convince firms that other firms
are interested in the same contract. They might exaggerate the competition's terms in an effort to lower your price. The novice might find these
gambits intimidating and manipulative, but a cat can look at a king, a
capitalist can parley with a Communist. Be polite, be open, but don't
defer to them and offer them second-rate terms simply because the cultural context is different. At the table, the Chinese are poker pragmatists,
and all maneuvering and entertainment is subordinate to one goal—to get
the best deal at the best terms with the least effort. Lenin said "negotiating
is one tool among many others in the conduct of the international class
struggle, to be judged by its utility in advancing Soviet objectives, but
without any inherent moral value in itself." Negotiation is more than that
to the Chinese. Not only is it a way to expand trade, it also provides the
ambience wherein China can achieve parity with other nations.

Preparation. Persistence. Patience. To these facets of successful negotiation, we might add another—payoffs. Tales of functionaries asking
for gifts before consummating a contract have circulated. While bribes
aren't a part of normal Chinese operations, traders wonder whether they
must grease palms to nail deals and meet competition. In many Asian
countries, such as Japan, Korea, and Malaysia, the government takes the
attitude that businessmen should not be hamstrung in their efforts to develop export markets. However, bribery saps political vitality and undermines a people's faith in the government. In an effort to stop corruption,
the U.S. Congress passed the 1977 Foreign Corrupt Practices Act, making
it a criminal offense to bribe foreign officials to secure or retain business
abroad. The practical effect of this has been to inspire CEOs to figure out
clever new schemes that are more difficult to spot, such as joining a foreign
company that is not prohibited from making payments, and letting them
do the dirty work. Perhaps to be honest is to be a fool in an imperfect
world. Yet, values are important. "Ethics in business is part of the American dream," William Safire of the *New York Times* explains. "America
stands for competition on the basis of quality, price, and service, and not
payola. If, in the short run, this costs us jobs and money, that's the price
for setting standards."

6 NAVI-GATING THE BUREAU-CRACY

The Problem

Bureaucracy in a country with vast spaces and a billion citizens is practiced on a grand scale. Two thousand years ago, the central government dispatched swarms of officers to the hinterland to build bureaus for dredging canals and collecting taxes. Boards of elders, mainly local merchants, ran the cities. Emperors Genghis and Kublai Khan and those of the late Manchu dynasty accepted the system and levied tributes on cities according to size to finance dynastic activities. Sun Zhongshan and Jiang Zhongzheng failed to unify the country partly because the city fathers wouldn't cooperate. Mao succeeded. He replaced the old system with a Soviet-style apparat, which he would dismantle periodically. His goal was to bind China together with "red" idealism, not red tape, and replace the Confucian ethic with Communistic ideals. The result was violent swings between anarchy and rigidity. During the Cultural Revolution, for example, three-in-one committees managed the plants. Activists who rose to prominence during the Cultural Revolution, older leaders who had been managers before the Cultural Revolution, and soldiers made up the committees. Management by junta brought industrial ferment and infighting. On economic grounds, it's hard to justify Mao's politicization of industry, the effects of which persist in present-day business.

The term "bureaucracy" conjures images of piles of memoranda and managers who "go by the book." A more formal definition could describe a bureau as a system of manpower and materials organized to attain some goal. Effectiveness is the ability of that bureau to attain its goal. The relationship between effectiveness and bureaucracy is parabolic. The more organized it is, the more effective it is, until it becomes bureaucratized. The bureau then is no longer a means to an end, but an end in itself. Original functions become peripheral and sometimes antagonistic to its new preoccupation—self-preservation and self-perpetuation. The exercise of detailed control of the Chinese economy requires an army of bureaucrats and a complicated chain of command. We would have to go back to the Ottoman Empire to find a similar array of elephantine satrapies. China's bureaucracy promotes and protects incompetence. It rewards party members and apparatchiks with the best jobs, schooling, and apartments. As former China resident James Kenneson notes, commoners react with cynicism: "Unable to express dissatisfaction, they simply do less work. We were told many times that there was kind of a nationwide slowdown strike constantly in progress."[1] Managers of foreign ventures in China confirm Kenneson's remarks. They report workers show frequent absenteeism and lack of interest in achieving production targets. Labor legislation aggravates these problems by not permitting dismissal of workers. One wonderful aspect of any rule-laden system is that people will always find a way around the rules. Party officials pull strings to obtain scarce goods. To do this, you need *guan-xi*—connections. Even state enterprises need *guan-xi* to get raw materials. They are called *cai gou yuan*—fixers.

Westerners—with pink ribbon on breast and green card in hand—are disinclined to be solicitous to bureaucrats. They find stock phrases as "it's inconvenient" or "there's no responsible person" cover-ups for indolence, negligence, malfeasance. Lack of coordination and communication between ministries and purchasing departments is particularly disturbing. Traders rarely get letters of acknowledgment in communicating with official organs other than trading corporations. Examples of poor communication are commonplace. When one procedure set by the Foreign Ministry directly contradicted another rule by the Public Security Bureau, a security officer proclaimed to the hapless foreigner in the middle: "They're right and we're right." Poor coordination has brought the collapse of some joint ventures. In 1982, for example, the American side of the 1,008-room Great Wall Hotel project, the largest U.S.-China joint venture to date, was forced to cede construction responsibilities for the $75 million hotel to the Chinese. A cumbersome and chaotic joint management system bogged down the project. The Chinese and Americans

[1]James Kenneson, "Letter from Abroad: China Stinks," *Harper's*, April, 1982, pp. 13–19.

planned to oversee the project through a five-member team, but no one was able to make decisions without first consulting their superiors in the U.S. or China's government.

China's sense of collective is rooted in its experience as a densely populated nation in which teamwork and compromise are essential. China seemed crowded to Marco Polo in the 13th century and to the Jesuit pioneer Matteo Ricci in the 16th. It has always been the world's most populous country. In short, living together produced the Chinese personality. It requires a feat of sympathetic imagination for Westerners to understand this. Western corporations encourage executives to be decisive, to act forcefully. Chinese decisions are reached by a tedious process of collective compromise that sometimes involves 80 individuals, each of whom holds a potential veto. Therefore, deliberation is not just a technical process, but a bargaining one. Although consideration of technical aspects and personal points of view is lengthy, once agreement is reached, no one tries to sabotage the project. A foreign firm must convince Chinese end-users of the effectiveness of their product. In turn, the end-user must persuade higher authorities that there is a need for the product, that it cannot be effectively produced in China, and that importing it should have priority over competing needs.

What China is Doing

The Chinese recognize the problem of bureaucracy. They are working to break what German sociologist Max Weber called its "iron cage." In 1982, for example, the leadership began to restructure the State Council—China's cabinet. Eight state agencies under the council's authority were merged into the remaining 19 to streamline the inflated bureaucracy. The State Council originally had 41 such agencies that administered a broad range of affairs, from earthquake control to Mao's mausoleum. A realignment earlier in the year reduced the number to 21. They are also trying to weed out lazy and corrupt officials who snarl China's middle levels. This effort to invigorate the bureaucracy is neither the first one since 1949, nor is it likely to be the last. No nation with 20 million civil servants working at five tiers of government (center, province, district, county, commune) can escape bureaucratism.

In agriculture, the production team (usually a small village) is taking charge of its own accounting and investment. This should improve the morale and livelihood of China's often dissatisfied peasantry without the need for investment from above. However, the government has issued warnings against dissolving production teams. Authorities feel attempts to return to private farming carry self-reliance too far. As the drive for efficiency continues, leaders will face resistance to capitalist techniques. Deng Xiaoping earned radical wrath when he argued for giving peasants a greater measure of private farming to produce more food. "For purposes of increasing agricultural production, any by hook or by crook method can be applied," he said after Mao's Great Leap Forward. "Black cat, white cat. As long as it catches rats, it's a good cat." Radical resistance to private initiative didn't die with the Cultural Revolution.

Since the 1950s, Beijing has accepted the need for local direction of industry. It's trying to prune inefficient bureaus, giving local managers more autonomy in planning, finance, and trade. Although Beijing will continue to determine major imports, it has granted increasing import power to provinces and localities since 1978. China has found no satisfactory way of retaining central control while leaving room for local initiative. Although party input is a significant factor in overall policy, Beijing is limiting its involvement, particularly at the enterprise level. To restore a more stable administration, China has abolished revolutionary committees. Professional principals and managers have replaced committees in schools and factories. China is establishing better auditing methods and is directing funds to sectors where returns are highest. Plans are underway to let factories set output quotas and prices. Some firms may keep up to 13 percent of pretax profits and foreign earnings. Wage increases and bonuses with the promise of more material incentives are meant to prod a workforce with a long record of slowdowns and absenteeism into working harder and more purposefully. Despite these reforms, China's economy remains complex and centralized. Yet, it's striking how much China has done. Not only has China mastered esoteric technologies (especially in defense-related sectors), it has shown remarkable capacity for innovation and improvisation. Modern industry demands individual initiative, self-reliance, risk-taking. It requires a belief in progress and the utility of a meritocracy. This view is essentially what the West can offer China in its present stage. On the response made by China rests much of its future.

What You Can Do

Bureaucracy short-circuits profitability. It also undermines morality because it segments deliberation and dilutes responsibility. We must be wary of abstractions. The "Nazi SS" didn't run Auschwitz, nor did the "Pentagon" drop the bomb on Hiroshima. Men did. It's a paradox. The best way of dealing with the bureaucracy is by refusing to deal with the bureaucracy. As Herb Cohen, negotiator *par excellence*, points out, people keep commitments, institutions don't: "Commitments are never kept with institutions. They're too big, too impersonal. A guy waffles on his commitment and you say, 'Look, you told me you were going to do this, and I told my boss. You're not going to let me down are you?' He answers: 'Hey, you're not taking this personally, are you?' You answer: 'Yeah, I am.'" To navigate the bureaucracy, you must insist on dealing with people—names, not titles or numbers. Try to build relationships with key people in China's trading establishment. Work to sustain that relationship. Any effort to get closer to the decision-makers will pay. China has a command economy. A small group makes most consumer decisions. They decree such-and-such, issue orders about thus-and-so, approve, disapprove, dispose, oppose, denounce, announce. They have the power to buy, sell, and distribute. Thus, your clients number not in the millions, but in the dozens. The problem is to find and win those people. Some firms are fortunate to have hired contacts within the bureaucracy. They can achieve breakthroughs by blazing back channels to bypass regular bureaucracies and arrange meetings for visiting executives.

Advertising is another way to reach purchasing agents. Plant managers are avid readers of Chinese-language journals, such as McGraw-Hill's monthly *American Industrial Report*. Published in Hong Kong with a controlled circulation, it's a joint venture of McGraw-Hill and China Consultants International. The *Report* is the first American-owned Chinese publication to use reader service cards for advertiser feed-back:

McGraw-Hill Publications Co.
1221 Avenue of the Americas
New York, NY   10020
Phone: (212) 997–2807
Telex: 0127960

Other avenues of promotion are: billboards, store displays, and radio and television advertising. Chinese publications such as *Renmin Ribao* (*People's Daily*), *Beijing Ribao*, and *Guangzhou Ribao* accept foreign advertisements. Advertising probably won't produce immediate results, although it may lead to inquiries from end-users. You should place emphasis on developing company and brand name recognition. These firms provide marketing services in China:

Beijing Advertising Corporation
190 Cheonei Street
Beijing
Phone: 553326
Cable: ADVERCORP BEIJING

China Trade Communications
Division of Dow Jones
22 Cortland Street
New York, NY   10007

Chinese Marketing Communications, Ltd.
84 Fifth Avenue
New York, NY   10011
Phone: (212) 929-5757

East-West Trade Publications
475 Fifth Avenue, Suite 1210
New York, NY   10017
Phone: (212) 889-5342
Telex: EASTWES 421077

Guangdong Advertising Corporation
2 Qiaoguang Road
Guangzhou

International Trade & Technology Research Associates
805-A Cheong K. Building
84–86 Des Voeux Road
Central, Hong Kong
Cable: INTTRASSOC HONGKONG
Telex: 63128 INSOC HX

McCann-Erickson International
485 Lexington Avenue
New York, NY   10017
Phone: (212) 697-6000

Shanghai Advertising Corporation
95 Yuan Ming Yuan Road
Shanghai
Cable: ADVERCORP SHANGHAI

Tianjin Advertising Corporation
345 Jie Fang Road
Tianjin
Cable: TJAC TIANJIN

The Chinese act out of self-interest. If it's in their interest to get your product, they will accommodate you. For this reason, you shouldn't be afraid to rattle cages when you're not satisfied. Like all bureaucracies, China's bureaucracy moves like a tiger when its interests are threatened. To paraphrase Mao, doing business in China is "not a dinner party, or writing an essay, or painting a picture, or doing embroidery. It cannot be so refined, leisurely, and gentle." If you want a higher official to examine your complaint, complain about his subordinate. Positioning your problem or project as unique will drive it up the hierarchy, because that situation isn't covered by the 'lowerarchy's' standard operating procedure. While you should have contacts in the trading establishment, government ties should be loose, preferably non-existent. Take on the local color by hiring nationals as executives. Avoid any display of home-country pride. As a matter of principle, missionaries will turn down embassy invitations to maintain their credibility. Companies also should have a code of strict political neutrality, for world executives are the kind of people revolutionary mobs like to hang. When political conditions in China take a turn for the worse, you must be able to show by your record that you are a true friend of China.

Signs of organizational inefficiency are epidemic in China's plants and offices:

> Too many meetings.
> Too many coordinators.
> Too many levels of organization.
> Too much paperwork.

The business ambience shaped by statist control produces a mindset marked by caution and conformity. It might be too much to expect someone reared in China's hierarchical culture to manifest great initiative. Foreign investors have resorted to different measures to overcome these problems, including the introduction of cash incentives and management by objectives. Perhaps what is needed most is not management, but leadership to bring out the greatness of people, regardless of background. Consider the words of Laozi: "A leader is best when he is neither seen nor heard. Not so good when he is adored and glorified. Worse when he is hated and despised. Fail to honor people, they will fail to honor you. But of a good leader, when his work is done, his aim fulfilled, the people will say, 'We did this ourselves.' "

China's Trading Establishment

The national government rations food, clothing, and other necessities and sets prices of most goods and services. It owns and operates all important plants and controls most employment and wages. The government also operates the banking system, long-distance transportation, and foreign trade. Since the establishment of the People's Republic, China has pursued a policy of total control of foreign trade. The function of its trading system is to design and implement import and export plans based on the requirements of the national economic plan. The following organizations are part of China's trading establishment. This isn't an exhaustive list, but these organizations are of most interest to traders. Organizations listed early in this chapter tend to play a part in making policy. Others play a more operational role. This distinction is sometimes ambiguous.

The National Party Congress

The National Party Congress is China's highest party organ. It elects the 210-member Central Committee, which elects the Politburo. As stipulated by the constitutions of the CCP and the PRC, the Communist Party is China's primary political force. The party makes nearly all major decisions. Its objective has been to build an industrial society in which production is consciously planned, the means of production are publicly owned, and the incentive to work is service to people rather than individual gain. Thirty-nine million Chinese belong to the party, the largest in the world. However, they make up only 4 percent of the total population. In 1982, the post of Party Chairman, created by Mao to preside over party affairs, was abolished to remove the aura of omnipotence that turned Mao into an autocrat. A General Secretariat of 11 in charge of policy-making and administrative organs heads the party.

The National People's Congress

The National People's Congress is China's highest organ of state power. Representatives to the congress are indirectly elected for a term of five years, with annual sessions. Its main function is to approve party decisions that pertain to constitutional amendments and economic plans.

The Politburo

Political power is concentrated in the 30-member Politburo. Removed from all but the most critical issues, it settles questions such as the construction of major plants and the role of foreign technology. The Politburo guides the import programs and resolves controversies over purchases. It elects the Standing Committee, the body with final decision-making authority.

The State Council

Cabinet responsibility is vested in the State Council, the highest organ of state power. Members include the premier, vice premiers, ministers, and heads of commissions. They are responsible to the Politburo for all important matters. The 1978 Constitution of the People's Republic of China (as translated by the Foreign Language Press) defines its functions and powers in article thirty-two:

> To formulate administrative measures, issue decisions and orders, and verify their execution, in accordance with the Constitution, laws, and decrees; to submit proposals on laws and other matters to the National People's Congress or its Standing Committee; to exercise unified leadership over the work of the ministries and commissions and other organizations under it; to exercise unified leadership over the work of local

organs of state administration at various levels throughout the country; to draw up and put into effect the national economic plan and the state budget; to protect the interests of the state, maintain public order, and safeguard the rights of citizens; to confirm the following administrative divisions: autonomous prefectures, counties, autonomous counties, and cities; to appoint and remove administrative personnel according to the provisions of the law; and to exercise such other functions and powers as are vested in it by the National People's Congress or its Standing Committee.

The council is the highest economic authority in the country. It irons out all but the biggest problems. Relatively small issues concerning raw materials or fuel supplies might consume council time. It also has a number of specialized bureaus dealing with economic matters. In general, they don't have daily control over production units, nor are they generally involved in direct talks with foreign companies. Nevertheless, they play a vital role in drafting foreign trade plans and authorizing important activities. Bureaus of the State Council:

Agricultural Bank of China

Central Meteorological Bureau

General Administration of Civil Aviation

General Administration of Industry and Commerce

General Administration of Travel and Tourism

People's Construction Bank of China

State Council Foreign Experts Bureau

State Council Government Offices Bureau

State Council Overseas Chinese Affairs Office

State Council Religious Affairs Bureau

State Council Special Economic Zones Office

State Commodity Prices General Bureau

State Customs General Administration

State General Administration of Foreign Exchange Control

State Oceanography Bureau

State Seismology Bureau

State Statistical Bureau

State Supplies General Bureau

Xinhua (New China) News Agency

The Communist Party, the military, and the State Council dominate China's government. Almost all leaders in the military and State Council also hold high positions in the party. Thus, the party strictly controls the political system.

The State Planning Commission

The State Planning Commission (SPC) is at the top of China's planning mechanism. Similar to the Soviet Union's GOSPLAN, it's charged with framing the national economic plan. The SPC draws a detailed blueprint to bring the overall objects established by the party to fruition. It collects voluminous amounts of data from a host of subordinate ministries. A tentative plan is then submitted to various administrative units for study, evaluation, and criticism. Local planning bodies receive the plan, by which they set detailed production targets. When the plans are completed, they are forwarded to the central ministries for cross-checking, balancing, and aggregating. When the plan is approved by the State Council and rubber-stamped by the party and state, it becomes the next Five-Year Plan. The SPC also controls all financial aggregates, including the money supply, balance of payments, and state budget. In some respects, it serves the function of the U.S. Office of Management and Budget. With the State Capital Construction Commission, the SPC determines China's investment and construction programs. The SPC also plays a key role in determining the outlines of foreign trade plans. It identifies gaps between targets and capacity and takes steps to overcome them through domestic investment or foreign imports. Other components of the bureaucracy advise the commission on relative merits of various technologies and foreign sources. With the initial approval of the commission, Foreign Trade Corporations investigate foreign equipment and vendors. Since the State Planning Commission approves major purchases of foreign technology, some firms have focused lobbying efforts at this level.

The State Economic Commission

The State Economic Commission (SEC) monitors the implementation of the SPC's plans. It draws up and coordinates annual plans with long-term plans created by the SPC. In short, the SEC's job is to ensure the economy runs smoothly once the SPC has made the plan. It has a consultative and even a preemptive relationship with the SPC in getting technologies to lagging sectors.

The State Science and Technology Commission (S&T)

The State Science and Technology Commission controls most scientific institutions and laboratories. It also shares responsibility for the research activities of various ministries.

The State Capital Construction Commission (SCCC)

The State Capital Construction Commission carries out China's investment program. It approves projects, assigns investment priorities, and monitors the progress of construction.

The State Machine Building Commission (SMBC)

The State Machine Building Commission manages activities of the eight machine building ministries.

The State Agricultural Commission

The State Agricultural Commission was founded in 1979 to take charge of the government's renewed enthusiasm to expand agricultural output.

The State Finance and Economic Commission

The State Finance and Economic Commission was also established in 1979. It provides guidance in formulating, coordinating, and implementing policies in China's drive to achieve the Four Modernizations.

Ministries

Ministries evaluate the need for foreign trade to make up production shortfalls. Plants or provinces submit requests for imports to industrial ministries. After becoming convinced of the merits of the request, the ministry explores domestic means of meeting the need. Finding them inadequate, it recommends purchase from abroad. Ministries also help decide what technical seminars should be held and what delegations should be invited. Within the ministries, they coordinate contacts between foreigners and various end-user enterprises.

In 1982, the Fifth National People's Congress placed all of China's foreign economic relations under one authority, the Ministry of Foreign Economic Relations (MOFERT). This ministry is a merger of China's Foreign Investment Control Commission (FICC), Import-Export Control Commission (IECC), Ministry of Foreign Trade, and Ministry of Economic Relations with Foreign Countries. (The FICC approved or disapproved joint ventures and foreign investment. The IECC approved or disapproved other types of foreign ventures, such as trade compensation arrangements.) MOFERT also supervises the China Council for the Promotion of International Trade and the China International Trust and Investment Corporation. The FICC previously guided both entities. While not affecting day-to-day trade operations, this reorganization will help separate ordinary business relations with foreign countries from overall trade planning. This ministry has 7 administrative and 13 regional and functional departments. Most are located in the old Ministry of Foreign Trade building on Chang An Road in Beijing. The departments:

1.   General Planning, of trade and investment.

2.   Finance and Accounting.

3.   Treaties and Law.

4.   Foreign Trade Administration.

5.   Import and Export, in charge of contract licenses.

6.   Foreign Aid.

7.   Foreign Economic Relations.

8.   Foreign Investment Administration, responsible for approving investments.

9.   Relations with International Organizations, serves as liaison to the United Nations and other multinational organizations.

10.   Technical Import and Export, responsible for technology transfer and supervises TECHIMPORT.

11.   First Department of Regional Affairs, in charge of Asia (including Japan), Africa, and Latin America.

12.   Second Department of Regional Affairs, in charge of Eastern Europe and the Soviet Union.

13.   Third Department of Regional Affairs, in charge of industrialized Western countries, including Western Europe and the United States.

In a manifestation of increasing central control, the number of ministries under the State Council has increased. In 1975, a single ministry was responsible for fuels and chemicals. Now, there are separate ministries for coal, chemicals, and petroleum. In 1982, there were 40 ministries, including eight separate ministries for machine building:

Ministry of Agriculture, Animal Husbandry, and Fisheries
Ministry of Aviation Industry
Ministry of Chemical Industry
Ministry of Civil Affairs

Ministry of Coal Industry

Ministry of Commerce (domestic retail trade)

Ministry of Communications (shipping and roads)

Ministry of Culture

Ministry of Education

Ministry of Electronics Industry

Ministry of Finance

Ministry of Foreign Affairs

Ministry of Foreign Economic Relations and Trade

Ministry of Forestry

Ministry of Geology and Minerals

Ministry of Justice

Ministry of Labor and Personnel

Ministry of Light Industry

First Ministry of Machine Building (general industrial equipment)

Second Ministry of Machine Building (administers China's nuclear program)

Third Ministry of Machine Building (aircraft)

Fourth Ministry of Machine Building (electronics)

Fifth Ministry of Machine Building (conventional weapons)

Sixth Ministry of Machine Building (shipbuilding)

Seventh Ministry of Machine Building (aerospace)

Eighth Ministry of Machine Building (precision machinery)

Ministry of Metallurgical Industry

Ministry of National Defense

Ministry of Nuclear Industry

Ministry of Ordnance Industry

Ministry of Petroleum Industry

Ministry of Posts and Telecommunications

Ministry of Public Health

Ministry of Public Security

Ministry of Radio and Television

Ministry of Railways

Ministry of Space Industry

Ministry of Textile Industry

Ministry of Urban and Rural Construction and Environmental Protection

Ministry of Water Conservancy and Electric Power

If you wish to write to a Chinese ministry, you can use this address:

Foreign Affairs Office
Ministry of...
Beijing
People's Republic of China

End-users

Several ministries have established import and export corporations to handle foreign trade and investment activities for product lines within their jurisdiction. These corporations have the authority to conduct technical and commercial negotiations with foreign firms and sign contracts, thus bypassing MOFERT's Foreign Trade Corporations. Foreign firms are dealing increasingly with ministerial corporations. Such corporations manage China's economic units and handle cooperation, countertrade, joint venture, and technical exchange activities involving the ministries. They also keep factories under the ministries aware of innovations in their fields and generally coordinate communication among factories. These end-users have engaged in foreign trade:

China National Aeronautical Technology Import-Export Corporation
P.O. Box 1671
Beijing
Phone: 442444
Cable: CAID
Telex: 22318 AERO TCN

China Agricultural Machinery Corporation
c/o First Ministry of Machine Building

China Automobile Components Corporation
c/o First Ministry of Machine Building

China Chemical Construction Corporation
He Ping Li
Dong Cheng Qu
Beijing

China National Chemical Fibers Corporation
c/o Ministry of Textile Industry

China Coal Industry Technology and Equipment Corporation
16 He Ping Road North
Beijing
Phone: 461223
Cable: CCITEC BEIJING

China Container Traffic Corporation
c/o Ministry of Communications

China National Electronic Component Corporation
c/o Fourth Ministry of Machine Building

China National Electronic Technical Import-Export Corporation
49 Fuxing Road, P.O. Box 140
Phone: 810910
Telex: 22475 CTEITEK CN

China Electronic Systems Engineering Company
c/o Ministry of Posts and Telecommunications

China National Feedstuffs Corporation
c/o Ministry of Commerce

China National Forestry Machinery and Equipment
Corporation
c/o Ministry of Forestry

China National Geological Exploration Corporation
c/o State Bureau of Geology

China Heavy Machinery Corporation
c/o First Ministry of Machine Building

China National Metallurgical Import-Export Corporation
54 Dongsi Dajie
Beijing
Phone: 556345
Cable: 2250 BEIJING
Telex: 6 DINM CN 22194

China National New Building Materials Corporation
Zi Zlu Yuan Road, P.O. Box 2815
Xi Jiao, Beijing

China Northern Industries Corporation
(conventional military weapons)
7A Yuetan Nanjie
Beijing
Phone: 812254
Cable: NORINCO BEIJING
Telex: 22339 CNIC CN

China Nuclear Energy Industry Corporation
c/o Second Ministry of Machine Building

China Nuclear Equipment Corporation
c/o Second Ministry of Machine Building

China Petroleum Corporation
P.O. Box 766
Beijing

China National Posts and Telecommunications
Appliance Corporation
13 West Changan Street
Beijing
Phone: 661245
Telex: 01681

China Posts and Telecommunications Industrial Corporation
c/o Ministry of Posts and Telecommunications

China National Precision Machinery Import-Export Corporation
c/o Eighth Ministry of Machine Building

China National Radio Equipment Corporation
c/o Fourth Ministry of Machine Building

China Railway Technical and Equipment Corporation
c/o Ministry of Railways
Cable: CRATECO

China National Road and Bridge Construction Company
c/o Ministry of Communications

China Seed Corporation
c/o Ministry of Agriculture, Animal Husbandry, and Fisheries

China Shipbuilding Corporation
10 Yuetan
Beiziaojie, Beijing

China National Textile Machinery Industry Corporation
c/o Ministry of Textile Industry

China Trade Consultation and Technical Service Corporation
c/o Ministry of Foreign Economic Relations and Trade

China National Underwater Cable and Construction
Corporation
c/o Ministry of Posts and Telecommunications

China Waste Materials Reclamation Corporation
c/o Ministry of Public Health

Great Wall Industrial Corporation
(computer technology)
c/o Seventh Ministry of Machine Building

Import-Export Corporation of the Ministry of Light Industry
c/o Ministry of Light Industry

Oriental Scientific Instruments Import-Export Corporation
Erligou, Xijiao
Phone: 866361, 868361
Cable: INSTRIMPEX BEIJING
Telex: 22242 CMIEC CN

Yan Shan Petrochemical Corporation
c/o Ministry of Petroleum Industry

Foreign Trade Corporations

Basic responsibility for carrying out foreign trade rests with Foreign
Trade Corporations. Under the direction of the Ministry of Foreign Economic Relations and Trade, FTCs draw detailed import and export plans,
carry out negotiations, draft and sign contracts, and represent China's producers and end-users. The target for your proposal will be the FTC re-

sponsible for the goods or services in which you wish to deal. FTC headquarters are in Beijing, but they have a network of branch offices in centers of export production. Since 1979, branch offices have had great autonomy in conducting foreign trade. Head offices still have the responsibility for passing on information and proposals to branch offices. Sometimes, one FTC won't be aware of a firm's dealing with another FTC. On the other hand, a firm may send an enquiry to one FTC and it may get a reply from another FTC. The China Council for Promotion of International Trade's *China's Foreign Trade* magazine is the best source of information on products handled by FTC branches. FTCs have representatives in their overseas embassies. They also have offices in New York and other cities.

China's FTCs:

ARTCHINA

China National Arts and Crafts Import and Export Corporation
Pottery and porcelain, drawn work and embroidered articles, ivory carvings, jade and semiprecious stone carvings, pearls and gems, jewelry, lacquer wares, cloisonné wares, Chinese paintings and calligraphy, antiques, straw, wicker, bamboo, and rattan articles, furniture, artistic handicrafts, and other handicrafts for daily use.

Head Office
    82 Donganmen Street
    Beijing
    Phone: 552187
    Cable: ARTCHINA BEIJING
    Telex: 22155 CNART CN

Beijing Branch
    1 Xijiaominxiang
    Cable: PEKARTCO BEIJING

Beijing Jewelry Branch
    No. 1 Building
    Fuwai Street
    Cable: PEKJEWECO BEIJING

Shanghai Branch
    16 Zhongshan Road E. 1
    Cable: ARTSCRAFT SHANGHAI
    Telex: 33053 ARTEX CN

Tianjin Branch
    135 Tangshan Road
    Cable: ARTS TIANJIN
            PORCELAIN TIANJIN
            STRAW TIANJIN

Guangdong Branch
 2 Qiaoguang Road
 Guangzhou
 Cable: CERAMICO GUANGZHOU
   ARTCANTON GUANGZHOU
  Telex: 44029 KCACB CN

Shandong Branch
 12–14 Baoding Road
 Qingdao
 Cable: CRAFT QINGDAO

Dalian Branch
 2 Hongyan Street
 Cable: ARTSALIEN DALIAN

Fujian Branch
 Foreign Trade Building
 Dongfanghong Street
 Fuzhou
 Cable: ARTCRAFT FUZHOU

Guangxi Branch
 Hongxing Road
 Nanning
 Cable: ARTCRAFT NANNING

Hunan Branch
 103 Wuyi Road
 Changsha
 Cable: HNARTS CHANGSHA

Hubei Branch
 75 Shengli Street
 Hankou
 Cable: INDUSTRY HANKOU

Jiangsu Branch
 50 Zhonghua Road
 Nanjing
 Cable: INDUSTRY NANJING

Hebei Branch
 8 Jichang Road
 Shijiazhuang
 Cable: INDUSTRY SHIJIAZHUANG

Guangzhou Ceramics Export Department
 China Export Commodities Fair Building
 Cable: POTTERY GUANGZHOU

Guangzhou Arts and Crafts Export Department
 China Export Commodities Fair Building
 Cable: 5050 GUANGZHOU

Jiangxi Branch
 Foreign Trade Building
 Nanchang
 Cable: POTTERY NANCHANG

Henan Branch
    6 Wenhua Road
    Zhengzhou
    Cable: 7671 ZHENGZHOU

Hong Kong Agent
    Chinese Arts and Crafts Ltd.
    Garley Building
    233–239 Nathan Road
    Cable: CRAFTS HONGKONG

Macao Agent
    Nam Kwong Trading Company
    Nam Tung Bank Building
    Rua Da Praia Grande, 65-A
    Cable: NAMKWONG MACAO

CEROILFOOD

China National Cereals, Oils, and Foodstuffs Import and Export Corporation

Cereals, edible vegetable and animal oils and fats, vegetable and animal oils and fats for industrial use, oilseeds, seeds, oil cakes, feedstuffs, salt, edible livestock and poultry, meat and meat products, eggs and egg products, fresh fruit and fruit products, aquatic and marine products, canned goods of various kinds, sugar and sweets, wines, liquors and spirits of various kinds, dairy products, vegetables and condiments, bean flour noodles, grain products, and nuts and dried vegetables.

Head Office
    82 Donganmen Street
    Beijing
    Phone: 558831
           528531
    Cable: CEROILFOOD BEIJING
    Telex: 22281 CEROF CN
          22111 CEROF CN

Beijing Branch
    No. 1 Building
    Funwai Street
    Cable: CIFCPB BEIJING

Shanghai Cereals and Oils Branch
    11 Hankou Road
    Cable: CHINAFAT SHANGHAI

Shanghai Foodstuffs Branch
    26 Zhongshan Road E. 1
    Cable: FOODSTUFFS SHANGHAI

Guangdong Foodstuffs Branch
48 Xiti Road 2
Guangzhou
Cable: FOODCO GUANGZHOU

Guangdong Cereals and Oils Branch
2 Qiaoguang Road
Guangzhou
Cable: CNCOFC GUANGZHOU

Shandong Cereals and Oils Branch
29 Wusong Road
Qingdao
Cable: NACEROIL QINGDAO

Shandong Foodstuffs Branch
70 Zhongshan Road
Qingdao
Cable: FOODSTUFFS QINGDAO

Tianjin Branch
134 Chifeng Road
Cable: CEROILFOOD TIANJIN

Dalien Branch
145 Stalin Road
Cable: TALOILFOOD DALIEN

Fujian Branch
Foreign Trade Building
Dongfanghong Street
Fuzhou
Cable: FOODCO FUZHOU

Hubei Branch
319 Zhaojiatiao Road
Hankou
Cable: CEROILFOOD HANKOU

Hunan Branch
103 Wuyi Road
Changsha
Cable: REDEAST CHANGSHA

Guangxi Branch
Hongxing Road
Nanning
Cable: CEROILFOOD NANNING

Yunnan Branch
148 Huashan Road S.
Kunming
Cable: CEROILFOOD KUNMING

Henan Branch
6 Wenhua Road
Zhengzhou
Cable: YUFOOD ZHENGZHOU

Jiangzi Branch
    25 Zhonghua Road
    Nanchang
    Cable: 1120 NANCHANG

Hebei Branch
    52 Beima Street
    Shijiazhuang
    Cable: CEROILFOOD SHIJIAZHUANG

Hong Kong Agent
    Ng Fung Hong
    115–119 Queen's Road, West
    Cable: NGFUNG HONGKONG
    Telex: 74054 NGFUN HX

Macao Agent
    Nam Kwong Trading Company
    Nam Tung Bank Building
    Rua Da Praia Grande, 65-A
    Cable: NAMKWONG MACAO

CHINAPACK

China National Packaging Import and Export Corporation
This FTC handles import and export of packaging materials, containers, machinery, and tools. It lists its principal business interests as follows: packaging materials, corrugating medium, white board with grey back, white lined folding box board, sack paper, white cardboard, art printing paper, cellophane, foil-laminated paper, decorative paper for packaging presentation, plastic film, metallized film, laminated materials, ink, coating, adhesive aluminum foil, hot stamping foil, bronze powder, jute cloth, etc.; packaging containers: paper, plastic and metal containers, packaging machinery and tools, corrugator, die-cutting machines, can makers, steel drum makers, glass bottle manufacturing machines, closure and cap makers, molds, printing machines, plate-making equipment, blow molding machines, injection molding machines, plastic foaming machines, blow and cast extruders, laminating machines, plastic bag makers, vacuum packers, shrink wrap, blister pack, forming, filling, sealing, casing, cartoning, strapping, labelling, marking and weighing machines, and testing instruments for packaging materials and containers.

Head Office
    2 Dong Changan Street
    Beijing
    Phone: 557610
    Cable: CHINAPACK BEIJING

CHINATEX

China National Textiles Import and Export Corporation
Cotton, cotton yarn, raw silk, steam filature, wool tops, rayon fibers, synthetic fibers, cotton piecegoods, woolen piecegoods, linen, garments and apparel, knitted goods, cotton and woolen manufactured goods, ready-made silk articles, drawn works.

Head Office
82 Donganmen Street,
Beijing
Phone: 550258
Cable: CHINATEX BEIJING
Telex: 22280 CNTEX CN

Shanghai Branch
27 Zhongshan Road E. 1
Cable: TEXTILE SHANGHAI
Telex: 33055 SHTEX CN

Shanghai Garments Branch
27 Zhongshan Road E. 1
Cable: GARMENTS SHANGHAI
Telex: 33056 GAREX CN

Shanghai Silk Branch
17 Zhongshan Road E. 1
Cable: CHISICORP SHANGHAI
Telex: 33059 CTSSB CN

Beijing Branch
No 1. Building, Fuwai Street
Cable: PEKITEX BEIJING
Telex: 22148 PKTEX CN

Tianjin Branch
114 Dagu Road
Cable: CHINATEX TIANJIN

Shandong Branch
78 Zhongshan Road
Qingdao
Cable: CHINATEX QINGDAO

Guangdong Branch
255 Yanan Road
Guangzhou
Cable: CANTEX GUANGZHOU
Telex: 44071 KTTEX CN

Dalian Branch
One 55 Road
Cable: CHINATEX DALIAN

Jiangsu Branch
    50 Zhonghua Road
    Nanjing
    Cable: CHINATEX SHIJIAZHUANG

Hong Kong Agent
    China Resources Company
    Bank of China Building
    Cable: CIRECO HONGKONG

Macao Agent
    Nam Kwong Trading Company
    Nam Tung Bank Building
    Rua Da Praia Grande, 65-A
    Cable: NAMKWONG MACAO

CHINATUHSU

China National Native Produce and Animal By-Products Import and Export Corporation
    Tea, coffee, cocoa, tobacco and cigarettes, fibers (hemp, jute, sisal, flax, etc.), rosin, manioc, starches, seeds, cotton linters and waste, timber, certain papers and forest products, waxes, spices, essential oils, aromatic chemicals, nuts, dried fruits and vegetables, patent medicines and medicinal herbs, fireworks, nursery stock and other native produce, bristles and brushes, horsetails, feathers, down and down products, decorative feathers, rabbit hair, goat hair, wool, cashmere, camel hair, casings, hides, leathers, fur mattresses, fur products, carpets, living animals.

Head Office
    82 Donganmen Street
    Beijing
    Phone: 554124
    Cable: CHINATUHSU BEIJING
    Telex: 22283 TUHSU CN

Beijing Branch
    52 Xijiaominxiang
    Cable: TUHSUBRAN BEIJING

Shanghai Tea Branch
    74 Dianchi Road
    Cable: NATIONTEA SHANGHAI

Shanghai Native Produce Branch
    18 Dianchi Road
    Cable: CHINAPROCO SHANGHAI
    Telex: 33060 CNPCS CN

Shanghai Animal By-Products Branch
    23 Zhongshan Road E. 1
    Cable: BYPRODUCTS SHANGHAI
    Telex: 33065 ANIBY CN

Tianjin Native Produce Branch
    33 Harbin Road
    Cable: NCNPC TIANJIN
            DRUGS TIANJIN

Tianjin Animal By-Products Branch
    66 Yantai Road
    Cable: BYPRODUCTS TIANJIN

Dalian Branch
    139 Stalin Road
    Cable: BYPRODUCTS DALIAN

Shandong Native Products Branch
    16 Baoding Road
    Qingdao
    Cable: CNSNP QINGDAO

Shandong Animal By-Products Branch
    24 Hubei Road
    Qingdao
    Cable: BYPRODUCTS QINGDAO

Fujian Branch
    Foreign Trade Building
    Dongfanghong Street
    Fuzhou
    Cable: NATIONTEA FUZHOU
            PROFUKIEN FUZHOU
            BYPRODUCTS FUZHOU

Guangdong Tea Branch
    486 Lohneesan Road
    Guangzhou
    Cable: NATIONTEA GUANGZHOU

Guangdong Native Produce Branch
    486 Lohneesan Road
    Guangzhou
    Cable: PROCANTON GUANGZHOU
    Telex: 44072 KTNB CN

Guangdong Animal By-Products Branch
    48 Zhujiang Road
    Guangzhou
    Cable: BYPRODUCTS GUANGZHOU

Guangxi Branch
    Hongxing Road
    Nanning
    Cable: PRONANNING NANNING

Hubei Branch
    766 Zhongshan Road
    Hankou
    Cable: PROWUHAN HANKOU

Hunan Branch
    34 Dongmao Street
    Changsha
    Cable: 0960 CHANGSHA

Hunan Tea Branch
    103 Wuyl Road
    Changsha
    Cable: HUNANTEA CHANGSHA

Yunnan Native Produce Branch
    148 Huashan Road
    Kunming
    Cable: TEAEXCORP KUNMING

Jiangsu Branch
    50 Zhonghua Road
    Nanjing
    Cable: CHINATUHSU NANJING

Hebei Branch
    52 Belma Street
    Shijiazhuang
    Cable: TUHSUBRAN SHIJIAZHUANG

Hong Kong Agent
    Tech Soon Hong Ltd.
    37–39 Connaught Road West
    Cable: STILLON HONGKONG

Macao Agent
    Nam Kwong Trading Company
    Nam Tung Bank Building
    Rua Da Praia Grande, 65-A
    Cable: NAMKWONG MACAO

COMPLANT

China National Complete Plant Export Corporation
This FTC is responsible for exporting complete factories, works, and production units under economic and technical cooperation agreements concluded at government level.

Head Office
    An Ding Men Wai
    Beijing
    Cable: COMPLANT BEIJING

EQUIPEX

China National Machinery and Equipment Import and Export Corporation

Machine tools, forging and pressing equipment, woodworking machinery, measuring and cutting tools, heavy-duty machinery, mining machinery, machinery for petroleum and chemical industries, general utility machinery, agricultural machinery, power-generating machinery, electric generating sets, automobiles, roller bearings, hoisting and transport equipment, building machinery, printing machinery, electric motors, electric devices and equipment, electric instruments and meters, physical instruments, optical instruments, complete equipment for hydroelectric power stations, refrigerating works, icemaking machinery, wood screw machinery, and rubber-making and plastic-making machinery.

Head Office
12 Fuxingmenwai Street
Beijing
Phone: 866442
866541

Beijing Branch
190 Chaoyangmennei Street
Cable: EQUIPBRANCH BEIJING

Shanghai Branch
27 Zhongshan Road E. 1
Cable: EQUIPEX SHANGHAI

Tianjin Branch
14 Zhangde Road
Cable: EQUIPEX TIANJIN

Hebei Branch
9 Hezuo Street
Shijiazhuang
Cable: EQUIPEX SHIJIAZHUANG

Dalian Branch
145 Stalin Road
Cable: EQUIPEX DALIAN

Jiangsu Branch
50 Zhonghua Road
Nanjing
Cable: EQUIPEX NANJING

Shandong Branch
127 Guanxian Road
Qingdao
Cable: EQUIPEX QINGDAO

Guangdong Branch
    510 Dongfeng Road 4
    Guangzhou
    Cable: EQUIPEX GUANGZHOU

Hong Kong Agent
    China Resources Company
    Bank of China Building
    Cable: CIRIMP HONGKONG

Macao Agent
    Nam Kwong Trading Company
    Nam Tung Bank Building
    Rua Da Praia Grande, 65-A
    Cable: NAMKWONG MACAO

Industry

China National Light Industrial Products Import and Export Corporation

General merchandise of all kinds, paper, stationery, musical instruments, typewriters, cameras, film, radios, refrigerators, sporting goods, toys, building materials (plywood, insulation board, tiles, glass sanitary ware, etc.) and electric appliances, clocks and wristwatches, fishnets, leather shoes, and leather products.

Head Office
    82 Donganmen Street
    Beijing
    Phone: 556749
    Cable: INDUSTRY BEIJING
    Telex: 22282 LIGHT CN

Beijing Branch
    76 Changan Street
    Cable: INDUSPK BEIJING
    Telex: 22142 LITPK CN

Shanghai Branch
    128 Huqiu Road
    Cable: INDUSTRY SHANGHAI
    Telex: 33054 INDUS CN

Tianjin Branch
    172 Liaoning Road
    Cable: INDUSTRY TIANJIN

Guangdong Branch
    110 Qiaoguang Road
    Guangzhou
    Cable: INDUKT GUANGZHOU
    Telex: 44078 LECKB CN

Liaoning Branch
    110 Stalin Road
    Dalian
    Cable: INDUSTRY DALIAN

Shandong Branch
    8 Tianjin Road
    Qingdao
    Cable: INDUSTRY QINGDAO

Fujian Branch
    Foreign Trade Building
    Dongfanghong Street
    Fuzhou
    Cable: INDUSTRY FUZHOU

Hunan Branch
    103 Wuyi Road
    Changsha
    Cable: HNARTS CHANGSHA

Hubei Branch
    75 Shengli Street
    Hankou
    Cable: INDUSTRY HANKOU

Jiangsu Branch
    50 Zhonghua Road
    Nanjing
    Cable: INDUSTRY NANJING

Hebei Branch
    50 Beima Street
    Shijiazhuang
    Cable: INDUSTRY SHIJIAZHUANG

Hong Kong Agent
    Tech Soon Hong Ltd.
    37–39 Connaught Road West
    Cable: STILLON HONGKONG

Macao Agent
    Nam Kwong Trading Company
    Nam Tung Bank Building
    Rua Da Praia Grande 65-A
    Cable: NAMKWONG MACAO

INSTRIMPEX

China National Instruments Import and Export Corporation
Telecommunication equipment, computers, television center equipment, radio broadcasting equipment, radio positioning and ranging equipment, electronic components, electronic instruments, nuclear instruments, electric instruments, physical-optical instruments, electron-optical

instruments, optical metrological instruments, geodesic and aerophotogrammetric surveying instruments, electron-magnetic analysis instruments, material testing machines and equipment, geophysical surveying instruments, pollution testing equipment, laboratory instruments and appliances, and industrial processing instruments.

Head Office
    Erligou
    Xijiao, Beijing
    Cable: INSTRIMPEX BEIJING
    Telex: 22242 CMIEC CN

MACHIMPEX

China National Machinery Import and Export Corporation

Machine tools, presses, hammers, shears, forging machines, diesel engines, gasoline engines, steam turbines, boilers, industrial and institutional refrigeration and air conditioning equipment, mining machinery, metallurgical machinery, compressors and pumps, hoists, winches and cranes, transport equipment (aircraft, railroad, automotive, ships, and parts thereof), power and hand tools, agricultural machinery and implements, printing machines, knitting and other textile machines, building machinery, machinery for chemical, rubber, plastics, and other industries, ball and roller bearings, tungsten carbide, and machinery and equipment.

Head Office
    Erligou
    Xijiao, Beijing
    Phone: 891974
          891243
    Cable: MACHIMPEX BEIJING
    Telex: 22242 CNMIEC CN

Shanghai Branch
    27 Zhongshan Road E. 1
    Cable: MACHIMPEX SHANGHAI
    Telex: 33066 SHCMC CN

Tianjin Branch
    14 Zhangde Road
    Cable: MACHIMPEX TIANJIN

Guangdong Branch
    61 Yanjiang Road 1
    Guangzhou
    Cable: MACHIMPEX GUANGZHOU

Shandong Branch
    82 Zhongshan Road
    Qingdao
    Cable: MACHIMPEX QINGDAO

Dalian Branch
    145 Stalin Road
    Cable: MACHIMPEX DALIAN

Beijing Branch
    190 Chaoyangmennei Road
    Nanjing
    Cable: MACHBRANCH BEIJING

Jiangsu Branch
    50 Zhonghua Road
    Fuzhou
    Cable: MACHIMPEX FUZHOU

Fujian Branch
    1 Jianbing Road
    Fuzhou
    Cable: MACHIMPEX FUZHOU

Hebei Branch
    52 Beima Street
    Shijiazhuang
    Cable: MACHIMPEX SHIJIAZHUANG

Hong Kong Agent
    China Resources Company
    Bank of China Building
    Cable: CIRECO HONGKONG

Macao Agent
    Nam Kwong Trading Company
    Nam Tung Bank Building
    Rua Da Praia Grande 65-A
    Cable: NAMKWONG MACAO

MINMETALS

China National Metals and Minerals Import and Export Corporation

Steel plates, sheets and pipes, steel sections, steel tubes, special steel, railway materials, metallic products, pig iron, ferro-alloys, non-ferrous metals, precious rare metals, ferrous mineral ores, non-ferrous mineral ores, non-metallic minerals and products, coal, cement, and hardware.

Head Office
    Erligou
    Xijiao, Beijing
    Phone: 890931
          892376
    Cable: MINMETALS NANNING
    Telex: 22241 MIMET CN

Shanghai Branch
    27 Zhongshan Road E. 1
    Cable: MINMETALS SHANGHAI

Tianjin Branch
   319 Heping Road
   Cable: MINMETALS TIANJIN

Guangdong Branch
   61 Yanjiang Road 1
   Guangzhou
   Cable: MINMETALS GUANGZHOU
   Telex: 44077 WUJIN CN

Shandong Branch
   9 Tangyi Road
   Qingdao
   Cable: MINMETALS QINGDAO

Dalian Branch
   143 Stalin Road
   Cable: MINMETALS DALIAN

Guangxi Branch
   Hongxing Road
   Nanning

Yunnan Branch
   248 Huashan Road S.
   Kunming
   Cable: 0674 KUNMING

Beijing Branch
   190 Chaoyangmennei Street
   Cable: MINMETBRANCH BEIJING

Jiangsu Branch
   50 Zhonghua Road
   Nanjing
   Cable: MINMETALS NANJING

Fujian Branch
   1 Jianbing Road
   Fuzhou
   Cable: MINMETALS FUZHOU

Hebei Branch
   52 Beima Street
   Shijiazhuang
   Cable: MINMETALS SHIJIAZHUANG

Hong Kong Agent
   China Resources Company
   Bank of China Building
   Cable: CIRECO HONGKONG

Macao Agent
   Nam Kwong Trading Company
   Nam Tung Bank Building
   Rua Da Praia Grande, 65–A
   Cable: NAMKWONG MACAO

PUBIMPORT

China National Publications Import Corporation
This corporation is mainly involved with the importation of foreign books, newspapers, periodicals, documents, and other materials.

Head Office
    P.O. Box 88
    Beijing
    Cable: PUBLIM BEIJING

SINOCHEM

China National Chemicals Import and Export Corporation
Organic and inorganic chemicals, chemical raw materials, rubber, rubber tires, and other rubber products, crude petroleum and petroleum and petrochemical products (except aromatics), chemical fertilizers, insecticides, fungicides, antibiotics and pharmaceuticals, medical instruments, apparatus and supplies, dyestuffs, pigments, and paints.

Head Office
    Erligou
    Xijiao, Beijing
    Phone: 891289
    Cable: SINOCHEM BEIJING
    Telex: 22243 CHEMI CN

Guangdong Branch
    61 Yanjiang Road 1
    Guangzhou
    Cable: SINOCHEMIC GUANGZHOU
    Telex: 44076 HAGON CN

Shanghai Branch
    27 Zhongshan Road E. 1
    Cable: SINOCHEMIS SHANGHAI

Shandong Branch
    82 Zhongshan Road
    Qingdao
    Cable: SINOCHEMAO QINGDAO

Tianjin Branch
    171 Jianshe Road
    Cable: SINOCHEM TIANJIN
           NOCIPHARM TIANJIN

Beijing Branch
    190 Chaoyangmennei Street
    Cable: SINOCHEMIP BEIJING

Dalian Branch
    135 Stalin Road
    Cable: SINOCHEMIR DALIAN

Jiangsu Branch
    50 Zhonghua Road
    Nanjing
    Cable: SINOCHEM NANJING

Fujian Branch
    1 Jianbing Road
    Fuzhou
    Cable: SINOCHEM FUZHOU

Hebei Branch
    52 Beima Street
    Shijiazhuang
    Cable: SINOCHEM SHIJIAZHUANG

Hong Kong Agent
    China Resources Company
    Bank of China Building
    Cable: CIRECO HONGKONG

Macao Agent
    Nam Kwong Trading Company
    Nam Tung Bank Building
    Rua Da Praia Grande 65-A
    Cable: NAMKWONG MACAO

TECHIMPORT

China National Technical Import Corporation
Industrial technological improvements and complete plants and factories.

Head Office
    Erligou
    Xijiao, Beijing
    Phone: 890931
    Cable: TECHIMPORT BEIJING
    Telex: 22244 CNTIC CN

The China Ocean Shipping Company

In general, China arranges for its own shipping. Three national corporations manage Chinese shipping: The China Ocean Shipping Company, the China National Foreign Trade Transportation Corporation, and the China National Chartering Corporation. The China Ocean Shipping Company (COSCO) is part of the Ministry of Communications. It operates China's flag vessels and controls Chinese ships operating under foreign flags and shipping firms in Macao and Hong Kong. This company also manages transshipment of cargo. For the United States, Hong Kong and Tokyo are the most common transshipment points:

China Ocean Shipping Company
6 Dong Changan Jie
Beijing
Cable: COSCO BEIJING
Telex: 22264 CPCPK CN

The China National Foreign Trade Transportation Corporation

The China National Foreign Trade Transportation Corporation (SINOTRANS) arranges customs clearance and delivery of all import and export cargos by land, sea, air, or post. It acts as agent for delivering goods through China's ports. Sinotrans can arrange marine insurance and make claims on behalf of cargo owners. It's subordinate to the Ministry of Foreign Economic Relations and Trade:

The China National Foreign Trade Transportation Corp.
Erligou
Xijiao, Beijing
Cable: ZHONGWAIYUN BEIJING
Telex: 22153 TRANS CN
       22154 TRANS CN
       22265 TRANS CN

The China National Chartering Corporation

China's Foreign Trade Corporations normally buy F.O.B. and sell C.I.F. Therefore, the China National Chartering Corporation (ZHONGZU) usually handles shipping. Most export contracts stipulate the buyer may not designate a particular vessel or shipping line. However, sometimes a buyer may submit a letter of preference specifying a carrier if ZHONGZU doesn't specify a carrier. ZHONGZU books shipping space for import and export cargoes. It provides a similar service for principals located abroad:

The China National Chartering Corporation
Xijiao, Beijing
Cable: ZHONGZU BEIJING
Telex: 22153 TRANS CN
       22154 TRANS CN
       22265 TRANS CN

The China National Import and Export Commodities Inspection Corporation

CHINSPECT must inspect all goods before they are shipped into or out of China. Chinese contractual language reflects this final right of inspection. It remains a hindrance in U.S.-China grain trade. Most U.S. exporters would not be willing to sell to China because final inspection is at China's port of destination. Now that China has started to stress various kinds of competitive schemes, Chinese producers are more willing to allow outside inspection and quality control before the product leaves China. Under many standard Chinese purchase contracts, CHINSPECT is given responsibility to test imported machinery. This provision is the usual Chinese basis for making a claim of faulty equipment. In many cases, manufacturers must submit their own certificates of inspection. Sometimes, Chinese engineers will visit the Western plant where the equipment is produced. However, the Chinese won't accept this kind of inspection as final. CHINSPECT has divisions that inspect agricultural and animal products, industrial and mining products, and light industrial and textile products. It's competent, exacting, and just in determining whether shipments conform to contractual requirements. The production unit performs the first check, the FTC the second, inland CHINSPECT officials the third, and dockside officals the final. China demands the power of final inspection. This demand stems from China's distaste of losing authority over customs, as it did in the last century. Sometimes, the Chinese have withheld 10 percent of the purchase price pending inspection. Sellers have marveled at the meticulousness of Chinese inspections and the particularity of Chinese claims. Where other buyers of vehicles are content to buy small parts by the volume, the Chinese count them one by one. Where other buyers of steel pipe X-ray the pipe at random for cracks, the Chinese may X-ray every inch to make claims for hairline cracks, which most buyers would ignore. The seller must be prepared for extraordinarily detailed inspections and for some uncommon, perhaps minor, claims:

> The China National Import and Export Commodities Inspection Corporation
> 2 Changan Street E.
> Beijing
> Phone: 553876
> Cable: CHINSPECT BEIJING

The China International Trust Investment Company

In 1979, the State Council established the China International Trust Investment Company (CITIC) to help set up joint ventures with foreign firms. It greets investors, finds their requirements, and matches them with a suitable Chinese firm. The CITIC may also sit in on negotiations:

> The China International Trust Investment Company
> 2 Qianmen Dong Dajie
> Beijing
> Phone: 558841
>   550905
> Cable: CITIC BEIJING
> Telex: 22305 CITIC CN

China International Trust Investment Company
Bank of China Building
Hong Kong

The China Council for Promotion of International Trade

Established in 1952, the China Council for Promotion of International Trade (CCPIT) maintains contacts with foreign firms. It sponsors foreign exhibits in China. CCPIT acts as a legal advisor to FTCs. It registers foreign trademarks with the Administration Bureau for Industry and Commerce, issues certificates of origin, and certifies documents. (Authentication of documents by non-Chinese consulates isn't acceptable.) CCPIT also deals with disputes through the Maritime Arbitration Commission and the Foreign Trade Arbitration Commission. Chinese officials prefer to use these commissions to settle disputes between Chinese organizations and foreign companies. If the CCPIT rejects a proposal, it transfers the proposal to the China International Trust Company for further consideration. CCPIT publishes China's most well-known foreign trade journal, *China's Foreign Trade*. This magazine has information on its foreign trade policies and organizations as well as advertisements for Chinese export commodities:

The China Council for Promotion of International Trade
4 Taiping Qiao Street
Beijing
Cable: COMTRADE BEIJING
Telex: 668981
       662835
       660436

CCPIT also contains a center for distributing samples and literature on new foreign products to Chinese end-users:

Center for Introducing Literature and Samples of New Foreign Products
P.O. Box 1420
Beijing

Professional Groups

Groups, such as the China Chemical Society and the China Civil Engineering Society, assess and sometimes select foreign technologies through contact with foreign counterparts. They also disseminate new ideas through seminars. Most groups represent research institutes or industrial ministries.

Delegations

Planners send delegations in a series of logically arranged groups to technologically superior firms in industries of interest. A survey group visits several vendors in different countries. The Chinese might decide one or two nations are leaders in a particular technology (Japan in electronics, West Germany in steel-making, the United States in oil drilling) and limit visits accordingly. A study group then visits firms on the basis of the previous reports. These secondary delegations are smaller and have a higher level of expertise than the first delegations. The report from this group is the basis for selecting a supplier. Once a decision is reached, a purchasing group might enter the picture. It has financial experts with authority to agree on contractual details. Purchasing delegations are unusual. Most negotiations and contract signings take place in Beijing. In 1977–78, 2,000 Chinese technicians and officials traveled to Japan, Western Europe, and the United States. Japan accounted for one-third of the delegations, the United States 30 percent, and West Germany 10 percent. In 1979–80, 1,398 Chinese delegations visited the United States for deals or information about American technology.

The Chinese Export Commodities Fair

Twice a year, foreign dealers, from Macy's, Neiman-Marcus, Fiat, and Hitachi, descend on Guangzhou, 75 miles northeast of Hong Kong. The Chinese Export Commodities Fair (CECF) is China's most important annual business event. It accounts for nearly half of its yearly export sales and a third of its total turnover. The fair continues to play a vital role in introducing first-time traders to China. FTCs and the CCPIT cosponsor the fair. It exports cereals, oils, foodstuffs, native produce and animal by-products, textiles, light industrial goods, chemicals, metals and minerals, machinery, and handicrafts. The fair also imports chemicals, synthetic fibers, pulp and paper, and steel. More than 25,000 businessmen and 50,000 visitors attend the fair. Attendance requires invitation. Businessmen who want to attend should get an invitation from the appropriate FTC, the CCPIT head office in Beijing, or CECF officials at the Guangzhou Foreign Trade Center. The fair is held from April 15th through May 15th and October 15th through November 15th at the Trade Fair Exhibition Hall located off Renmin Road in a large area between the Guanzhou Railway Station and the Dong Fang Hotel. Business is conducted Monday through Saturday, with the exception of May 1st, a national holiday, and from 8:30 to 11:30 a.m. and 2:30 to 5:30 p.m. While the fair is in progress, CECF operates liaison offices at a number of hotels. Each liaison office is responsible for a group of nationalities:

Chinese Export Commodities Fair
Guangzhou Foreign Trade Center
Renmin Bei Lu
Guangzhou
Phone: 30849
      61149
Cable: CECFA
Liaison Office Number One: Dong Fang Guest House
Liaison Office Number Two: Guangzhou Guest Office
Liaison Office Number Three: People's Mansion
Liaison Office Number Four: Li Hua Guest House
Liaison Office Number Five: Bai Yun Guest House

Upon arriving in Guangzhou, executives should present their invitation to the Fair Reception Office in their hotel. The Liaison Office will issue you a numbered ribbon, which is a door pass to the fair. You should ask the office to set an appointment for you with FTC officials. If you plan to stay in Guangzhou more than 48 hours, you must register with the Guangzhou Public Security Bureau (GPSB). You can arrange registration by handing your passport or travel document for transfer to the GPSB to the China Travel Service counter at the hotel. Businessmen may also make appointments by approaching FTC officials on the floor of the exhibition hall. Each of the major exporting FTCs has permanently assigned quarters in the exhibition hall. FTC representatives may be found at tables near product exhibits in their designated areas. Discussion may take place at these tables or in rooms on the second and third floors. FTCs supply interpreters. It's not unusual to find competitors sitting at adjacent tables. FTC representatives often adopt a passive attitude, behaving more like order-takers than salesman. Because the variety of goods on display will tempt window-shopping, you should have a clear idea of what you want before you go. An impulsive decision can be counter-productive, as it can take two or three days to find the appropriate Chinese agent to discuss the product's availability. Some traders dislike the fair's hurley-burley atmosphere. They prefer to make exploratory contact at Guangzhou and then promote further discussions at Beijing. Take up such special arrangements with the FTC.

Guangzhou's first fair was held in 1957. It attracted 1,200 visitors from 20 countries and regions to view 12,000 products. Most guests were compatriots from Macao and Hong Kong. At the time, China was recovering from the Korean War. Agricultural production had reached record levels, but commercial links with the West were limited because of the embargo. Most transactions involved exchanges of chemicals and machinery for produce. The fair grew despite hard times induced by the Great Leap Forward. Then came the Cultural Revolution. The situation was so far out of hand by 1967, the autumn fair had to be delayed. Throughout the Cultural Revolution, the fair remained the focus of China's foreign trade. As domestic conditions improved, trade delegations spread across the globe. Machimpex and Techimport, China's main corporations for importing capital goods, held technical seminars with foreign firms at the fair. In 1974, the Chinese opened a new complex. By 1975, 40,000 items were on display. The 1978 fair saw great participation of Third World participants and overseas Chinese. It attracted 25,000 visitors from 110 nations. Seventy-seven North Americans, representing 300 firms, sold $83 million in commodities (mainly industrial chemicals) and bought $62 million in crafts, metals, and textiles. Future fairs will be scaled down and more true to their exporting function; importers will deal in Beijing. Since 1975, China has also held mini-fairs that specialize in a single group of commodities. Fairs are usually held for two or three weeks in major cities and concentrate on products such as carpets, feathers, furs, and crafts. Although they are scheduled in an ad hoc manner and often on short notice, mini-fairs seem destined to become regular events. Interested persons should contact FTC branch offices to obtain information and invitations.

Local Administrations

The Chinese are decentralizing foreign trade. In 1980, they announced that the cities of Beijing, Shanghai, and Tianjin, and the provinces of Guangdong, Fujian, and Liaoning have established units to negotiate with foreign firms. Firms interested in small (less than $3 million) ventures should contact officials in these regions. Any venture involving more than $3 million requires approval at the national level. These local administrations have some authority over production facilities. They are also forming local Foreign Trade Corporations. These firms will manage the affairs of the local offices of national foreign trade organizations. With authority focused more at the local level, foreign buyers will find it less difficult than in the past to make contact with local manufacturers. Names and addresses of local organizations playing this role are as follows:

Beijing Foreign Trade Corporation
190 Chanonei Street
Beijing
Phone: 554871
Cable: JINGRTA BEIJING
Telex: 22470 BFTCC CN

Shanghai Foreign Trade Corporation
27 Zhongshan Road E. 1
Shanghai
Phone: 217350
Cable: SHANTRA SHANGHAI
Telex: 33034 SIMEX CN

Tianjin Foreign Trade Corporation
57 Hubei Road
Tianjin
Phone: 34872
Cable: JINTRA TIANJIN

Fujian Foreign Trade Corporation
Gengin Road
Fuzhou
Phone: 34018
Cable: 6319

Guangdong Foreign Trade Corporation
2 Qiaoguang Road
Guangzhou
Guangdong
Cable: COMTRADE GUANGZHOU

Liaoning Foreign Trade Corporation
135 Stalin Road
Dalian
Calbe: LIAOTRA DALIAN
Telex: 23041

Finally, local corporations have been established to encourage foreign investors to find Chinese partners for joint ventures, trade compensation, or other projects. The functions of these companies are much like those of the China International Trust and Investment Company for the country as a whole:

Beijing Economic Development Corporation
3 Taijiang
Beijing
Phone: 551071

Tianjin International Trust and Investment Corporation
36 Hubei Road
Tianjin
Phone: 36394
       31767
Cable: 2094 TIANJIN

Fujian Investment Enterprise Corporation
185 Bayiqi Road, North
Fuzhou
Phone: 33093
Cable: 8199 FUZHOU

Guangzhou Municipal Foreign Trade Bureau
Changti
Guangzhou
Phone: 20945

Shanghai International Trust Service Corporation
521 Henan Central Road
Shanghai
P.O Box 3066
Phone: 226650
Cable: SINTRUST SHANGHAI

7

LAW

China's legal system is a combination of native concepts, civil and common law, and Communist theory. It evolved over a millennia, uninfluenced by foreign jurisprudence. China's legal tradition is the longest of any enduring community. In the early years of the People's Republic, it experimented, with varying degrees of commitment and intensity, with a Soviet-style legal system. The Cultural Revolution destroyed many of China's legal institutions. In the wake of the overthrow of the Gang of Four, China's leadership has used law to strengthen its administration. The reemergence of Chinese law as a legitimate academic discipline at Beijing University's Department of Law and publication of rules to guide Western participation and guard Chinese interests is proof of this. China's present laws regulate shipping, banking, investments, foreign exchange, offshore oil, taxation, etc. You must understand these laws to engage in business with China.

The Contract

Strict adherence to the contract is the expected norm. Since the Chinese tend to interpret contracts literally, you should exclude anything you cannot abide and include clauses important to you even though they may be customary under other contracts. You should carefully define assurances about product performance. The

Chinese sometimes buy only a section of a processing line, preferring to substitute more labor-intensive methods for the remainder. Such substitution can affect the performance of the entire system. Contracts are not unique to the Western legal tradition. In China, such formal agreements existed before Han times. They covered marriage, land transfers, and transactions involving sale of goods, tenancy, and labor. Chinese attach great importance to contracts and expect compliance by all. Contracts are binding and must be honored to the last letter. Canceling a contract will reduce chances of a future trading relationship. Negotiations of major plant sales to China, with provisions for onsite personnel and training, involve complexities that require detailed contracts. Addenda describing specific provisions and responsibilities of each party are sometimes more explicit than would be necessary in commercial transactions in other parts of the world. You should make sure all possible areas of misunderstanding are settled before completing the contract. Settlement of a dispute can be a lengthy and costly process, disregarding the damage it may cause the reputation of your firm. You should also ensure versions of all official papers agree completely. Remember to specify in the contract conditions verbally agreed to during negotiations. Importers should repeat such stipulations when opening letters of credit. The best protection in dealing with the Chinese is to see that genuine agreement exists on all points. A letter of intent or a handshake won't seal an agreement.

Contract forms are usually the same in essence (appendix eight). They are short, covering two sides of one sheet of paper, and are issued in either French or English and Chinese. Each language is equally valid. Chinese contracts are weighted toward protection of Chinese interests. Sales contracts thus contain more protection in the case of failure by the seller than do purchase contracts. In general, Chinese sales contracts are less stringent than Chinese purchase contracts. Hence, sellers to China generally have to meet more exacting requirements than Chinese sellers. FTCs have standardized two-page sales and purchase contracts that they prefer to use. They are ordinarily more willing to revise their forms in the case of Chinese purchases than Chinese sales. Chinese organizations, however, have become more flexible on many aspects of the contract. Therefore, you should consider all apsects of the contract negotiable. Nevertheless, be prepared to meet stiff Chinese resistance to suggestions for contract modifications. Western equipment sellers have encountered difficulties associated with delivery. Since FTCs tend to buy F.O.B., they determine the shipping arrangements. In a number of cases, ships have arrived considerably later than expected. This delay has resulted in substantially increased interest and warehousing costs for Western firms. Another problem has been crowding at Chinese ports. Unloading delays have resulted in demurrage costs for Western shippers in some cases in which China bought on C.I.F. terms. Chinese export contracts tend to be vague about the shipment date.

They don't contain provisions for penalties, if there are delays. This has caused problems for Western importers—especially those who have had imported goods whose demand is seasonal. In contrast, Chinese purchase contracts are specific about delivery dates and penalties. One typical formulation from a machinery purchase contract called for a penalty at a fixed percentage of the contract to be assessed for each seven days to a specified maximum of delay. The Chinese side usually retains the right to cancel the contract for late delivery.

The *force majeure*—an uncontrollable force compelling modification or cancellation of the contract—has a narrower meaning in China than in the rest of the world. The Chinese will resort to such a clause if their interests so warrant. In 1981, for example, China's State Council postponed a steel project in Shanghai by invoking an economic *force majeure*, a cancellation clause based entirely on its ability to pay—something unheard of in past dealings with China. The second phase of the $5 billion Baoshan steelworks was tabled, effectively annulling seven major contracts with Japanese and West German firms. Ironically, the affair occurred amid an effort to establish a legal code to govern business in China. However economically sensible it may have been to pare down an overambitious project, a blemish now marred China's once perfect record of painstaking observance of contractual arrangements. But China's willingness to renegotiate and settle most remaining issues showed sensitivity to the consternation its actions caused. Another cause of consternation has been cancellation of contracts by higher authorities after lower authorities signed contracts with foreign firms. In the past, you could assume that your negotiations with Chinese companies were executed pursuant to prior authorization by Chinese planning authorities. Now the assumption that higher ratification of these contracts is *pro forma* is wrong.

Both import and export contracts have clauses stating that the seller won't be responsible for non-performance. There is usually no penalty clause for delay in delivery by Chinese sellers, for the Chinese are often late in making delivery. China's internal transportation system and ports are so congested, delivery deadlines are often unmet. *Force majeure* clauses in Chinese contracts are vague. The Chinese have resisted foreign efforts to specify acceptable instance of *force majeure* and have, for ideological reasons, been unwilling to specify acts of God or labor unrest. Only export contracts may specify certain natural disasters and "any other causes beyond their control" as mitigating factors. The Chinese seldom enforce the 5 percent penalty for fulfillment delay if the seller can show he acted in good faith. Although the formal language of Chinese penalty clauses is strict, FTCs in some cases have chosen to extend the delivery date without penalty. Although a liberal policy cannot be assumed, Chinese corporations have accepted the explanations of Western firms that natural disasters and strikes caused delays and have waived penalties. A more difficult problem for exporters of sophisticated equipment is to get a clause that the export must be approved by the Western government. In their hearts, Chinese businessmen regard a business arrangement as a matter of honor between men of honor. They regard *force majeure* as a legal smokescreen. Thus, Western firms should consider accepting an occasional loss in an individual transaction to preserve their good name. Some exporters have modified parts of the standard form, including a more acceptable *force majeure* clause. The prevailing attitude of Western firms is that attempts to negotiate changes in this clause are more trouble than they are worth, since the end result of any dispute and claim will generally be the same.

Trademarks

In contrast to Western law, Chinese law affords little protection for industrial property rights. However, China is studying international conventions for trademarks, patents, and copyrights. As it establishes a comprehensive legal system, investors will find China's working environment more palatable.

Firms may register a trademark in China, if they meet straightforward preconditions of the Trademark Registration Agency of the Administration Bureau for Industry and Commerce, an organ of the China Council for the Promotion of International Trade. Submit:

- A separate application, in duplicate, for each trademark.
- A power of attorney, in duplicate, authorizing the CCPIT to act for the firm. The Chinese embassy must notarize the original copy of the power of attorney.
- A certificate of nationality. This certificate shows where the firm was organized.
- Twelve prints of the trademark for each application. This should be accompanied by an explanation of the mark's derivation.

Marks registered by local enterprises have no fixed duration. They are valid until the registrant withdraws them. Marks registered by foreign firms are valid for 10 years, renewable at the end of that time. The owner of a registered trademark acquires the exclusive right to use it in China. In 1979, the United States and China recognized the right of nationals of each country to apply for trademark registration in the territory of the other. Reciprocal agreements also exist with Canada, Britain, Sweden, Denmark, West Germany, Switzerland, Finland, Italy, Belgium, Luxemburg, New Zealand, Australia, East Germany, Greece, Norway, Hungary, Czechoslovakia, the Netherlands, and France. If a foreign subsidiary has registered a trademark in China, that subsidiary may reassign it to its parent company. This should be done if the parent firm wants to deal with China directly. Firms may not register markings similar to China's national flag or other emblems, to national flags or emblems of other countries, the Red Cross or Red Crescent, or marks having "ill effect politically." Firms cannot register medical trademarks without a certificate from China's Health Ministry authorizing the product's manufacture. China may cancel a trademark if the product's quality is unacceptable, if the mark is altered without permission, if it hasn't been used for one year and permission for non-use hadn't been obtained, or if a third party persuades China to cancel it.

Patents

The transfer of technology raises the question of protection of patent and proprietary rights. The Chinese demand all available technical documentation to understand your product's technology thoroughly. With practice and an increased supply of parts, they will be able to make your product without tutelage. "You sell them an aircraft, and two years later they've got an airline factory," said a Soviet diplomat, reflecting on Soviet aid to China in the 1950s. China will try to copy some foreign products and processes, but engineering problems involved in gearing for production are considerable. The process of developing from prototype to mass production will deter replication of all but the most simple technology. Nevertheless, complaints from foreign businessmen and subsequent denials of information forced Beijing to reconsider its stand on "intellectual property rights." Citing China's unauthorized duplication of imported technology, firms refused to discuss available technology without some guarantee of protection. According to provisions of the U.S. Trade Act of 1974, the conclusion of most favored nation status depended on China's protection of patents no less than that provided in the Paris Convention for the Protection of Industrial Property. (See Appendix 7: 1979 *Agreement Between the United States of America and the People's Republic of China,* article VI.) In 1978, Foreign Trade Minister Li Qiang said China might join the Paris Convention to avoid patent problems involved in technology transfer. It has already joined the World Intellectual Property Organization:

> World Intellectual Property Organization
> 32 Chenmin des Colombettes
> 1211 Geneva 20, Switzerland
> Phone: (022) 34.63.00
> Telex: 22 376

While China is drafting a patent code, firms should stipulate patent protection in their contracts. Each company must assess the utility of such contractual assurances.

Copyrights

Chinese going abroad are told to get as much written material as possible. The Chinese National Publications Import Corporation has ordered thousands of technical titles from Western booksellers. In 1978, it spent $6 million on U.S. books and periodicals, one-third of its foreign literature purchases. China clearly wants to be an educated consumer of technology. Its attitude toward Western literature has changed since the radical era. China has reversed a longstanding policy against recognizing foreign copyrights. Until China adopts a copyright law along the lines of the Universal Copyright Convention, however, Western books, plays, music, and other literary and artistic works are vulnerable to copying, translation, and reproduction without authorization from or compensation to the original copyright owner.

Arbitration

Almost all Chinese contracts have arbitration clauses of three types: arbitration in China, arbitration in the country of the defendant, and arbitration in a third country. Both the first and second clauses involve artibration in China, for if the foreign party is the plantiff, the country of the defendant is China. The Chinese will sometimes permit arbitration in a third country. Switzerland and Sweden are the most common countries, but Canada, Singapore, and others have been used in U.S.-China commercial contracts. The Chinese side has also agreed to use non-Chinese arbitration procedures. It has even accepted the use of the third country's law to govern a handful of transactions. In the past, China had been reluctant to endorse Western claims of impartiality. The Chinese side in contract negotiations will press for a clause requiring that arbitration will take place in China. The Foreign Economic and Trade Arbitration Committee (FETAC) of the China Council for the Promotion of International Trade will govern proceedings. The Provisional Rules of Procedure, adopted in 1956 and effective today, feature stipulations that have made the prospect of arbitration in China unattractive to foreigners. For example, the rules provide that Chinese be the official language of the arbitration commission (article 36) and that arbitrators be selected from among members of the FETAC (article 4). On January 1, 1982, China's Provisional Regulations on Lawyers went into effect. These regulations state by implication that foreign counsel is not qualified to practice law in China, and therefore cannot represent the foreign party during arbitration. To qualify as a lawyer, an individual must be a Chinese citizen (article 8) and one of the "State's legal workers" (article 1), who "must serve the cause of socialism and the interests of the people" (article 3) in "litigation and nonlitigation matters" (article 5). We might be wrong to suppose this regulation applies to foreign counsel as well as Chinese lawyers. However, as Eugene Theroux, partner in the office of Baker and McKenzie and frequent commentator on Chinese law, notes: "Until this issue is clarified and foreign parties are reasonably certain their claims in arbitration will be properly advocated, another reason has evolved for resisting arbitration in China."

From the Chinese viewpoint, a reasonable objection to Western arbitration is that the Chinese language—spoken by one-quarter of mankind—is not one of the languages used in such arbitration proceedings. Furthermore, Western arbitration arises from the adversarial tradition, in contrast to the Chinese ideal of resolving disputes through consultation and conciliation. Even in such lawyer-ridden societies as the United States, only a small percentage of contracts ever need resort to the court of law. In practice, the Chinese prefer to settle disputes through informal discussion rather than arbitration. Disputes are often resolved by adjusting new contracts rather than invoking penalty clauses. Such practices require trust on both sides and would be ineffective if the two parties didn't have a long-term relationship. Some business firms are reluctant to bring disputes to formal arbitration for fear that this would be considered an "unfriendly" act and would undermine the development of long-term relations with China. Contrary to this belief, China isn't reluctant to go to arbitration, nor does it consider it unfriendly on the part of foreign trading partners to ask for arbitration. In fact, China encourages the use of its arbitration procedure. It's less costly and less complicated than involving a third country in the dispute. Because amicable conciliation is frustrating, time-consuming, and not always entirely amicable, it's still best to try to settle disputes without invoking arbitration.

Article 14 of China's joint venture law says that "disputes arising between parties to the joint venture...may be settled through...arbitration by an arbitral body of China or through arbitration by an arbitral body agreed upon by the parties." Arbitration clauses, however, generally call for negotiations in Beijing under terms set by the Chinese Foreign Economic and Trade Arbitration Committee. There have been instances when proceedings were begun before this tribunal and then were settled out of court. In maritime disputes, the Maritime Arbitration Commission of the CCPIT handles the matter. Any party needing arbitration should write to one of these two commissions. Indicate:

- The name and address of the claimant and the party against whom the claim is being made.
- Details of the claim and supporting evidence.
- The name of the arbitrator representing the claimant or, in the absence of a nominee, a request to the director of the Arbitration Commission for the appointment of an arbitrator.

A deposit to cover the estimated cost of the arbitration is required on application. The cost of foreign trade arbitration is usually one-half percent of the disputed amount and 1 percent for maritime arbitration. The successful party is entitled to a refund of the deposit.

In the Chinese arbitration system, friendly negotiations and arbitration form a continuous process; neither should be considered in isolation without reference to the other. Even after formal written reference to arbitration has been made to the relevant commission, the initial approach to the commission is still through friendly negotiations. The Arbitration Commission conducts independent investigations into the facts of the case and explores possible avenues of conciliation. An award has three parts: the facts of the case, the determination of liability, and the principal part of the award. The principal part of the award is read to the parties at the closing session of the hearing. The full award with reasons for the decision is delivered in writing within fifteen days from the date of hearing. Awards are final and no appeal for revision before a court of law or any other organization is possible. However, an explanation of the award or reasons for the award will be made, if clarification is sought. If the award isn't satisfied within the time specified, the People's Court will enforce it by motion of the party in whose favor the award has been made.

Commerical disputes arising from international transactions may be referred to alternative arbitration procedures. Under terms of the 1979 U.S.-China Trade Agreement, both sides agreed that:

> If such disputes cannot be settled promptly by any of the above-mentioned means, the parties to the dispute may have recourse to arbitration for settlement in accordance with provisions specified in their contracts or other agreements to submit to arbitration. Such arbitration may be conducted by an arbitration institution in the People's Republic of China, the United States of America, or a third country. The arbitration rules of procedure of the relevant arbitration institutions are applicable, and the arbitration rules of the United Nations Commission on International Trade recommended by the United Nations, or other international arbitration rules, may also be used where acceptable to the other parties of the dispute and the arbitration institutions (article VIII).

The International Chamber of Commerce and the American Arbitration Association are recognized sources of international commercial arbitration assistance:

> United States Council of the International Chamber of Commerce
> 1212 Avenue of the Americas
> New York, NY   10036
> Phone: (212) 582–4850

> American Arbitration Association
> 140 W. 51st Street
> New York, NY   10020
> Phone: (212) 977–2000

A most pervasive concept in China is harmony. In arbitration, harmony is preserved by friendly discussion until compromise is reached, not by litigious proceedings. Accommodation concerning the interpretation of terms in a Chinese contract settles disputes rather than a victory for the "right." There is no single right in a harmonious world, nor are there rights in the Western sense. Harmony demands friction be avoided by elaborate sensitivity for the feelings of others. This accounts for the importance of "face." It's not an alien idea. In Western society, face translates as pride, dignity, ego, personal prestige, self-respect. To avoid insulting a guest, the Chinese cultivate a habit for euphemisms. If the Chinese don't wish to conclude a deal, for example, they will say, "We'll think about it." That is probably the most negative response you will hear, for they are reluctant to respond directly to any situation. Where face is involved, form is superior to substance. Courtesy has an esthetic value that means more than mere good manners. In fact, face is more virtuous than honesty—hence the wide-spread acceptance of bribery and the sense of ruffled dignity in Asian countries when Westerners rail at the practice. With Chinese friends, you must remember the principle of reciprocity. If you give them a gift that is beyond their power to repay in equal measure, you put them in a serious bind. Jerome Alan Cohen, Professor of Law at Harvard Law School, is one person close to Chinese thinking. In 1979, he lectured Beijing municipality officials on Western commercial law. Cohen has frequently advised China's government on legal reforms. "No Chinese would understand Shylock's claim to a pound of flesh in *The Merchant of Venice*," Cohen says. "The important thing is human relations. When you allow for disputes in contracts, you imply a lack of trust."

Negotiations can only succeed if all parties assent to a common standard transcending the dispute. For Westerners, that standard is the adversary system, built on a Roman-Germanic legal heritage. For the Chinese, that standard is trust, arising from collective, ethical behavior. To an extent not conceded by Chinese Communists, Chinese law is still based on Confucian ethics, wherein right action is a meld of custom and propriety demonstrated by the sage. It is seemingly a paradox—to be law-abiding without law. Yet, these doctrines produced people who had a sense of duties and limits. China didn't develop a philosphy of civil liberties and individual rights after the Western manner. The Western concept of the individual, upholding and upheld by law, has little meaning. But China did inherit a profound moral sense of justice and proper conduct and an admiration for the integrity of the lone individual against the group from tradition. The individual exercised his responsibilities and passions within the context of conscience and civilization rather than the precepts of a constitution. Written contracts are often mere pieces of paper. When the Chinese put ink to paper, Westerners frequently misread the documents. It's hard to find a Chinese-English translation that any four experts agree is accurate. The Chinese have contempt for literalism. They are more interested in impressions that go unspoken, the nuances of conversation that can never be written down, relationships, the spirit of the law. In the absence of commercial law, the Chinese have transacted business in the spirit of trust. China has an excellent reputation for reliability and honesty, but the need for a code and contracts is clear. The word of a Chinese is as good as his bond, and well may he prefer one handshake to ten written contracts. Unfortunately, handshake deals too often wind up in court. A man's honor is sometimes better than his memory. He may not have the slightest intention of going back on his word, but there could be a difference of opinion about what his word was. This accounts for the proliferation of boilerplate—court-tested legal language—in Western contracts. Sometimes, his health or luck isn't as good as his word. To reassure foreigners, the Chinese have accepted the presence of foreign lawyers during contract discussions.

For information and interpretation on current developments on particular Chinese laws, contact:

Trade Development Assistance Division
U.S. Department of Commerce
Washington, DC   20230
Phone: (202) 377-2835

China Council for the Promotion of International Trade
Legal Counsel Office
4 Taipingqiao Street
Beijing
Cable: COMTRADE BEIJING

Coudert Brothers, Attorneys
200 Park Avenue
New York, NY   10017
Phone: (212) 880-4400

Eugene Theroux, Attorney
Baker and McKenzie
815 Connecticut Avenue, N.W.
Washington, DC   20006
Phone: (202) 298-8290

Stanley B. Lubman, Attorney
Heller, Ehrman, White and McAuliffe
44 Montgomery Street
San Francisco, CA   94102
Phone: (415) 772-6000

8 Banking

FINANCE

The Ministry of Finance administers China's financial affairs. Domestic banking activities are the province of the People's Bank of China. The People's Bank has 10,000 branches and 20,000 sub-offices in China. The bank receives deposits from state enterprises and other organizations. It provides credit to meet seasonal or temporary cash problems and mobilizes resources for investment. The government is distributing loans rather than grants for capital investment so that authorities can better monitor performance. The other side of the bank's work—mobilizing savings—brings it into daily contact with the public. China's scarcity of capital forces the People's Bank to use every means to attract investment resources. Although appeals to increase savings are strong, private saving through the bank is voluntary. In 1979, the People's Bank raised interest rates to just over 5 percent per annum for five-year deposits and just under 4 percent for one year. Overseas Chinese get slightly better rates. By Western standards, rates are low, but savings alternatives are few and interest is tax free. The People's Bank also directs such specialized entities as the Construction Bank of China and the China Agricultural Bank. The Construction Bank manages capital investment on a contractual basis and the Agricultural Bank coordinates agricultural investment. In 1979, the Agricultural Bank reopened its doors after 14 years of inactivity.

All commercial transactions with foreign countries must be settled through the Bank of China, the foreign exchange arm of the People's Bank of China. No foreign banks may establish branches in China, but a number of foreign banks enjoy full correspondent relations and manage commercial transactions much as they would with any bank. (Two British banks have had branches in Shanghai since 1949, but the amount of business they are permitted to transact is small.) The First National Bank of Chicago was the first U.S. bank to establish expanded correspondent relations with China, allowing it to handle commercial letters of credit, payments, collections, and foreign exchange transactions for customers. In 1978, First Chicago announced it would no longer do business in Taiwan. In 1979, the bank announced two separate loans of $18 million and $20 million to the Fujian Investment Enterprise Corporation, a provincial Chinese development agency. In 1980, the Bank of China, taking another step to expand its international financial activities, formed a joint-venture merchant bank. First National Bank of Chicago, the Industrial Bank of Japan, and the China Resource Company, China's primary Hong Kong agent for imports and exports, are partners in the venture. The Bank of China is a joint state and private enterprise with limited liability. The government owns two-thirds of the operation, and shareholders control the remaining third. It enjoys special status as an agency of the State Council. The Bank of China both supervises the budget and the monetary system and acts as a commercial bank and savings institution. In addition to its head office in Beijing, the bank has domestic branches in major Chinese cities, Hong Kong, Singapore, London, Luxemburg, and New York City. The London branch manages China's hard currency portfolio. In the late 1960s, China sent 213 tons of gold to London. It shipped another 80 tons in 1976. Reserves of gold and foreign currency stood at about $9 billion in 1981.

China's principal financial outlet is its Hong Kong branch. The Bank of China controls 12 other banks, four of which are on the 407 square-mile British Crown Colony:

Name of Bank	Location of Head Office
Bank of China	Beijing
Bank of Communications	Beijing
China and South Sea Bank	Shanghai
China State Bank	Shanghai
Chiyu Banking Corporation	Hong Kong
Hua Chiao Commercial Bank	Hong Kong
Kincheng Banking Corporation	Shanghai
Kwangtung Provincial Bank	Guangzhou

Nanyang Commercial Bank	Hong Kong
National Commercial Bank	Shanghai
Po Sang Bank	Hong Kong
Sin Hua Trust, Savings & Commercial Bank	Shanghai
Yien Yieh Commercial Bank	Shanghai

Investment capital is scarce. Foreign exchange is ever rarer. As China is anxious to increase foreign currency earnings, Hong Kong is becoming more important than ever. China's largest port is a capitalist enclave of 5.5 million people. From 1976–80, its economy grew 12.75 percent annually, while unemployment was a modest 2 percent despite influxes of refugees. Per capita real income increased 25 percent during the same time. In 1981, it produced a gross domestic product of $22 billion and ranked in the top 20 of the world's trading nations. China earns about a third of its currency from remittances from overseas Chinese and Hong Kong's mainland-controlled banks, stores, shipping firms, and real estate investments. It maintains teams of negotiators, economists, and technicians to watch over its varied interests. Throughout the 1960s and 70s, Hong Kong was consistently the leading market for China's exports and its second largest partner in overall trade. In the late 1970s, Hong Kong received 22 percent of Chinese goods sold abroad, but supplied only 7 percent of its imports. Hong Kong is a major market for Chinese foodstuffs and serves as a link with much of the world. Many goods sent from China to Hong Kong are re-exported to other countries. Britain's lease on 373 square miles of the South China colony expires in 1997. Prime Minister Margaret Thatcher launched negotiations in 1982 to assure the continued stability and special nature of Hong Kong's business environment. China's leaders insist they don't recognize the treaties that gave Hong Kong to Britain. They demand full sovereignty of the entire colony. Reinforced by victory in their war of sovereignty over the Falkland Islands in 1982, the Thatcher government adopted an equally tough stand. China intends to regain Hong Kong. It's doubtful, however, whether China can socialize Hong Kong's institutions without jeopardizing its main source of foreign exchange and capitalist expertise. From China's viewpoint, sovereignty means Communist administration. China might have to settle for a kind of joint rule by a two-nation committee on a gradual transfer of power over a lengthy period under supervision by the United Nations or even symbolic recognition of sovereignty that precludes the actual exercise of authority. Britain could recognize Beijing's claim, fly the Chinese flag alongside the Union Jack over Government House, and make similar gestures while preserving its present administrative structure. In 1977, a senior Chinese official told a Hong Kong trade delegation that China wouldn't try to take the colony back until Taiwan had been liberated. China's handling of Macao suggests how it may deal with Hong Kong. When leftists came to power in Portugal in the 1970s, they tried to return this enclave of 400,000 people to China as part of its decolonialization effort. Beijing rejected this offer, because Macao is a cash cow the way it is. Since the 1840s, legalized gambling has flourished on these six square miles of Chinese territory that Lisbon "temporarily administers." The *Sociedade de Tourismo e Diversoes de Macau,* usually called "the Syndicate," rakes in $200 million in annual profits from its four casinos. Some of this money finds its way back to China.

Credit

China pursues a highly conservative international financial policy. Generally, it finances imports with export earnings, attempting to achieve a balance of trade on a multilateral basis. Since liquidating its debt in 1965, China has avoided long-term credit. However, it has availed itself of short-term credits and deferred payments. Chinese banking emphasizes maintenance of economic stabililty, promotes thrift, discourages deficit spending, and supervises adherence to the national economic plan. The Bank of China was established in 1948, during one of the most severe periods of inflation suffered by an economy. The black market exchange rate was about one U.S. dollar to $12,000,000 in Chinese currency. Since then, China has seen little inflation, although it has experienced production bottlenecks and black markets. Throughout the 1960s, China's per capita imports were among the lowest in the world, on the scale of Finland's. Under these conditions, China was usually able to maintain a balance of trade and a cash on the barrelhead posture.

Trading expansion in the 1970s forced China to modify its refusal to incur long-term indebtedness. In 1974–75, China borrowed a half billion dollars from Western and Japanese banks. Although officials dislike using expressions like "debt" and "foreign investment," they are nevertheless willing to accept medium-term deposits through the Bank of China. China has solicited government-supported export credits. It has also accepted government-to-government economic aid at low interest rates and easy repayment terms. Finally, China has joined the International Monetary Fund (IMF) and the World Bank. (The IMF, attempting to maintain a stable international financial system, lends money to countries with problems repaying debts to private and government lenders. It also bolsters a country's reserves to cover balance of payments. The World Bank finances development projects, primarily in poorer countries.) China's participation in such global clubs makes it a more welcome partner. In the past, some types of U.S. loans to China were prohibited by provisions of the Johnson Debt Default Act. However, an amendment to the act states that countries belonging to the IMF and World Bank are not subject to the strictures of the act.

China has also become a more active participant on the international money market. The Bank of China (BOC) has taken a number of Euro-currency dollar loans and has participated in loan syndications. Moreover, the BOC has made a large number of agreements with various foreign banks for lines of credit. Such credit lines are linked to government-supported credit programs. China's reliance on commercial loans over the next 15 years will require that it maintain its credit rating on the international money market. Although credits and other forms of import financing can smooth repayment obligations, ultimately higher levels of exports are needed. China's failure to invest in mining and agriculture at an appropriate level has forced it to import many goods it should be able to export. Financial considerations might prevent China from attaining all its import goals, but China will be able to finance much of its major capital import program. Short-term financing through suppliers meets most of China's present needs. Deferred payment arrangements will continue. However, a trend toward syndicated direct buyer credits will cover large-scale projects. In 1978, Beijing got a commitment from France for government-backed loans totaling nearly 30 billion francs (U.S. $6.6 billion). Seven British banking groups have also arranged for up to $1.2 billion in credits, guaranteed by the British Export Credits Guarantee Department. As of mid-1979, Beijing had reached major credit agreements with Western government credit agencies and private banks totaling $23 billion. The Japanese Exim Bank extended a $2 billion credit line to help finance Chinese resource development. China will repay the untied loan in Japanese yen with an annual interest rate of 6.25 percent over 10 years. A syndicate of 22 Japanese commercial banks also provided another loan totaling $2 billion, denominated in U.S. dollars. The loan has a 4½ year term and an annual interest rate of 0.5 percent above the prevailing London interbank offer rate.

Opening China to Export-Import loans and guarantees enhances the ability of U.S. firms to compete with suppliers from Japan and Europe. In 1980, President Carter gave Eximbank authority to extend $2 billion in credits to China. The bank offers direct loans for large projects and equipment sales that usually require longer-term financing. It provides export credit guarantees to commercial banks that in turn finance export sales. Due to charter limitations, Exim may not be able to offer interest rates as favorable as those offered abroad. However, without Exim's help, it's unlikely U.S. commercial banks can offer rates close to the 7.5 percent China currently deems acceptable:

Export-Import Bank of the United States
811 Vermont Avenue, N.W.
Washington, DC   20571

Other government credit organizations will finance trade directly through loans to China or work indirectly by subsidizing or guaranteeing export firms or commercial banks:

Canada

Export Development Corporation

This government-owned corporation provides export financing and insurance to foreign purchasers of Canadian goods and services. However, the EDC doesn't use credit subsidies to promote exports.

Federal Republic of Germany

HERMES-Kreditversicherungs

This private company is authorized by the federal government to administer the country's export insurance system. In cases where credit is linked to a clearly defined project, HERMES covers 95 percent of the buyer credits at the request of the bank involved.

France

Compagnie Francaise d'Assurance pour le Commerce Exterieur

This quasi-governmental agency provides export credit insurance to French firms. COFACE doesn't extend credit directly but guarantees such credit.

Italy

Mediocredito Centrale

This organization refinances loans made by other financial institutions.

Japan

Export-Import Bank of Japan

This government-established organization provides financing for heavy industrial exports, loans, and commerical bank guarantees.

Netherlands

Nederlandsche Credietverzekering Maatschappij

NCM extends credit insurance to Dutch exporters and commercial banks.

United Kingdom

Export Credits Guarantee Department

ECGD works through clearing banks by subsidizing their loans to promote British exports.

In addition to Eximbank, the U.S. Department of Agriculture's Commodity Credit Corporation operates an export credit sales program. Under this program, U.S. exporters may apply for export financing of eligible commodities of a deferred-payment sale to a foreign importer. Each month, the department announces commodities eligible for financing under this program and the rate of interest:

The Assistant Sales Manager
Commerical Export Programs
Foreign Agricultural Service
U.S. Department of Agriculture
Washington, DC   20250
Phone: (202) 447-6301

The U.S. exporter can also secure financing through the Private Export Funding Corporation, which provides credits to purchasers of U.S. exports:

Private Export Funding Corporation
280 Park Avenue
New York, NY   10017
Phone: (212) 557-3100

Major banks routinely assess the credit risks of countries. The *Institutional Investor*, a U.S. monthly for moneymen, regularly publishes a summary of world credit rankings. Although China has relaxed its policies toward debt, its financial policies are still among the most conservative in the world and its credit rating is good. Out of 93 nations, China ranked 27th with a credit rating of 7.11 out of 10.00, according to the 1979 analysis. This journal polled 90 leading international bankers on a confidential basis to assess "country risk" on a 1 to 10 scale. By comparison, other nations ranked: Japan, 9.69; Singapore, 7.89; South Korea, 7.12; Malaysia, 7.03; Taiwan, 6.58; and Thailand, 5.47. Western bankers have generally found socialist nations to be good credit risks, because of their stability and repayment record. Nevertheless, China has never dealt in the lofty sums now under discussion and it could borrow more than it could absorb. Its 1979 readjustment suggests how easily it can over-extend itself. A $2 billion buying spree in the early 1970s for Western plants left Beijing with repayment obligations of $1.3 billion in 1977. In the credit market, China is a spring chicken and many are clamoring to pluck it. China needs an institution in Hong Kong, Singapore, or Tokyo to regulate credit flow to China, to allocate funds based on performance, and ensure it doesn't draw too much credit from developing countries. China will perceive such an organization as an infringement on its sovereignty. However, if China cannot pay its debts, it could withdraw from the world again.

Pricing

Pricing is the fundamental revenue-producing element in the marketing plan. Marketing must carefully consider demand, cost, and competition in setting prices. It must also consider the cost of manufacturing, export commission, foreign freight forward, freight to port, consular invoice, packing, marine insurance, and ocean freight. When talks turn to price, Chinese negotiators usually ask foreign firms to quote first. Then they seek concessions, implying a competitor will provide them. The Chinese often invite competing bids. At the Spring fair in 1974, lack of world demand and disenchantment with Chinese delivery performance forced Chinese negotiators to abandon their "non-negotiable fixed prices" policy. Official prices became "negotiable reference prices." The price of minerals, metals, and other products moved down to world levels. This was even true of commodities in which China had a powerful world position, such as antimony, cassia, and anise oil. Since 1974, China's export pricing has been based on a careful analysis of world markets. When the Chinese state a price, it's a reasonable one, one they expect to pay. They choose their words carefully and assume their counterparts do the same. Avoid inaccurate or hypothetical examples. The Chinese show less flexibility in export dealings than in import negotiations. Export prices are keyed to China's evaluation of the market rather than production costs. Thus, importers show no hesitation about demonstrating the availability of similar goods at better prices. China has supported higher oil and raw materials prices. It has moved oil prices in tandem with OPEC. This isn't surprising since China relies heavily on raw materials and agricultural exports. The worst mistake foreign negotiators can make is to give too liberal a deal to get a quick sale. The Chinese will snap it up—and expect the same price on future deals. When that price doesn't materialize, they could blacklist the firm. China's bureaucracy, like the lumbering creature it resembles, never forgets. Trust can only be built up over time. That's why the Chinese have such high regard for well-established firms such as East Asiatic and Krupp. It's better to agree to disagree than to create an unrealistic precedent.

Both parties should agree on deliver terms. Contact the Chamber of Commerce of the United States or the National Foreign Trade Council for their *Revised American Foreign Trade Definitions—1941* for a more comprehensive definition of the following terms. Sellers and buyers may agree to accept these terms as part of the contract. The definitions will then become legally binding on all parties, Adoption of the revised definitions will impress all parties with their respective responsibilities and rights.

C.I.F.

Cost, insurance, and freight to named overseas port. Under this term, the seller quotes a price, which includes the goods, insurance, and all transportation and miscellaneous charges to the point of debarkation from vessel or aircraft.

C. & F.

Cost and freight to named overseas port. Under this term, the seller quotes a price, which includes the cost of transportation to the point of debarkation.

F.O.B.

Free on board. The price quoted includes loading the product onto the carrying vessel, but not shipping it.

In general, Chinese exports are sold C.& F. or C.I.F. and imports are purchased F.O.B., as China can conserve foreign exchange by using its own insurance companies and carriers. Although certain standard contract forms don't use the term F.O.B., the clauses on these forms spell out the responsibilities of the parties in a manner consistent with the common understanding of the term. For instance, these contracts specify the documents, including a "clean on board ocean bill of lading marked freight to collect." The seller must present this to the Bank of China when he wants to negotiate a draft drawn on the letter of credit opened by the bank. Another common clause states that the risk passes when the goods have "passed over the vessel's rail and been released from the tackle." Standard forms used by the chemicals, minerals and metals, and machinery corporations contain clauses clearly identified as F.O.B. terms. These require the China National Chartering Corporation, the Chinese shipping agent, to notify the seller of arrival of the vessel a fixed number of days before the arrival date. The machinery and metals and minerals corporations require the seller to notify them 30 days before the agreed time of shipment, together with details that will allow ZHONGZU to book shipping space accurately. F.O.B. clauses may vary according to the calculation of liability for storage expenses, if a seller has delivered cargo to the port of shipment as agreed, but the Chinese vessel arrives late. The standard chemicals corporation form states that such losses are to be calculated from "the 16th day after expiry of the free storage time at the port." The standard machinery corporation clause simply states that if the Chinese vessel "fails to arrive at the port of loading within thirty days after the arrival date advised by the Buyer, the Buyer shall bear the storage and insurance expenses incurred from the 31st day." In negotiations on this clause, the Chinese may show some flexibility. The seller should be particularly attentive to demurrage. When the Chinese purchase on F.O.B.

terms, they provide that the seller is liable for demurrage if the goods are not ready when the vessel arrives at the port on time. However, the C.I.F. terms are silent on demurrage. Sellers under these terms who have not insisted on demurrage clauses have suffered great losses when unloading of their vessels was delayed at congested Chinese ports. The value of imports for calculating duty payable is the C.I.F. value at port of importation in China. Customs assess this value as the total landed cost of the import, including export duty, packing charges, and other miscellaneous charges involved in the transfer of goods to the Chinese port. Having found Chinese insurance to be a good value, importers prefer C.I.F. to C.&F. terms.

Two laws issued in 1951 (as amended) are the basic regulations governing customs duties and related matters—the Provisional Custom Law and the Customs Import and Export Tariff. Custom duties in the Chinese tariff distinguish between countries having MFN agreement with China and those that do not. Goods shipped from those countries with which China has concluded reciprocal commercial treaties (including the United States) are subject in China to minimum duties, ranging from 5 to 200 percent of taxable value. Goods from countries that don't extend such preferences enter under higher rates, ranging from 7.5 to 400 percent of taxable value.

Payment

In the matter of payments, Chinese contracts are distinctly biased to favor the Chinese. When it is importing, the contract will precisely enumerate documents the foreign party must present before the FTC makes payment. When China is exporting, this information is often missing. Engineering and service contracts often call for lump-sum payments for technology plus commissions on equipment purchases. China unofficially follows the Uniform Customs and Practice for Documentary Credits. Contact the Department of Commerce or the Chamber of Commerce for a copy of these articles. Beneficiaries in China don't normally signify acceptance of amendments to credits. They do advise nonacceptance. In the absence of any advice to the contrary, you may assume beneficiaries have accepted the amendments. Credits may be opened in U.S. dollars, if the contract so stipulates. All charges in connection with documentary credits, such as advising amendments, confirmation, negotiation, and postal and cable expenses, must be borne abroad. Trade transactions usually demand payment by irrevocable documentary credit against presentation of shipping documents and a sight draft. Drafts are a popular and common method of financing exports. A draft is a written instrument drawn by one party (the overseas importer) ordering a second party (the bank) to pay a sum of money to a third party (the exporter) at sight or at some definite future time. Authorization of payment to an exporter is made only after the Bank of China receives all proper shipping documents. Foreign buyers usually have to open letters of credit much earlier than Chinese buyers. Foreign buyers also often have to give immediate notice of completion of loading, while Chinese buyers are apt to be given more time. Foreign buyers are required to have their letters of credit confirmed. Chinese L/Cs are usually not confirmed. Sometimes, letters of credit contain a requirement for a certificate from a Chinese consulate that the steamer carrying the goods is in conformity with Chinese regulations. The consular office will issue this certificate, upon receipt of a non-negotiable copy of the bill of lading. These regulations also apply to drafts sent to China for collection. Depending upon the type of goods being sent, sanitary or quality certificates may also be required. This is especially true for scientific or professional items. The L/C will note these requirements.

These documents are required for all shipments regardless of value or mode of transportation:

Commercial invoice

The invoice should include a detailed description of the goods, the name and address of the supplier or manufacturer, place and date of shipment, name and address of consignee, gross and net weights, and cost. Exporters should be guided by the Chinese importer for other particulars regarding the format of the invoice, number of copies, and any other information required.

Certificate of origin

May be required by the importer or letter of credit. If requested, two copies of the certificate are required. A recognized chamber of commerce must certify the certificate of origin. The chamber of commerce will usually require an additional notarized copy for its files.

Packing list

Usually required. The packing list shows the weights and contents of each shipment.

Bill of lading

There are no special requirements for the bill of lading. It customarily shows the name of the shipper, name and address of the consignee, port of destination, description of goods, listing of freight and other charges, number of bills of lading in the full set, and date and signature of the carrier's official acknowledging receipt on board of the goods for shipment. The information should correspond with that shown on the invoice and packages. The air waybill replaces the bill of lading on air cargo shipments.

Insurance certificate

Imports are usually insured by the foreign trade organization with the state insurance company in China. When the exporter can effect insurance coverage, then he should rely on instructions from the importer or insurance company.

Labeling/packing of hazardous and/or restricted materials

Most United Nations members have adopted the UN recommendations for labeling and packing of hazardous materials in a standardized manner and style. Exporters to China should ascertain from their importers whether or not China currently adheres to these requirements. Shippers must also take into consideration any special Chinese requirements in this regard.

The Chinese normally discharge their obligations under turnkey contracts by payment in cash. A typical contract may provide for payment of a total of 20 to 30 percent of the contract price at two stages prior to the first shipment of equipment, one at the signing of the contract, the other at an agreed-upon date some months thereafter. Most of the balance of the contract price would be paid as agreed percentages of the invoice value of each shipment. The last two payments, often 5 percent each, would be paid respectively upon Chinese acceptance of the plant and expiration of the guarantee period. The buyer's receipt of notification from the seller that the plant is ready for operation is another point at which the Chinese will make payments.

Buyers of Chinese products are usually required to open an irrevocable letter of credit payable to the Bank of China. A letter of credit is a financing instrument opened by a foreign banker with a bank in his locality. It stipulates the purchase price agreed upon by the buyer and seller, the quantity of merchandise to be shipped, and the type of insurance coverage to protect the merchandise in transit. Finally, the letter of credit directs the buyer's bank to transmit credit (payment) to the seller's bank via cable or airmail when all the stipulated conditions have been met. A letter of credit assures the seller of the solvency of the buyer. Most letters of credit are "irrevocable and confirmed" by the seller's bank before they are accepted by the seller. An irrevocable letter of credit is a letter of credit that can neither be modified nor cancelled without the agreement of all concerned. Chinese payment terms usually require that the buyer deliver the L/C by a certain date after the goods have been shipped. In the case of some large import transactions, the FTC may have a L/C opened for only 90 percent of the F.O.B. value of the merchandise, with the remaining 10 percent to be paid, if there are no claims against the exporter. The rate of exchange for each transaction is determined by the Bank of China on the date of negotiation of documents. It's a good idea to arrange for the validity of the L/C to extend 15 days beyond the anticipated date stated in the contract. Since the shipping date is often uncertain and payment may be required a month before the earliest possible shipping date, the foreign buyer may suffer the inconvenience of having his credit tied up while no goods have been received. In the case of Chinese purchases, there will be a time when goods have been shipped and documents sent to the BOC and the foreign seller will not have goods, documents, or payment. Despite China's unusual business practices, the BOC has a reputation for efficiency and integrity and an impeccable payment record. In terms of receiving payment, exporting to China involves little risk.

Will the relevant Chinese organization have any foreign exchange to pay you? The answer will depend to a large extent on the Provisional Regulations for Foreign Exchange Control of the People's Republic of China, promulgated by China's State Council on December 18, 1980 (appendix nine). Its major provisions: The State General Administration of Foreign Exchange Control (SGAFEC) administers control over foreign exchange transactions. The Bank of China is the specialized foreign exchange bank in China. No other financial institution may engage in foreign exchange business, unless approved by SGAFEC. Chinese nationals, foreign organizations, and individuals residing in China must surrender foreign exchange proceeds to the BOC, which will allocate foreign exchange as required. Chinese and foreign nationals and stateless persons may keep foreign exchange in China. Such exchange may not be remitted or carried out of China. If the owners want to sell the exchange, they must sell it to the BOC. They may keep a portion as convertible foreign currency according to the percentage prescribed by the State. Application must be made to the BOC for remittances abroad from such accounts as net profits and other legitimate earnings. Application must be made to SGAFEC for remittances abroad from such accounts covering capital repatriation. These regulations leave many questions unanswered and raise other questions. China has deferred until the publication of future regulations many issues, including specific approval procedures for foreign currency loans to Chinese borrowers.

In many Chinese contracts, payment is made by telegraphic or mail transfer after the BOC branch that opened the L/C got the shipping documents. Exporters who want to be paid as soon as possible may be able to find a bank that is willing to pay the exporter the value of the discounted sight L/C. Hand delivery of shipping documents by firm representatives to China will shorten the length of time it takes for the BOC to get the necessary documents. In negotiating L/C transactions, the BOC uses a network of correspondent banks throughout the world. The foreign correspondent bank opens a Renminbi account in Beijing. The Bank of China opens a hard currency account with a foreign bank. The purchase of Renminbi is then allowed as required by contracts between clients of the foreign bank and the Chinese. Limited correspondent relationships exist with many banks. In the United States, these banks service almost every region and include some of the nation's largest international banks. As of January, 1978, the Bank of China had begun to establish full correspondent relations with these U.S. banks:

American Express International Banking Corporation

American Security Bank

Bankers Trust Company

Bank of America

Chase Manhattan Bank, N.A.

Chemical Bank

Citibank

First National Bank of Boston

First National Bank of Chicago

Manufacturers Hanover Trust

Morgan Guarantee Trust

Ranier National Bank

United California Bank

Wells Fargo Bank

China shows a preference for government-guaranteed export credits. A foreign government, to support its export sector, agrees to insure the private bank against nonpayment or default. These credits are alluring because they can provide longer rates of maturity than those otherwise offered by commercial banks. They are also interest subsidized, can provide a fixed interest rate, and can be denominated in U.S. dollars. Until 1967, China's foreign trade contracts were usually denominated in British pounds sterling. In November, 1967, sterling was devalued 17 percent. China then started to use French francs for trading purposes. In 1968, the franc weakened and sterling regained part of its previous role. Chinese sellers prefer to denominate contracts in their own currency, Renminbi. There are exceptions. China National Chemical Import and Export Corporation has signed contracts for crude oil exports in U.S. dollars. The Renminbi tends to follow movements of the strongest European currencies. The New China News Agency broadcasts daily rates. The Chinese insist on a fixed price in a currency acceptable to the seller. Prices are usually stated in RMB, but may be quoted in other currencies, including the French franc, Swiss franc, Belgian franc, West German deutschmark, Dutch guilder, and U.S. dollar.

Insurance

FTCs usually arrange insurance through the People's Insurance Company
of China (PICC), a state-owned agency:

People's Insurance Company of China
108 Xijiaomingziang
P.O. Box 2149
Beijing
Phone: 335150

Previously, Chinese goods were sold on a C.I.F. basis. Foreign importers
now may handle their own insurance. The official policy reads: "The People's Insurance Company of China holds that transport insurance on imports and exports should be arranged by the cargo owners, so China's
imports are generally insured with the People's Insurance Company of
China, whereas insurance on China's exports is generally arranged by the
foreign importers." Chinese insurance coverage for C.I.F. shipments is
regulated through the Ocean Marine Cargo and Ocean Marine Cargo War
Clauses. Ocean Marine Cargo Clauses cover Total Loss Only, with Average, All Risks, and War Risk. That cover is referred to as the China
Insurance Clause. The PICC also underwrites compensatory trade insurance, insurance for foreign goods to be processed in China, insurance for
engineering projects and installation of foreign equipment, property insurance for joint ventures, property and liability insurance for foreign exhibitions, and personal accident insurance for foreign nationals working
in China. The PICC has also made insurance against contract failures and
political risks available to foreign interests operating in China. China has
agents in most major ports to handle claims. These agents make on-the-
spot surveys. They can make settlements locally for claims that fall below
a prescribed amount. PICC also accepts appointments by foreign insurance companies to conduct surveys and handle claims. The Ming An Insurance Company in Hong Kong, the Tai Ping Insurance Company in
Hong Kong and Singapore, and the China Insurance Company in Hong
Kong, Singapore, and Macao are China's overseas agents. These firms
write normal transport and shipping policies. FTCs arrange for insurance
to cover 110 percent of the invoice value. Claims for damage should be
filed within 30 days of arrival of goods. PICC rates, terms, and conditions
generally concur with international standards.

If the People's Insurance Company isn't specified, the trader may
arrange his own insurance. In 1980, the U.S. Overseas Private Insurance
Corporation (OPIC) signed an agreement with the China International
Trust and Investment Corporation that will make OPIC political risk in-

surance and other programs available for U.S. investors in China. The Overseas Private Investment Corporation, an independent government agency formed in 1954 to foster trade with Third World nations, offers the cheapest political risk insurance. It insures investors against war damage, incontrovertability of earnings, arbitrary drawings of letters of credit, or on-demand bonds required as bid, performance, or advance payment guarantees:

> Overseas Private Investment Corporation
> Contract Administration Section
> 1129 20th Street, N.W.
> Washington, DC   20527
> Phone: (202) 632–7825

The Export-Import Bank of the United States offers insurance coverage for political risks associated with the underlying construction or service contract. Coverage applies specifically to the protection of American firms from expropriation and confiscation of physical assets or bank accounts, damages to a firm's property due to war or insurrection, or non-payment of arbitral awards. Exporters can also turn to the Foreign Credit Insurance Association (FCIA). The FCIA covers commercial credit risks (mainly insolvency or prolonged payment default by an overseas buyer) as well as political risks, including such hazards as war, confiscation, and expropriation:

> Foreign Credit Insurance Association
> One World Trade Center, 9th Floor
> New York, NY   10048

The American Institute of Marine Insurance doesn't write insurance. Its functions are informative and advisory. The institute publishes recommended marine clauses:

> American Institute of Marine Underwriters
> 14 Wall Street
> New York, NY   10005

Lloyd's of London will underwrite political risk in virtually unlimited amounts in any country, but premiums are high. A few private underwriters can fill other gaps for premiums that start at 0.1 percent for the safest places and run up to 6 percent or more for the most dangerous places. But no policy can cover a firm's entire foreign exposure.

Joint Ventures

A significant development in Chinese business law was the 1979 enactment of The Law of the People's Republic of China on Joint Ventures Using China and Foreign Investment. In general, this law outlines the minimum terms the Chinese seek in a joint venture. It will undoubtedly encourage more foreign investment in China. The law, however, is intentionally vague. Chinese officials urge foreigners to fill in the gaps in the law with contractual clauses. Under the joint venture system, the Chinese will supply land, factory, infrastructure, labor, and some materials and machinery. Foreigners will provide technology, capital equipment, marketing expertise, management, and possibly raw materials. The formula most desirable to China has the Western company providing the technology, manufacturing know-how, and capital investment for facilities, equipment, and materials as well as responsibility for marketing the end-product outside the country. China accepts the technology and facilities; the Western firm assumes most of the risk. For firms that don't find this formula palatable, one compromise might be sharing capital expenses. Another might be a guarantee of consumption of part or all of the end-product within China.

The law allows remittance of profits, protects equity and intellectual property, and provides for a board of directors, marketing opportunities, and reinvestment incentives. It establishes the administrative machinery to deal with firms wishing to take advantage of this law. Unlike other nations, China puts no ceiling on the degree of foreign ownership in a joint venture. Instead, it has a 25 percent minimum. While equity participation is unlimited, authority is restricted, both through the application of regulations and through the constitution of the venture's board. For example, the chairman must be Chinese. Unsuitable or surplus workers may be discharged, but punishment by firing must be reported to the appropriate level of the government's labor management department for approval. In 1980, the Chinese government promulgated a law covering taxation of income from joint ventures. The tax on joint venture profits won't be applied to ventures exploiting petroleum, natural gas, and other resources. Taxes on such undertakings are fixed separately. The income tax rate is a flat 30 percent plus a local surtax of 10 percent on that. Thus, the joint venture will pay a 33 percent tax on income. Profits repatriated by foreign partners are subject to a further 10 percent tax. However, preferential allowances are provided in special economic zones, including an income tax rate of 15 percent. China provides favorable tax treatment for reinvestment and for investing in forestry and farming. Joint ventures that are scheduled to operate more than 10 years may have their income exempt from taxation in the first year and pay taxes at reduced rates in the second and third years. (See appendix ten for more information on China's income tax regulations.) One objective of the joint venture is to keep the foreigner involved in a project until it is firmly established. Joint ventures may range from 7 to 10 years for light industry and up to 15 years for hotels and resource development. Although there is no special time limit, the Chinese intend to own the enterprises as soon as possible. The China

International Trust and Investment Corporation will help arrange suitable joint venture partners for foreigners.

Here is our interpretation of an unofficial version of the law:

Article 1
With a view to expanding international economic co-operation and technological exchange, the People's Republic of China permits foreign companies, enterprises, other economic entities, or individuals (hereinafter referred to as foreign participants) to incorporate themselves, within the territory of the People's Republic of China, into joint ventures with Chinese companies, enterprises, or other economic entities (hereinafter referred to as Chinese participants) on the principle of equality and mutual benefit and subject to authorization by the Chinese government.

Foreign participants apparently include foreign governments. Chinese participants will generally be large governmental agencies, but will include production units, mines, oilfields, refineries, research institutes, communes, forestry stations, port authorities, and provincial units. Branch operations won't fall under the auspices of joint ventures. The principle of equality and mutual benefit is a key factor in developing a relationship. Both parties must have each other's understanding and confidence to share a common interest in the profitability of the enterprise.

Article 2
The Chinese government protects, by the legislation in force, the resources invested by a foreign participant in a joint venture and the profits due him pursuant to the agreements, contracts, and articles of association authorized by the Chinese government as well as his other lawful rights and interests.

This clause protects the investor and his profits. The "legislation in force" presumably includes this law. Protection for "other lawful rights and interests" is unclear, but may include proprietary industrial information, patents, and copyrights.

All the activities of a joint venture shall be governed by the laws, decrees, and pertinent rules and regulations of the People's Republic of China.

The joint venture law must be interpreted against the backdrop of Chinese law. This means accepting China's banking regulations (including exchange control) and system of central economic planning. Questions raised by the law will largely be answered by how China applies the law.

Article 3
A joint venture shall apply to the Foreign Investment Commission of the People's Republic of China for authorization of the agreements and contracts concluded between the parties to the venture and the articles of association of the venture formulated by them, and the Commission shall authorize or reject these documents within three months.

This article establishes some of the superstructure and schedule for administering joint ventures. The Foreign Investment Control Commission, a part of the Ministry of Foreign Economic Relations, must approve all venture contracts within three months.

> When authorized, the joint venture shall register with the General Administration for Industry and Commerce of the People's Republic of China and start operations under license.

Practice will tell whether the operating license is merely a formality.

> Article 4
> A joint venture shall take the form of a limited liability company. In the registered capital of a joint venture, the proportion of the investment contributed by the foreign participant(s) shall in general not be less than twenty-five percent.

Important is the lack of an upper limit on foreign equity ownership. The Chinese have indicated they will take a flexible approach to foreign equity and, in some cases, may permit up to 99 percent foreign ownership. However, the Chinese partner will always maintain effective control of the enterprise through the appointment of a chairman of the board of directors (article six). Firms should try to finance ventures with Chinese money to the greatest possible extent. If anything happened to the investment, the Bank of China would have to take the brunt of the loss. In the event of turmoil short of expropriation, a firm's low equity profile will give the Chinese an incentive to keep the business running as smoothly as possible.

> The profits, risks, and losses of a joint venture shall be shared by the parties to the venture in proportion to their contributions to the registered capital.
> The transfer of one party's share in the registered capital shall be effected only with the consent of the other parties to the venture.

Limited liability allows the shares held by foreign participants to be transferred.

> Article 5
> Each party to a joint venture may contribute cash, capital goods, industrial property rights, etc., as its investment in the venture.

A partner can count property rights as part of his share in a venture. This ends a longstanding Chinese legal view denying the individual's right to monopolistic control over intellectual property.

> The technology or equipment contributed by any foreign participant as investment shall be truly advanced and appropriate to China's needs.

China's insistence on getting state-of-the-art technology is an unusual feature of the law, unique to joint venture codes of less developed countries. This clause could prove problematic given an honest difference of opinion on what constitutes the latest technology. In view of labor costs and availability, cheaper, modern equipment that is not necessarily "truly advanced" would serve China's needs better.

> In cases of losses caused by deception through the intentional provision of outdated equipment or technology, compensation shall be paid for the losses.

This rather alarmingly worded sanction could be used as a switch to beat the partner whenever goals of the enterprise were not being met.

> The investment contributed by a Chinese participant may include the right to use a site provided for the joint venture during the period of its operations. In case such a contribution does not constitute a part of the investment from the Chinese participant, the joint venture shall pay the Chinese government for its use.

Chinese land can either be contributed as part of the joint investment or rented. Assessing land values could cause problems.

> The various contributions referred to in the present article shall be specified in the contracts concerning the joint venture or in its articles of association, and the value of each contribution (excluding that of the site) shall be ascertained by the parties to the venture through joint assessment.

Partners will negotiate the value of inputs, such as labor and operating costs.

> Article 6
> A joint venture shall have a board of directors with a composition stipulated in the contracts and the articles of association after consultation between the parties to the venture, and each director shall be appointed or removed by his own side. The board of directors shall have a chairman appointed by the Chinese participant and one or two vicechairmen appointed by the foreign participant(s).

China intends to maintain firm control over decision-making. The Chinese will appoint the chairman of the venture.

> In handling an important problem, the board of directors shall reach a decision through consultation by the participants on the principle of equality and mutual benefit.

Basic decisions will be made by consensus rather than majority vote. Chinese managers have a tradition of collective responsibility, a process of compromise and communality nurtured by centuries of development in isolation. Westerners will have to adjust to this system of never-ending discussion and consultation.

The board of directors is empowered to discuss and take action on, pursuant to the provisions of the articles of association of the joint venture, all fundamental issues concerning the venture, namely, expansion projects, production and business programs, the budget, distribution of profits, plans concerning manpower and pay scales, the termination of business, the appointment or hiring of the president, the vice-president(s), the chief engineer, the treasurer, and the auditors as well as their functions and powers and their remuneration, etc.

The president and vice-president(s) (or the general manager and assistant general manager(s) in a factory) shall be chosen from the various parties to the joint venture.

Procedures covering the employment and discharge of the workers and staff members of a joint venture shall be stipulated according to law in the agreement or contract between the parties to the venture.

Chinese managers have less control over planning, marketing, hiring, and firing that do Western managers. Most Chinese directors have trouble with methods of foreign management, and most Chinese workers find taking direction from foreign managers difficult. But China wants practical experience in Western managerial techniques. Partners may thus come to a satisfactory compromise. China is wary of anything smacking of labor exploitation. Under existing regulations, firms must have a government-appointed manager. Such managers usually have little technical training or interest in accepting supervisors sent from Hong Kong. Worker absenteeism also causes concern. Foreign investors have used various incentives to surmount these problems.

Article 7

The net profits of a joint venture shall be distributed between the parties to the venture in proportion to their respective shares in the registered capital after the payment of a joint venture income tax on its gross profit pursuant to the tax laws of the People's Republic of China and after the deductions therefrom as stipulated in the articles of association of the venture for the reserve funds, the bonus and welfare funds for the workers and staff members, and the expansion funds of the venture.

Profits of the venture are allocated to partners according to their share in the venture. The proportion of profits disbursed in foreign exchange will vary. China may let investors recover expenses quickly with returns diminishing thereafter. (The repatriation of profits and the taxation of remitted profits is discussed in appendixes nine and ten.) Although the law provides for reserves for workers, it's unclear whether these funds are negotiable or stipulated.

A joint venture equipped with up-to-date technology by world standards may apply for a reduction or an exemption from income tax for the first two to three profit-making years.

A firm with modern technology qualifies for tax relief or a tax holiday for up to three profitable years—a welcome carrot.

A foreign participant who reinvests any part of his share of the net profit within the Chinese territory may apply for the restitution of a part of the income taxes paid.

The foreign partner may recover taxes if he reinvests his profit.

Article 8
A joint venture shall open an account with the Bank of China or a bank approved by the Bank of China.
A joint venture shall conduct its foreign exchange transactions in accordance with the foreign exchange regulations of the People's Republic of China.

A joint venture can use its own foreign exchange for imports. This will ease the problem of supply through Chinese channels.

A joint venture may, in its business operations, obtain funds from foreign banks directly.

Though subject to Chinese exchange control, foreign banks may directly finance the venture.

The insurance appropriate to a joint venture shall be furnished by Chinese insurance companies.

China doesn't require firms to carry insurance. Those wishing coverage must seek it at their own discretion.

Article 9
The production and business programs of a joint venture shall be filed with the authorities concerned and shall be implemented through business contracts.

Article six empowered the directors to take action on "all fundamental issues concerning the venture." Article nine, however, requires bureaucratic authorization before proceeding.

In its purchase of required raw and semi-processed materials, fuels, auxiliary equipment, etc., a joint venture should give first priority to Chinese sources, but may also acquire them directly from the world market with its own foreign exchange funds.

Ventures may import materials from abroad, but preference must be given to Chinese supplies.

A joint venture is encouraged to market its products outside China. It may distribute its export products on foreign markets through direct channels or its associated agencies or China's foreign trade establishments. Its products may also be distributed on the Chinese market.

The world marketing of the venture's end-product through China's FTCs could produce most hard currency profits.

Whenever necessary, a joint venture may set up affiliated agencies outside China.

Since one of the principal aims of ventures is to earn foreign exchange, they are expected to export most of their production overseas.

Article 10
The net profit which a foreign participant receives as his share after executing his obligations under the pertinent laws and agreements and contracts, the funds he receives at the time when his joint venture terminates or winds up its operations, and his other funds may be remitted abroad through the Bank of China in accordance with the foreign exchange regulations and in the currency or currencies specified in the contracts concerning the joint venture.

Foreign partners may transfer abroad net profits, wages, and part of the original capital at the end of the venture's life.

A foreign participant shall receive encouragement for depositing in the Bank of China any part of the foreign exchange which he is entitled to remit abroad.

The foreign investor is encouraged to bank his earnings in China, receiving interest at LIBOR rates.

Article 11
The wages, salaries, or other legitimate income earned by a foreign worker or staff member of a joint venture, after payment of the personal income tax under the tax laws of the People's Republic of China, may be remitted abroad through the Bank of China in accordance with the foreign exchange regulations.

Foreigners are subject to China's income tax law, passed by the National People's Congress in September 1980. Under the terms of the law, wages and salaries in excess of 800 yuan per month will be taxed at progressive rates ranging from 5 to 45 percent. Other categories of income, such as royalties, interest, dividends and bonuses, and income from lease of property, are to be taxed at the flat rate of 20 percent. The personal income tax on foreign workers is a new departure for China, and one which could seriously inflate operating costs. Employers have paid a high tax on employee salaries in lieu of a personal income tax. Locally registered non-state firms have been subject to a 5.05 percent tax on gross receipts and to a profit tax calculated on a sliding scale starting at 34.5 percent.

Article 12
The contract period of a joint venture may be agreed upon between the parties to the venture according to its particular line of business and circumstances. The period may be extended upon expiration through agreement between the parties, subject to authorization by the Foreign Investment Commission of the People's Republic of China. Any application for such extension shall be made six months before the expiration of the contract.

China intends ventures to be temporary undertakings. It won't permit permanent foreign ownership of land. Product and investment size will determine the venture's duration.

Article 13
In case of heavy losses, the failure of any party to a joint venture to execute its obligations under the contracts or the articles of the venture, *force majeure*, etc., prior to the expiration by consultation and agreement between the parties and through the authorization by the Foreign Investment Commission of the People's Republic of China and registration with the General Administration for Industry and Commerce. In cases of losses caused by breach of contract(s) by a party to the venture, the financial responsibility shall be borne by the said party.

In case of failure, China is still in control, and the burden of proof will rest with the foreign party.

Article 14
Disputes arising between the parties to a joint venture, which the board of directors fails to settle through consultation, may be settled through conciliation or arbitration by an arbitral body agreed upon by the parties.

Arbitration within China or forums such as the International Chamber of Commerce can resolve disputes. The Chinese have concluded joint venture agreements that allow arbitration in third countries, including the United States.

Article 15
The present law comes into force on the date of its promulgation.

The joint venture law was adopted July 1, 1978, at the second session of the Fifth National People's Congress. It became effective on January 8, 1979.

The power of amendment is vested in the National People's Congress.

The National People's Congress is China's highest legislative organ.
Although this law goes a long way toward meeting investor expectations, it provides only a vague guide for operating ventures. However, it's a clear statement on China's willingness to let Western firms share in its development. In fact, joint ventures are a major departure from China's rejection of foreign influence in its economy. One element in Lenin's New Economic Policy of the early 1920s was Russia's attempt to enlist the aid of foreign capital through joint ventures in developing raw materials. Although this policy failed, it provides partial ideological justification for Chinese joint venture. Questions, such as the role of the chairman and the calculation of taxes, remain unanswered. Much depends

on how authorities complete details of the law through regulations and negotiations.

Countertrade

Trade with China has expanded to include an array of financial arrangements. These include leasing, switch, buy-back, licensing, processing, consignment, and compensation. The Chinese language has several ways to say "business," but when dealing with China, the most appropriate expression is *mai mai*—"buy and sell." If, while attempting to sell your product, you can also buy something in China, your chances of concluding a transaction will increase significantly. Countertrade (CT) is an agreement under which the seller gets goods or services instead of cash. Such arrangements allow you to make a sale that might otherwise be lost, given China's shortage of hard currency. Many Western firms are reluctant to engage in CT. The Chinese realize smaller or specialized firms aren't organizationally equipped to act as export agents for their products. They ask that these firms review the products they already buy in great quantity and investigate the possibility of selecting China as a source of these goods. You should determine at the outset whether the transaction under discussion will involve CT. If your firm is amenable to countertrade, you must verify the quality and quantity of goods to be traded before you sign the contract.

How do we do business with a country that is hungry for Western goods, but which doesn't have the money to pay for them? Many firms have learned to barter to secure an export market and minimize use of hard currency. Barter is the direct exchange of goods having offsetting values, without flow of money taking place. It's characterized by the following:

- It's a one-time transaction rather than an on-going dynamic relationship.
- Only two parties are involved in the transaction.
- Only one contract is drafted covering the offsetting deliveries between the two parties.
- The goods to be exchanged are specified at the time the export contract is signed.
- It takes place over a relatively short time (i.e., up to two years). Hence, there is relatively little time-lag between offsetting deliveries of goods.

Barter arrangements are used less frequently than counterpurchase and compensation in China trade. Figure 8-1 presents an analytic illustration of a barter transaction. The following steps are involved:

1.   The Western firm contracts with the Chinese Trade Organization (CTO) for the exchange of mutually desired goods.

2.   The Western firm delivers its goods to the CTO.

3.   As payment for those goods, the CTO delivers goods of equal value to the Western firm.

If a competitor is willing and armed to accept payment on a barter basis, he might find himself meeting competition with price cuts. The Japanese frequently pay for oil and gas imports with advanced technology exports. China's exchange of coal for Danish help in port modernization is another example. While a few barter deals have been made, the difficulty in coordinating two or more Chinese units remains a significant hurdle. Local planning bodies and supraministerial coordinating bureaus can help alleviate this problem.

One important Chinese trade practice involves the exchange of Western equipment and technology for a certain share of output over an ex-

Figure 8-1
MODEL OF A BARTER TRANSACTION

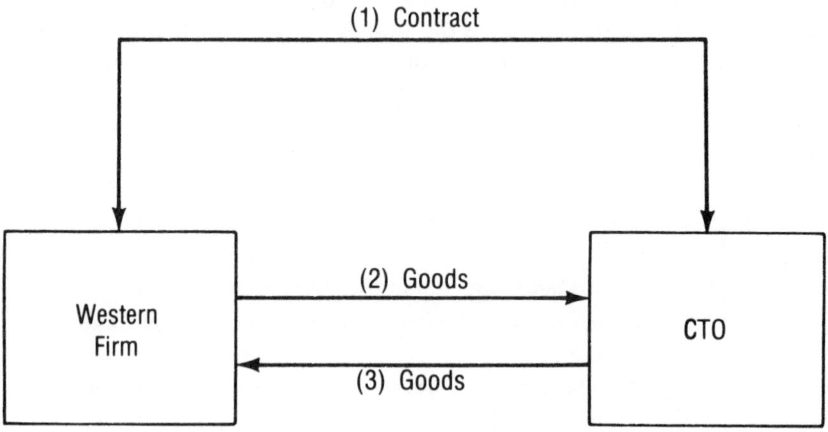

Source: Department of Commerce. *East-West Countertrade Practices: An Introductory Guide for Business*. Washington, D.C., 1978, p. 8.

tended period of time. China has entered into joint developments with foreign firms in the form of compensation trade, whereby the supplier agrees to take payment from the output of the plant, making the purchase self-liquidating. If the seller is paid totally in merchandise, the arrangement is similar to barter. The difference is that each partner pays for what is received. The Chinese use the term compensation trade *(bushang maoyi)* to refer only to instances in which they, the buyers, pay the cost of capital equipment imports by delivery of subsequent products. Compensation trade includes direct product compensation. This refers to repayment of the cost of imported equipment with products produced directly with the equipment. It also includes indirect or mixed product compensation, which refers to repayment with goods wholly or partially produced with equipment other than the imported equipment. Indirect product compensation occurs in cases where the Chinese import equipment against periodic payments of raw materials such as minerals. In a compensation agreement, a foreign firm sets up a plant in China and the firm's capital outlay is repaid in the form of an annual processing fee, in goods produced, or in periodic cash payments, or in a combination of all three. Compensation allows repatriation of capital investments made in China, such as buildings, machinery, and fixtures. Investment in the form of capital equipment is paid for in goods. Depending on the industry, compensatory trade arrangements may offer a better opportunity than direct equity investment.

Some countertrade transactions involve Chinese counterdeliveries of goods that are normally "non-resultant products," i.e., they aren't derived from or related to the Western export of technology, product plants, or equipment. These goods may consist of manufactured goods, raw materials, or machinery. This type of countertrade arrangement is known as a counterpurchase transaction. Although similar to compensation deals, counterpurchase involves signing two separate contracts. One covers the sale of goods. The second commits the seller to buy certain products within a specified time period. Counterpurchase deals are preferable to compensation deals because the seller gets paid for deliveries made and then has some time to select and buy the specified goods in return. Under a compensation agreement, by comparison, the seller obtains payment only for the portion that has been designated for cash. There is usually a much greater lag between reciprocal deliveries than is the case with counterpurchase agreements. The exchange of goods under a counterpurchase agreement generally takes place over a relatively short time frame—one to five years. The value of Chinese goods offered as counterdeliveries is generally less than 100 percent of the original Western sales contract value. Each side pays cash for the products and services it receives. Figure 8–2 is a model for a counterpurchase and compensation transaction. Steps illustrated don't

Figure 8-2
MODEL OF A COUNTERPURCHASE/COMPENSATION TRANSACTION

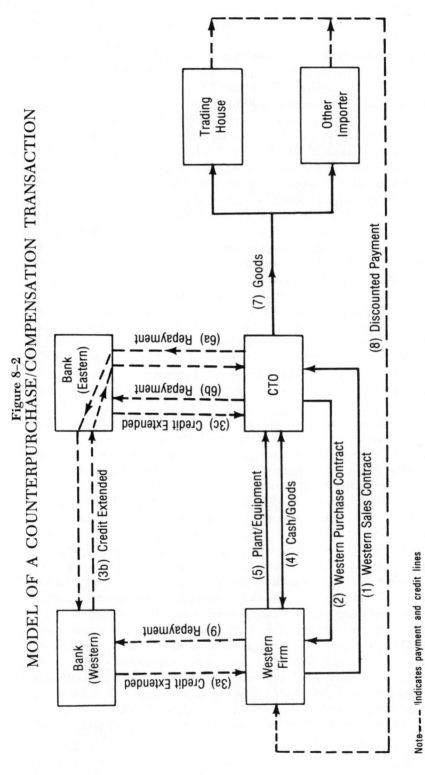

Source: Department of Commerce. *East-West Countertrade Practices: An Introductory Guide for Business.* Washington, D.C., 1978, p. 6.

Note --- Indicates payment and credit lines

182

necessarily occur in this sequence. However, each step is an element in the complete transaction:

1.   The Western firm contracts with the CTO for the sale of plants and equipment, denominated in cash, against the full or partial payment in goods.

2.   The CTO contracts to sell goods to the Western firm, generally under a separate contract from the original export contract.

3a.   The Western bank extends credit to the Western firm for the hard currency necessary, against promissory notes from the CTO with guarantees from the Chinese bank: or

3b.   The Western bank extends bank-to-bank credit to the Chinese bank to finance the hard currency portion of the transaction on behalf of the CTO: or

3c.   For projects that are only partially funded under national plans, the Chinese bank itself provides the budgeted hard currency funds to the CTO for the down payment and a percentage of the transaction. For these projects, countertrade exports are expected to provide the balance of the cost.

4.   The CTO may provide the Western firm with a cash down payment in hard currency for the Western export. Countertrade goods will also be provided by the CTO, in accordance with the provisions of the CT contract. The Western firm pays the CTO hard currency for the goods.

5.   The Western firm provides the CTO with the plant and equipment contracted.

6a.   The CTO remits payment of the outstanding credit to the Chinese bank, which in turn repays the Western bank: or

6b.   The CTO repays the credit received from the Chinese bank.

7.   If the Western firm cannot use the Chinese goods internally or sell them, it may transfer its rights to these goods to a third party, such as a trading house or importer, at discount.

8.   The Western firm receives payment for the goods transferred to the third party.

9.   The Western firm, if it received supplier credit from the Western bank, repays the outstanding credit to the bank.

The first factories operating under compensation trade began in 1978. By the end of the year, there were 38 such arrangements, mostly with local firms in Hong Kong and Macao. A number of foreign firms, including a major British toy manufacturer and an internationally known Japanese fashion designer, also participated in Chinese compensation trade arrangements. A typical example of one such project occurred in 1978. Itoman, the Japanese trading house, signed a deal with China's National Textile Import and Export Corporation. Itoman would supply 100 sewing machines and 15 technicians to a Shanghai apparel plant. In return, it would get 300,000 suits of pyjamas every year for five years. China's compensation trade has found its widest application in the manufacture of light industrial products, such as knitwear, electronic watches, and processed foods. A few significant deals, however, have been concluded for motor vehicles and marine containers. Compensation trade has great appeal in China since it will enable the Chinese to import modern technology without having to pay the full cost in valuable foreign exchange. Yet, this method is not without its difficulties. For example, some investors have had trouble getting Bank of China guarantees on foreign bank loans for equipment destined for compensation trade projects in China. Trade compensation can also include material processing and component assembly, which are particularly prevalent in textiles and other light industrial sectors.

China is experimenting with other more flexible approaches. In one approach, China accepts raw materials or components supplied by foreign firms and then receives processing fees. In another experiment, foreign firms supply some of the materials and parts with China providing the remainder. In a third variation, foreign firms also supply equipment, and China will eventually own the equipment through deducting its cost from processing fees over a period of several months to five years. China is eager to enter co-production to pay off debts. The investor gets payment in the form of finished products or other commodities or a combination of goods and cash. Variations on this theme are endless. They all have the common denominator of reliance on Chinese land, labor, and, sometimes, access to raw materials and local markets. In textiles, garments, food processing, toys, and electronics, Chinese authorities hope countertrade ventures will stimulate the inflow of capital and technology.

9 This chapter reviews areas of interest and concern to those who will work in China.

Land

With 3,691,506 square miles, China is the third largest nation (after Russia and Canada). Its frontiers abut North Korea, the Mongolian People's Republic, the Soviet

CHINA PROFILE

Union, Afghanistan, Pakistan, Nepal, Bhutan, Burma, Laos, and Vietnam. Superimposed on North America, China's northernmost point (in Heilonjiang province) would lie over James Bay, Canada. Beijing would lie near Cleveland and Wuhan close to New Orleans in the United States. Kashigar, in far western China, would lie over San Francisco, while Shanghai would lie in the Atlantic Ocean some two-hundred miles east of South Carolina. Xinjiang covers the far northwest and Xizang (Tibet) the far southwest. Inner Mongolia lies in the north. The eastern third of China, south of Manchuria, northeastern China, and Inner Mongolia, is China Proper, consisting of the 18 historic provinces of Imperial China. China's leaders are promoting a two-phase grand plan. In the first stage, China will build a comprehensive economic system. In the second stage, it will be divided into six administrative regions (north, northeast, east, central-south, southwest, and northwest), each a separate economic entity.

China's land is as varied as it is vast. Its natural features range from tundra and desert to mountains, rainforests, and ricelands. Some of the world's youngest and loftiest mountains, including Mt. Everest (29,028 feet) in the Himalayas, one of the lowest points on earth, the Turpan Pendi (505 feet below sea level), and two of the world's great rivers, the Huang He and Chang Jiang, make up China. In the far west and northwest are icy stretches as severe as Siberia. Two-thirds of China is mountainous or desert-like. Forty percent of China is grassland, 8 percent forest. Only 13 percent is cultivated. Ninety percent of China's people live on one-sixth of the land, mainly in the fertile plains and eastern deltas. Industrial centers are mostly in the northeast and near the coast. China has 11,250 miles of coastline and many large ports. It has a great diversity of animal life. Creatures now found only in China include the giant salamander, the giant panda, and the great paddlefish of the Chang Jiang. Dragons, believed to exist by many Chinese, are symbols of beneficent power, fertility, good fortune. In glittering gold and jeweled scales, they crouch atop temple roofs, defenders against evil demons. The imperial dragon has a camel head, rabbit eyes, cow ears, snake neck, frog belly, scales of a carp, palms of a tiger, and a beard of pearl. The dragon embodies China's diversity.

Climate

China's climate ranges from continental to tropical. Northern Manchuria, a part of China lying on the same latitude as southern Labrador, shares the biting cold of Siberia. At the other extreme, Hainan Dao lies well within the tropics and grows coconut palms, coffee, and rubber trees. China lies almost entirely in the temperate zone. The typical China trader won't have to worry about braving the conditions of the Gebi Shamo (Gobi desert), where temperatures in the summer daytime exceed 100°F and fall to negative 30°F in the winter. Frost is common as far south as Shanghai. The southern part of the country is hot and humid for six summer months. Monsoon winds dominate China's climate, accounting for much of the timing and amount of rainfall. Rainfall is less than four inches a year in the deserts; more than 80 inches in the subtropical areas on the southern coast. Beijing gets about 25 inches of rainfall each year, Guangzhou 75 inches. Winter temperatures can drop to a few degrees above freezing as far south as Shanghai. Beijing is on the same latitude as Philadelphia, and the range of temperature is comparable. Spring can be pleasant in Beijing. However, for most of the year, the capital is dry and dusty and many will wear protective masks. As the summer drags on, the heat will get worse. In August, the prevailing winds shift, bringing in humid air from the Pacific, pushing the mercury another few notches. During winter months, Beijing's dry conditions are accompanied by biting winds that sweep across the North China plains. Guangzhou has a subtropical climate, with warm weather throughout most of the year. During the spring fair, temperatures will range from 65°F to 85°F with humidity averaging 74 percent. The autumn temperature range is 67°F to 85°F, with humidity at about 52 percent. Visitors to the fair dress informally. Mosquito repellent and netting are advised.

In old China, clothing color distinguished rank. The emperor, empress, and prince wore yellow. State officers wore blue. Officers of lower rank wore red. The general public wore black or some dark shade. Today, most Chinese dress in dark colors, primarily blues and greens. Only children wear bright colors and patterns, although changes in fashion are evident in larger cities. Informality prevails in Chinese dress. They dress for comfort and practicality rather than style. Both men and women wear Western-style shirts and loose-fitting trousers. Even top Chinese businessmen may wear baggy, white shirts without jackets or ties. Foreigners should wear what is effective in their home business environment.

People

China's numbers defy the imagination. Many of its provinces have populations larger than all but a few countries. In 1982, Chinese officials estimated China's population had passed the 1 billion mark. Foreign demographers have long contended that Chinese population and birthrate estimates are too low. China's economic plans are predicated on holding the population to 1.2 billion by the year 2000. If that cannot be done, leaders will have to rethink development strategy and brace for the political fallout. Because China's richest resource is people, leaders were disposed to view a large population as an asset. But the liabilities of a growing population became apparent to the leadership. However, it wasn't until several years after Mao's death that the party was able to act on the premise that population control was necessary for economic growth and improved living standards. In 1978, China had an urban population of 110 million, about 13 percent of the total population. Other estimates suggest this percentage could be as high as 20 percent. Although China has 13 of the world's 50 most populous cities, more than 80 percent of the Chinese live in rural areas. In terms of population, Shanghai is the largest city, with 12.5 million in 1979. Beijing has 8.5 million denizens, and Tianjin has over 7 million. Three million people live in Guangzhou. Ninety-four percent of China's people are Han, as ethnic Chinese have termed themselves since the Han dynasty (206 B.C.–A.D. 220). Sharp regional and cultural differences, including major variations in the spoken form of Chinese, exist among the Han, who are a mingling of many peoples. Fifty-five separate national minorities, totaling 60 million, make up the remaining 6 percent. These include 1.7 million Mongols, once ruled by Genghis Khan, 1.3 million Tibetans, 500,000 Kazakh nomads, 7 million Thai-speaking Chuang, and Miao and Puyi peasants in the southwestern provinces. Minority areas have strategic significance. Some minorities have kin across the frontier in Russia and Mongolia. Xinjiang, Xizang, and Nei Mongol constitute nearly 40 percent of China's land, yet they support only 2 percent of its population. China has tried to win the allegiance of minority races by making concessions to their cultures and feelings and by getting them influential government and professional positions.

The Chinese are known for their industriousness, patience, frugality, kindness, and tolerance. As 19 centuries of the ethics of Kongfuzi still exercise an influence on the Chinese, they regard loyalty, filial piety, benevolence, love, righteousness, harmony, equity, scholarly discipline, and civic responsibility as high moral principles. Visitors are often amazed at the honesty of the Chinese. Even the smallest coin will be returned. The punishment for infractions is severe and population pressure ensures that few crimes remain unsolved. Thieves are sentenced to hard labor at state farms, mines, or plants, and must undergo an Orwellian regimen of "self-criticism." Crime exists in China, as it does in any country. However, visitors are rarely molested, materially or physically. Communist dogma and Western ways are undermining the traditional ideals of the Chinese. During the Cultural Revolution, the party encouraged revolt against customs and kindness. These attitudes persist in the surly demeanor of lower-level bureaucrats. Along with the Four Modernizations, the leadership is pushing the Five Emphases to improve China's "spiritual civilization": 1. Being cultured; 2. Being hygenic; 3. Being polite; 4. Being orderly; and 5. Being ethical. Officials attribute the rise of corruption and discontent to exposure to Western decadence. For example, a government directive prohibited families living in Guangdong province from watching Hong Kong television. Authorities considered many of the colony's programs vulgar, leading to perverted crimes.

Chinese usually don't understand physical contact, such as back-slapping and public affection. Behave with reserve and politeness. How should a trader conduct himself? Sage Li Zhongyun penned this admonition: "Keep a quiet heart. Sit like a tortoise. Walk sprightly like a pigeon. Sleep like a dog."

Religion

China has declining numbers of Muslims, Taoists, Confucianists, Christians, Buddhists, and adherents to tribal religions. Before the 1949 revolution, China had perhaps 3 million Catholics and 700,000 Protestants. In

1979, 2 million Catholics were members of the Patriotic Catholic Association. Protestants are members of the All-China Conference of Protestant Churches. Since the 13th century, Roman Catholic missionaries have attempted to establish their church in China. Jesuits contributed greatly to Chinese knowledge in such fields as cannon casting, calendar making, geography, mathematics, cartography, music, art, and architecture. Despite great difficulties, missionaries from many denominations helped ease the ravages of typhoid and starvation among some of the hinterland. They also channeled Western ideas to youngsters who attended their schools. Missionary organizations encouraged and subsidized the brightest to attend universities in Paris, London, and Boston. After the revolution, believers receded into a social framework where religion was equated with "superstition." The party banished ministers to the countryside, burned Bibles, expelled missionaries, and sealed churches. Despite sometimes violent attempts to suppress religion, Mao observed, "We cannot abolish religion by administrative order nor can we force people not to believe in it." In essence, he felt only education and the success of the new order could erase religious faith. Article 46 of China's 1978 constitution says "citizens enjoy the freedom to believe in religion and the freedom not to believe in religion and to propagate atheism." Chinese Communists especially oppose what we call Confucianism, because it emphasizes the past and justifies inequality. Authorities today tolerate religion within strict limits. In Beijing and Shanghai, Catholics, Protestants, and Moslems may worship within a few churches and mosques. The state has restored some Buddhist temples that for years served as warehouses, museums, or garages. Although the Church of Rome isn't in communion with China's Latin church, the Vatican has sent envoys to re-establish ties. Visiting ministers sometimes conduct services at embassies.

Language

The government has based the official language of China on the Northern Chinese dialect. Non-Chinese refer to this dialect as Mandarin. Chinese prefer to call it *Putunghua* (common language). Other dialects such as Cantonese, Fukienese, Wu, and Hakka are spoken, especially in the south and east. Chuang, Uigur, Yi, Tibetan, Miao, and Mongol are major tribal tongues. Each group uses its own language in its schools and publications. Most members of China's minority groups learn Chinese as a second language. English is the most widely studied foreign language in China. The Chinese language doesn't have an alphabet. Instead, the written language consists of more than 40,000 characters (including variants) that look like sketches to the Western eye. Chinese characters are commonly divided into six classes according to their etymology. Two of these classes are pictographs—pictures of objects, such as a drawing of a horse or of the sun, and ideographs—attempts at the graphic portrayal of an idea such as "up" or "down." But by far the largest category of characters are phonetic in origin, though the phonetic elements were originally pictographs or ideographs. Abbreviations have simplified many ideographs. Chinese can be written or printed either vertically, reading from right to left, or horizontally reading from left to right. Every Chinese character is monosyllabic. However, there are a vast number of disyllabic words, when we are speaking of semantically meaningful units. The predominance of homophones in Chinese is partly responsible for this. This has led the Chinese to often combine two syllables into one word, the new word then being less ambiguous when spoken. This has also affected the written language. Chinese verbs do not indicate tense or number by conjugation, nor do the nouns indicate case by declension. However, other words are usually added to a sentence to indicate tense, and the syntax serves to indicate noun functions. The language has four tones and 420 syllables. Therefore, each syllable must serve many words. The tone or pitch of the voice can drastically alter the syllable's meaning. For example, four different Chinese characters can represent the sound *ma—mother, hemp* or *numb, horse,* and *to scold.*

The Wade-Giles system, named after two professors at Cambridge University in the 19th century, was the most common method of transliterating Chinese words. Since January 1979, China has adopted *Pinyin* as the exclusive system of transliterating Chinese words in Western languages. *Pinyin* comes from the expression *Han yu pinyin fang-an,* which literally translated means "Chinese language transcription proposal." This refers to the official scheme put forward in 1958 for a Chinese phonetic alphabet. The new reform is part of a gradual effort to make the cumbersome language easier to read and write and to increase literacy. Pinyin has been used for years on street signs and in elementary textbooks as an aid in learning Chinese characters. The Pinyin alphabet is meant to standardize Chinese spellings in English, French, German, and other languages. The United Nations and most newspapers in the English-speaking world use Pinyin. However, almost every organization makes one or more exceptions. For example, most use the word *China* instead of *Zhongzua.* Pinyin is easy to master if we remember that the *j*-sound is sometimes rendered *zh*; the Pinyin *x* is like the English *sh*; and the English *ch* is spelled *q* before the letter *i.* Under the Pinyin system, *j-, x-,* and *q-* symbolize dentalized sounds, with the tongue against the bottom teeth. Their counterparts *zh-, sh-,* and *ch-* symbolize retroflex sounds, with the tongue curled back. When precision is of utmost importance, as in contractual negotiations, you must deal exclusively with Chinese characters rather than some kind of transliteration. The plethora of homophonous words in Chinese, errors in the presence and placement of diacritical marks, and romanization of different pronunciations can change or obscure meaning. Consider, for example, the name *Chiang Kai-shek*. That is the romanization of the Cantonese pronunciation of *Jiang Jieshi* in Pinyin. Similarly, *Sun Yat-sen* is Cantonese for *Sun Yixian*. Of course, it's by their Cantonese names these men became known to the West. However, they are better known in China as *Jiang Zhongzheng* and *Sun Zhongshan* respectively.

In China, given names are not merely a means of address, as in English. They also have meanings, such as "strong and capable" or "cool and upright." Chinese family names are almost always of one syllable and therefore easy to remember. Whenever possible, secure the full name of your Chinese counterpart. You should also try to get his given name, the name of his branch corporation, and details of his responsibilities. Never resort to the use of nicknames. Calling someone "master" or "madam" is obsolete. The friendly address "comrade" *(tongzhi)* for men and women has replaced the older forms. Foreigners are usually addressed as *pengyou* (friend), *xiansheng* (Mr.), *furen* or *taitai* (Mrs.), or *xiaojie* (miss). Where the surname is used, the form of address follows it, for example *Li tongzhi*—Comrade Li. First names aren't freely used except among family members or close friends. Friends or colleagues often use *xiao* (young) or *lao* (old) before the surname, depending upon the age of the person addressed.

As in other languages, there are formal and familiar pronouns. *Ni* and *nin* both mean "you," but the latter is more formal and polite. However, rules about usage aren't as strict as in some languages, and an acquaintance won't be offended, if you address him *ni*. The most common form of greeting, used at any time of the day, is *ni hao*—meaning more or less "You're well?" It doesn't require a literal answer, nor do such other traditional greetings as "Have you eaten?" and "Where have you been?" The Chinese word *wei* (usually translated "hello") is only used in answering the telephone. The Chinese are unlikely to be offended by undiplomatic references. Nevertheless, you should avoid discussion of Taiwan. Also, eschew demonstrations of radical chic. Communists distrust foreign displays of revolutionary zeal and associate home government disgruntlement with disloyalty.

Interpreters are always used during presentations, even though Chinese negotiators may speak fluent English. (Japanese businessmen complain they face a greater language barrier than Americans, since more Chinese speak English than Japanese.) Traders should bring their own interpreter, if they can find one skilled in both Chinese and Western business terms. The importance of having someone who can speak Chinese cannot be overestimated. Without such a person, you're at the mercy of Chinese translators, whose skills can be poor. Better still, learn Mandarin yourself. The Chinese will view this as a significant cultural concession. Even the most limited grasp of Chinese subtly changes the chemistry of relationships. It speeds negotiations and makes the Chinese more comfortable about dealing with you. Minimally, the foreign resident should be able to satisfy routine social demands and work requirements. The discipline needed for professional proficiency differs only in kind from the effort needed to win that contract. An intimate knowledge of Chinese can be crucial in winning accord. The Diplomatic Service Bureau of China's Foreign Ministry supplies interpreters and collects their wages. During the presentation, express only one thought at a time. Pause while the interpreter makes the point. Proceed when the audience shows it's ready for the next point. Avoid slang and sarcasm. Use the time employed by the translator in interpreting to prepare your thoughts. Be concise, and give your counterpart time to speak. If the translation seems inadequate during negotiations, discreetly request additional assistance from the Chinese head official. One way to avoid language pitfalls is to compile a list of all technical terms likely to arise and have a well-qualified source translate them before leaving for China. Dispatch a copy of this list to the Chinese side before arriving. You may also wish to brief the translator on the contents of the talk before the presentation starts.

Housing

The influx of businessmen is straining housing capacity. Accommodations are thus limited and spartan. Most hotels don't have air conditioning or private baths. Furnishings are adequate but old and threadbare. Walls, ceilings, and floors are often unfinished concrete or cinder block. Because of crowding, the CITS or the host FTC cannot make a reservation at Beijing's better hotels until one or two days before the guests arrive. Except for the new wing of Beijing Hotel on East Chang An Avenue, Chinese hotels are below international standards. Those lucky enough to snare a room will find luxuries unobtainable elsewhere: air conditioning, television, even electrical devices to open and close curtains. The hotel does regular duty for state functions and private meetings of officials with foreigners. The Beijing Hotel has 900 rooms and 54 banquet rooms and restaurants. Its 17 floors made it the highest building in the Imperial City in 1979. In times of pressure for shelter, visitors can stay at the Friendship Guest House, northwest of the city. Extra facilities are reserved for Japanese and overseas Chinese. While 13 hotels are set aside for foreign guests in Guangzhou, most Western businessmen stay at only two: the Dong Fang and the Bai Yun. The Dong Fang (North Renmin Road opposite the fair) is a bustling, 2,000 room place with a new, air-conditioned wing. Rooms are large, comfortable, and antless. The Dong Fang has some of the best service facilities in China, including three restaurants (the dining room on the eighth floor of the old wing is best), a coffee shop serving hamburgers and hot dogs, four retail shops, a bank, a post office, and telegraph and telex facilities. A snack room—affectionately known among traders as the "Top of the Fang"—serves Chinese beer and spirits. The Bai Yun (Huan Shi Road East, about three miles from the fair) is a 33-story, 776-room hotel with a restaurant that overlooks a pleasant inner yard.

Office space isn't available in Beijing. However, some firms have hotel suites on a semi-permanent basis. Firms with rented suites include Caterpillar Tractor, Fluor, Pullman, M. W. Kellogg, Pan American, Sumitomo, ENI, and Mercedes-Benz. The International Club, the San Litun Restaurant Building, the Palace of Nationalities, and house in the former Legation Quarters have offices. Leases are six months or one year.

The relatively small number of foreigners permitted to take up residence in the People's Republic of China are mostly accommodated in special apartment blocks in the eastern and northeastern parts of Beijing. In 1981, rents were about $1,000 per quarter for a two-bedroom apartment, with central heating and water charged at a flat rate. Electricity is expensive and may be inadequate for larger models of washing machines or air conditioners. Current is A.C. 220/380 volts, 50 cycles. Plugs are normally two or three pin flat (five amps). In hotel rooms, there is usually one connection for a two pin round continental-type plug. These outlets aren't suitable for western appliances, but you can buy conversion kits in Tokyo or Hong Kong before entering China.

Food

Beijing and other cities have restaurants offering all specialties in rooms set aside for foreigners. Quality ranges from delicious to disappointing. You may eat in plainer restaurants frequented by locals, but there could be a communications problem. Cuisines are exquisite. Lightly cooked to save fuel, dishes make use of every available food. Stir-frying, dry-frying, steaming, poaching, boiling, and baking, the great chefs of China make even pig ears, fish lips, and dog chops succulent. China's cooking, with its sensuous appeals and subtleties, is a gastronomic wonder of the world, matched only by France as a producer of culinary marvels. By no means is every dish firecracker hot, and there is enough variety for even the most timid Occidental palate. Rice is the favorite grain among people of south China. In the north, Chinese prefer wheat, which they make into bread and noodles. Meals generally have few calories, little meat, lots of cooked vegetables, and fresh fruit. Every area has its fruit specialties, such as bananas and oranges in the south and peaches and apples in the north. Dishes vary with the seasons, with casseroles and soups prevalent in the chilly winters and less oily concoctions favored during summer months. All hotels for foreigners offer both Western and Chinese food. When taking a party to a restaurant, some meals may need to be ordered 24 hours in advance to allow for proper preparation. Hotel and CITS representatives can recommend good restaurants and make reservations. Note that tipping is considered an insult. And, because there's no incentive to please the guest, there may also be minimum service.

Sometimes, hosts will arrange a banquet in the foreign delegation's honor. Dinner starts at 7 p.m. Your host will meet you on arrival. He will usher you to lounge chairs, for which you will exchange banter and platitudes. Political discussion and untoward quips are taboo. After 10 minutes, your host will seat you. A banquet consists of several dozen delicacies, orchestrated for flavor, texture, color. The host will start the feast by serving you food with long chopsticks set before him. He will make a short speech, and you, as the guest of honor, will reply. A guest should make the first move to depart. You will know when the meal is over when a large bowl of fruit is served. Your host will rise to utter a gracious valedictory and escort you not just to the door but down to the street.

Fastidious travelers should bring their own instant coffee, marmalade, and other requirements. You may also want to import packaged food and canned goods. Supply of fruit is seasonal. Store frozen lemon or orange juice when they become available. The most popular soft drinks are orangeade (*juxi shui*) and natural mineral water (*laoshan* or *kuangquan shui*). Larger hotels sell imported wines and spirits. Westerners find some Chinese beer, vodka (*futeka*), grape wines, and brandy acceptable. But caution must be exercised with grain spirits, such as the fiery 160-proof *mai tai* (common at banquet toasts) and *shaoxing jiu*, a warm, bitter rice wine.

Visitors in Northern China sometimes suffer from stomach upsets and disturbances of the respiratory system, especially in autumn. People sensitive to such afflictions should import a stock of favorite medicines. Lomotil or some other anti-diarrhetic is a must. Notify your guide if unusual medical problems persist. In case of illness, officials will instantly summon a doctor. Medical treatment for foreigners is meticulous, though some modern equipment is lacking. In major cities, hospitals are partially staffed with Western-trained, English-speaking personnel.

Money

China's basic unit of currency is the yuan. The term *kuai* is generally used when speaking about sums of money. Although the yuan has no material backing, it has proved stable. In April 1982, it had an exchange rate of

U.S.$1 = ¥1.85. The amount of money in circulation varies with the seasons, the peak being at Chinese New Year in January. The slowest circulation is in June. About 85 percent of China's financial transactions are carried out by bank transfers. The largest note is the 10 yuan, written ¥10. Other notes: ¥5, ¥2, ¥1, ¥.50, ¥.20, and ¥.10. The yuan is divided into 10 chiao (pronounced *mao*), and one chiao into 10 fen. Chiao and fen are available in notes of one, two, and five denominations. The Reminbi (People's Currency) is principally an accounting unit. It may not cross state lines and it isn't traded on international exchanges. Upon exiting China, RMB may be changed into foreign currency. China accepts American credit cards, including Mastercard, Visa, and American Express, but a 4 percent commission is charged for each purchase. Sometimes, the billing process takes months. Credit cards can also be used to cash personal checks in Shanghai and Guangzhou. You can exchange foreign currencies and travelers checks at banks and larger hotels. There is no limit on the amount of travelers checks, letters of credit, foreign notes, and drafts that you may bring into China. Currency taken into the country must be declared, and the declaration form retained. This declaration is necessary for the exchange of travelers checks or cash into RMB. The Bank of China and its branch offices in Hong Kong issue RMB travelers checks. Travelers checks in major currencies, such as U.S. dollars, German marks, British sterling, Swiss francs, and Japanese yen, are all acceptable. As of 1979, China accepted 41 types of travelers checks.

Chinese regulations, which became effective on April 1, 1980, limit the use of foreign currency for conducting most transactions in China. Under this system, foreign exchange certificates (FXC) replace RMB for a wide range of transactions, although RMB can still be used in some Chinese stores and restaurants. FXCs may be bought from offices of the Bank of China. Hotels, restaurants, and stores that normally cater to foreigners accept only FXCs as payment. When foreign currency is used to buy FXCs, foreigners are given BOC exchange memos. These memos should be retained and may be used to reconvert the FXC back to foreign currency for a period up to six months.

Foreign businessmen, already confounded by protracted negotiations, are increasingly upset over fantastic price increases. In 1981, telephone installation charges jumped overnight from $20 to $1,400 and telex installation went from $100 to $2,800. Because of the scarcity of accommodations, lodging is expensive. One American firm rented a house used for foreign diplomats at $5,000 a day. Lacking office space, some firms have been content to pay $200 a day for a back room in a restaurant. Sometimes, foreigners are asked to pay extra for turning on an electric fan, or opening a window. With a business acumen that dates back thousands of years, the Chinese also foster competition among nationalities. In 1981, Japanese journalists paid $310 a month for a translator. Americans paid up to $470. U.S. diplomats paid nearly $600 and Western business-men were charged up to $670 a month. The multi-tiered price structure extends even to the cost of food. A small can of mushrooms at Friendship Stores costs three times as much as the same size can in a Chinese market two blocks away. Business trips to China are often longer than antici-pated. Chinese officials might assure you the trip will take only twelve days to complete the transaction when it takes three months. In 1979, Strategic Business Service, a San Jose, California market research firm, estimated the cost of a delegation to China at $2,000 a day. All the po-tential expenses—salesmen, engineers, consultants, training, documenta-tion, travel expenses—add up to a sizeable figure. Small and medium-size firms are hardest hit. The major firms simply swallow the increase within their operating budget. Many development projects are in isolated regions with harsh weather. The climate, scarcity of adequate housing and amen-ities, and lack of Western-style entertainment facilities makes it hard to entice Westerners to live in China. Those who do come must be provided with substantial incentives. Their salaries and other benefits are often many times the amount of compensation they would get for comparable work in their home country. These costs must be taken into account when your firm is preparing its bid and negotiating the contract. In 1979, one firm estimated it spent about $100,000 a year for a three-man office, in-cluding a locally-hired manager.

Transportation

The Public Security Bureau (PSB) must approve all changes in itinerary. If you are visiting more than one city, the PSB will give you a green card specifying destinations and mode of transport. On arrival at the last city on your itinerary, the card will be collected and your passport returned a short time afterwards. Normally, when you stay in an area more than 24 hours, the local PSB must "chop" your passport. China's travel service is both rigid and costly. It refuses to make a hotel booking unless a visitor agrees to bear the expense of hiring an interpreter to escort him from the airport to the hotel. Of course, many visitors do need such a service, but those who do not must take it anyway.

Long-distance transportation in China is mainly by air. The Civil Aviation Administration of China (CAAC) handles 545 domestic flights a week. Internal routes cover about 45,000 miles, with major traffic centers at Beijing, Shanghai, Guangzhou, Wuhan, Zhejiang, Xian, Lanzhou, and Urumqi. There is daily service between Beijing, Shanghai, and Guang-zhou. It operates flights to Japan and Europe, as well as Hong Kong, North Korea, and Burma. Trips to smaller cities may be lengthy because of multiple stops. Reservations on the national airline are difficult to make. In-flight service on CAAC is spartan.

Like the Soviet Union, China is essentially a railroad nation. Fifteen percent of China's 27,000 miles of railroads is double-tracked and 2 percent is electrified. International and domestic train services link cities and towns in China, and major cities with capitals in other countries. International train services are available twice a week between Beijing-Hanoi, Beijing-Pyongyang, Beijing-Ulan Bator, and Beijing-Moscow. Trains have comfortable accommodations with restaurant cars serving Chinese and, in some cases, European food, but they tend to be slow and crowded. It takes 24 hours to travel from Guangzhou to Shanghai, 19 hours from Shanghai to Beijing, and 33 hours from Guangzhou to Beijing.

Buses and taxis are available in most large cities at reasonable rates. If you have an appointment, ask the taxi driver to wait. The charge is small, and it could be hard to get other transport. In Beijing, you can summon taxis from the hotel's front desk, at the International Club, and outside the Sanlitun foreigner's compound. In Guangzhou, Beijing, and Shanghai, restaurants and Friendship Stores will call taxis for their patrons. Pedicabs—three-wheeled vehicles driven by motorcycle engines and capable of carrying two passengers—are cheaper than taxis. Foreigners can import cars through Xigang near Tianjin. Duty isn't levied on a car brought in for personal use. Non-diplomatic residents can sell their car only to the Friendship Store, which will buy almost all used goods at fair prices. Chinese gas is acceptable, but you should import anti-freeze. Repair facilities are sub-standard. Larger embassies have mechanics who might do spare-time work. Chinese cars aren't for sale, but you may rent the Honqui or Red Flag limousine. It boasts jumpseats, cushions, curtains to block the stares of the curious, and a color range of gray to black. Chauffeur-driven cars and small buses are also available for rental through Beijing's Capital Car Rental Company. The Beijing Friendship Service Corporation will provide drivers.

Telecommunications

Airmail is reasonably quick. Surface mail takes six to eight weeks for delivery. Air mail takes 8 to 10 days. Sending packages out of the country could involve complications. Foreigners may have to pay duty and handling charges for packages mailed from abroad. Visitors may also receive medicine, liquor, or cigarettes through the mail, but the total value shouldn't exceed 50 RMB. Parcels should conform to the following restrictions: The combined length and girth must not exceed six feet. The length must not exceed 3½ feet. Parcels may measure up to 4 feet in length, if parcels over 42 and under 44 inches in length don't exceed 24 inches in girth, parcels over 44 and under 46 inches in length don't exceed 20 inches in girth, and parcels over 46 inches and under 4 feet do not exceed 16 inches in girth. If these restrictions are not followed, Chinese authorities will either return the parcel to the sender or dispose of it in accordance with their laws.

China has good telephone, telegraph, and telex links between Beijing, Guangzhou, Shanghai, and overseas points. In other cities, facilities are marginal. Since the installation of a coaxial cable, telephone service to Hong Kong has been excellent.

Common Beijing telephone numbers are as follows:

Ambulance	555678
Airport	
Arrival/departure inquiries	552515
CAAC freight office	552945
Domestic bookings	553245
International bookings	557878
Bank of China	330887
Capital Hospital	553731
China Council for Promotion of International Trade	660436/668981/662835
China Travel Service	557558
Fire brigade (emergency)	119
Foreign Languages Book Store	554783
Foreign Ministry	
Main switchboard	553831
Americas and Oceania	552167
Information Department	555505
Protocol Department	552642
Friendship Store	593531
Hotels	
Beijing	556231/556531
Chianmen	338731
Friendship	890621
Xinqiao	557731
Huaqiao	558851
Minzu	668541
Peace	553310

International Club	550602
Post office	665900
Railway station	
Inquiries	554866
Customs	556242
Telephone operator	
International calls	337431
Information	114

Pleasure

"In Xanadu did Kubla Khan/A stately pleasure-dome decree. . . ." Although China's first Mongol emperor enjoyed a life of besotted delectation, foreigners may see China as a hardship post. Their sense of isolation is great, for the Chinese, though considerate and courteous, refrain from mixing socially. Although there's no night life, businessmen can get tickets for a film or stageshow. The International Club in Beijing has facilities for tennis, swimming, badminton, table-tennis, billiards, bowling, and dancing. Generally, the initiative for entertainment should be left to Chinese officials. However, when you are entertained at a banquet, it's desirable to host a return banquet before departing for home. Shanghai's Jing Jiang Club, with its 150-foot heated pool, billard tables, and reading rooms, provides an oasis of pre-revolutionary ambience, although for some traders, it more resembles the delegate's lounge at the UN or, more severely, the bar scene of "Star Wars." Some embassies have swimming pools, to which they may invite guests. Westerners are limited to a dozen or so cities, factories, communes, and schools whose reason for being seems to be impressing friendly visitors. While it's naive to think such places are indicative of China's true stage of development, they provide insights unattainable elsewhere. Having received permission to visit a different Chinese city, foreigners may wander freely within its urban limits. Sometimes, inquisitive crowds are a problem, and the guide will urge visitors to accept a car tour. The larger cities have Friendship Stores, carrying items of everyday use, Western periodicals, and souvenirs and antiques. In larger cities, they have a limited line of imported wines and liquors, soft drinks, cigarettes, film, and cosmetics. Best buys are Chinese silks and brocades. Cashmere garments are of superb quality and are probably the lowest-priced in the world. Wool garments, particularly sweaters, are also of excellent value. Shops are generally open from 9 a.m. to 7 p.m. every day, including Sunday:

Beijing Friendship Store,
21 Jian Guo Men Wai Da Jie
Beijing
Phone: 593531
Cable: 4952 BEIJING

Photography is allowed throughout China except in restricted zones, such as military areas, water supply and power installations, bridges, and naval yards. Taking pictures from aircraft and of people against their will is forbidden. Ask permission before shooting wall posters. Kodak film for 35mm and 110 cameras is available in many cities. The Chinese also make their own film. They allow undeveloped film to be taken out of China, but reserve the right to make exceptions. If asked to surrender film, insist the authorities return the developed shots.

Notable points of interest or diversion near Guanzhou include the Cultural Park, Seventy-two Martyrs Mausoleum, Zenhai Park, the Island of Sha Mian, and the Peasant Training Institute. In Shanghai, visit the Bund (waterfront and site of former foreign offices), Mandarin Garden of Yu, Children's Palace, and Temple of the Jade Buddha. In Beijing, the Valley of the Ming Tombs, the Forbidden City, Zhon Shan Park, Coal Hill Park, Temple of Heaven, Temple of Azure Clouds, the Tian An Men Square are worth seeing. The climax of any visit is the Great Wall, 40 miles from Beijing. Built over the bodies of 1 million slaves to no ultimate military purpose, the 2,480 mile-long stone serpent is the largest construction executed by man and, astronauts say, the only manmade object visible from the moon. Recently, hotels have organized evening fun (?) for businessmen, including revolutionary song and dance troupes, acrobats, and music ensembles. Otherwise, entertainment will be in the visitor's own room, wherein he may sip his choice of poison, puzzle over where negotiations stand, or yak until yawn.

10

Unless we change, the Westerners will co-operate with each other and we shall stand isolated. They will be strong and we shall be weak.
—Xue Fucheng (1838–1894)

Will China's pragmatic course continue? The National Committee of American Foreign Policy posed that question to U.S. Ambassador Leonard Woodcock, following the opening of the American Embassy in Beijing in 1979. He said: "Deng told me, 'I know you're concerned about what will happen when I'm no longer around. Well, I intend to be here for a good while yet, but don't worry, I'm taking care of things.' "

WILL IT LAST?

Deng Xiaoping has staked China's future on modernizing with Western help. His economic strategy includes decentralization of decision-making, profit and loss accounting, and incentives for efficient workers. He has undercut efforts to thwart modernization by locking China into long-term commitments, such as development of oil fields. Although Deng commands loyalty from a broad base of people—commoners, officers, bureaucrats, technocrats, the intelligentsia—his power will someday pass to the younger generation that fared well during the Cultural Revolution. But, when that happens, thousands of young people will have been exposed to foreign ideas from studying abroad. Mao wrote, "The youth of today and of those to come after them should assess the work of the revolution in accordance with values of their own. A thousand years from now, Marx, Engels, and Lenin could possibly appear rather ridiculous." In the afterglow of the Cultural Revolution, China's youth are finding Maoism ridiculous. Deng's incentives appeal to the average Chinese, but many cling to attitudes prevalent in Mao's time. The Chinese have had to make wrenching changes of allegiance. Because policy shifts brought disastrous repercussions, officials will shy from initiatives that could backfire. Inertia in the middle could yet disrupt Deng's dream. The leadership's toughest job may be to convince people that the consumer society is here, that it's safe to be ambitious.

"The Chinese people's march toward the great goal of the Four Modernizations has aroused world-wide attention," the *People's Daily* proclaimed in 1978. If China triumphs, other Third World nations may adopt its formula: nationalism accommodating capitalism. Foreign trade, college exams, wage increases: these and other programs suggest China's populace is moving in lockstep to policy drumbeats of a unified leadership. The truth is more complex. The party and Politburo are by no means monolithic in their support for Deng's programs. Pressures from within to relax control and right the wrongs done during the Cultural Revolution will persist, provoking reaction and instability. A new Gang of Four could seize power, reversing China's westward orientation overnight. Witness Iran. Mao saw that possibility. In a letter to his wife at the start of the Cultural Revolution, he warned: "After my death, rightists may seize power. They will use my words to raise their own banner." He ventured, however, "they will not rule for long." Mao could be right. Rapid modernization threatens the leaders, practices, and institutions that emerged from the Cultural Revolution. It connotes automation, job transfers, the obsolescence of skills. It fosters social and political inequality. China won't be able to sustain high productivity without providing regular increases in living standards. Thus, the continuation of China's high investment rates is in doubt. The central government is just as worried about the loss of control over individuals as over economic affairs. Corruption, embezzlement, and tax evasion are on the rise. Communist sources claim juvenile delinquency is 10 times higher in 1980 than in 1960. That almost 30 percent of urban young people were jobless in 1980 surely is one factor that contributes to China's crime wave. One area in which the government is trying to clamp down is the tendency to give equal bonuses to all workers or to maintain bonus levels even when profits decrease. Managers are learning accounting tricks, such as adding bonus payments to production costs, rather than deducting them from profits. The success of the Four Modernizations will hinge critically on China's ability to expand agricultural output faster than population growth. The Chinese will look to the United States in particular for expertise in developing agriculture. The Chinese farmer averages a crop of 2,200 pounds of grain each year. The American farmer averages a crop of 110,000 pounds per year—50 times as productive. Other sectors, especially electric power and transportation, are major impediments brought about by years of neglect in investment allocation; slow progress in these areas will constrain China's industrial growth. If its *Wirtshaftswunder* (economic miracle) doesn't materialize, a political *Gotterdammerung* (twilight of the gods) will. And China will swing back into a state of rigidity, isolation, xenophobia.

In an article written for the *Encyclopedia Britannica 1980 Book of the Year*, Deng said there have been "even skeptics among the Chinese people themselves" about China's ability to meet its goals. He said there are four reasons why these doubts are groundless: China's natural resources; development of a basic industrial and technical system; encouragement of different schools of thought; and China's openness to foreign visitors and investment. Reassurances notwithstanding, China is no place to invest pension funds. No other sizeable nation has seen such upheavals in the last 30 years. Mao ran the country as though he were executing a succession of military assaults. Unable to abolish contradictions, he fed on them. Mao's actions brought harassment, incarceration, and death to thousands. China satisfactorily completed only its first Five-Year Plan. Mao's Great Leap Forward overturned the second plan, the Cultural Revolution the third, and the Gang of Four the fourth. Even since Mao's death, China's economy has moved fitfully, sometimes retrogressively. It abandoned the plan Huo Guofeng championed in 1977 less than a year later. China changed the fifth plan to "three years of readjustment" to resolve imbalances and priorities. In 1982, China issued a list of 130 projects requiring $900 million in foreign investment, and negotiations resumed on basic transportation, manufacturing, and mining projects that had been shelved in 1978. Nevertheless, we should be skeptical as to whether that is the final turn of the wheel. The 1977 Communist Party Constitution made an alarming prediction:

> China's Great Proletarian Cultural Revolution was a political revolution carried out under socialism by the proletariat against the bourgeoisie and all other exploiting classes to consolidate the dictatorship of the proletariat and prevent the restoration of capitalism. Political revolutions of this nature will be carried out many times in the future.

China's plans are feasible only under the most auspicious conditions. The size and speed of its grand design will create bottlenecks. China's infrastructure must keep pace with technological change. At the same time, it cannot industrialize at the expense of food and clothing. As problems mount, leaders will postpone targets and impose austerity budgets, which will spark political unrest. Progress will improve living standards and real incomes, but it won't create anything resembling an affluent society. Even if China were able to sustain its historic growth rate of 6 percent yearly, by the year 2000 its GNP would still be 15 percent below the United States'

1975 GNP. In 1976, the five major powers combined accounted for 70 percent of the world's GNP. Of these, China's share was only 6.7 percent. It produced less than one-fifth of the level of the world's largest producer, the United States, and 60 percent of Japan's level, the fourth largest producer. A successful modernization drive could increase China's share to 10 to 14 percent by 2000. With the most optimistic estimate, its GNP would still rank last among the five major powers by the end of this century, but could reach over half of the U.S. level and more than 70 percent of Japan's level.

We do have cause to be bullish. China's overall performance has exceeded the performance of all but a handful of less developed countries. If we compare present China with pre-1949 Republican China—a comparison Beijing likes to make—even small achievements have significance. Droughts, floods, and insects ravaged the land. Famine killed millions. Millions of others fled to cities, where they pulled rickshaws through teeming streets for pennies a week. Behind Shanghai's gleaming Bund were slums where beggars fought for crumbs. Corruption was so rampant China's allies despaired of its survival. Landlords, who controlled most of the land, exacted from peasants one-third of their production. Warlords levied taxes on what remained. They often collected 50 years in advance. Sale of children was common, child labor unrestricted. For all but a few, it was a wretched life. In 1949, China had uncontrolled inflation, vast destruction, restless armies. The Communists made China a united entity with secure borders, a nearly-common language, and improved communications. Mao's revolution demonstrably improved the lot of the average Chinese. The Communists have provided widespread employment opportunities, job security, and a more even distribution of income. Of China, Edgar Snow could write in 1973 that "all epidemic and contagious diseases had been exterminated or brought under control and reduced. Venereal disease had disappeared, while polio, measles, typhoid, and typhus were prevented by vaccines and hygienic measures." Today, China's ability to feed its people, absence of infant mortality, and elimination of disease are on par with—and in some cases better than—many developed nations. Grain output was three times that of 1949, and China has entered the orbit of the Industrial Revolution. It's still one of Asia's poorest countries in per capita terms. Yet, the Chinese economy is the sixth largest in the world, and basic achievements have been won in irrigation, flood control, and economic diversification. The People's Republic has outpaced LDCs in preventing disruptive rural-to-urban migration, in mobilizing labor, and in avoiding foreign debt. In general, the Chinese have been spared unemployment, inflation, abject poverty, conspicuous consumption, and foreign payment crises. Before 1949, China imported most of its machinery from Japan, Europe, and the United States. Now it produces its own high-grade steel and makes its own cars, ships, trains. Prospects for growth of China's economy are favorable. The country has enough mineral and fuel resources to become one of the greatest nations. Already, China is the world's largest and most powerful developing country and—after Japan—Asia's largest economic power. It accounts for a significant part of the region's industrial and agricultural output and is an important market for raw materials and manufactured products. China has embarked on a massive program to modernize agriculture, industry, science and technology, and defense in a way to propel it into the front ranks of industrialized nations by the turn of the century. To achieve these goals, China must import substantial quantities of complete plants and related technology. Beijing's promulgation of an array of economic laws, its favorable balance of payments, and efforts to streamline its bureaucracy have helped assure foreign firms of China's commitment to a new business environment.

It is absurd, however, to reduce an analysis of Italian Fascism to the punctuality of Italian trains. We needn't rhapsodize over the New China Man to sustain what should be friendly, fruitful relations that are free of illusions. We see China as it is: a thermonuclear superpower ruled by an unregenerate creed predicated on the inevitability of wars of national liberation and global conflagration. Its economic strides cannot hide the totalitarianism with which it maintains discipline. China still has its gulags, thought police, and rectification campaigns. The labor camp population is between several hundred thousand and several million. The Cultural Revolution has ended, but authorities still keep a dossier on each Chinese citizen. "Rich" peasant families of 30 years ago are still stigmatized. Pressures are universal and unceasing to be red first and right second. The worker is tied to his job. He can be moved at the whim of the state, even if this means rustication to a frontier area or separation from his spouse. He isn't free to travel, to buy or sell on his own, or to ignore indoctrination. A crackdown in the winter of 1979 on demonstrations in Shanghai and at Beijing's now-extinct Democracy Wall challenged some assumptions about the regime. In 1980, the Central Committee cut the Four Greats from China's constitution: "The right to speak out freely, air views fully, hold great debates, and write big character posters." People cannot put up wall posters without official approval. Dissidents who demanded freedom in the first years after the overthrow of Maoism have been jailed or otherwise silenced and all their publications halted. It's possible the thaw was a sham aimed at lulling gullible Westerners into accepting China's new relationship. Authorities also could have permitted the brief period of free expression in the late 1970s as a way of identifying those harboring dissenting opinions. This recalls Mao's Hundred Flowers movement in 1957, in which he urged open criticism before the State Council. Many who took him at his word were forced to recant. Today, security forces hold key spots in the party and state apparatus, and youth, labor, and women's organizations cast a tight web over the nation. The *Pao wei*, or secret police, remain at the Politburo's beck. Despite the omnipresence of China's Orwellian machinery, it's less repressive than it was in Mao's day. At least China has the rudiments of a criminal and civil code. China will never become a constitutional democracy, for it has been a totalitarian state for 2,000 years. Most Chinese feel uncomfortable with extreme demands. For them, the important thing is that the distortions of culture and behavior imposed by the Maoists, the repression, the incessant campaigns, everything that filled the lives of ordinary people with so much tension, are gone.

China's economic and political conditions continue to churn. The political consensus behind China's modernization is shaky, but don't let that paralyze corporate action. The search for stable markets is a false goal. If the business opportunity is sufficient, firms will cope with the political realities. The greatest potential for profit often arises from the hurley-burley of political turmoil. For example, in 1981, Iraq and Iran were at war. Yet, U.S. sales to Iraq were just under $1 billion. In Chinese calligraphy, the word *crisis* consists of two characters: the first means *danger* and the second means *opportunity:*

As long as we understand how Chinese politics and economics intersect— the finance of politics and the politics of finance—we can turn dangers into opportunities. China is so vast that no calamity can encompass the whole of it. There will always be havens for talent and capital in the worst of times. We would do well not to sell short the latent pragmatism of the Chinese, a spirit of optimism and moderation sustained through periods of incredible hysteria. (A comment made by a Hong Kong trader at the height of the Cultural Revolution reflects this attitude. He averred that he backed "Chiang Mao-shek.") Even if political upheaval should strike China again, there's no reason why your firm cannot continue to operate profitably. In such an environment, you should blend into the woodwork and carefully analyze the forces that lead to the turmoil. These forces often represent unfulfilled economic needs that the savvy entrepreneur can address.

China and the West have entered a marriage of convenience. Once China becomes strong, it might turn on us. There is a Chinese proverb to the effect that "you can get two people to share the same bed, but you cannot get them to share the same dream." We cannot assume China shares our dreams—or that we know China's dreams. China describes trade as "a weapon of international political struggle" and it can be ruthless when partners fall from grace. China won't hesitate to delay or cancel projects it had felt essential. In 1962, for example, China cancelled all Czechoslovakian contracts after Sino-Soviet relations broke. This caused catastrophic unemployment in Czechoslovakia. In China's long history, foreign trade has never played an important role. In 1793, the emperor informed a British trade mission: "Our Celestial Empire possesses all things in prolific abundance and lacks no product within its own borders. There is, therefore, no need to import the manufacturers of outside barbarians." China's policy is to aim for self-sufficiency in as many products as possible with the result that its importance to world trade is small. The operation of China's planned economy, which has stressed import substitution whereever possible to stretch exchange earnings and the export of marginal surpluses, has made China an unreliable market. Of course, a small trade sector is expected of such a vast and populous country. Yet, the share of trade in China's GNP, only about 5 percent, is low by world standards, reflecting the residual role assigned trade by planners and attitudes toward trade due to historical experiences. The national myth of its experience since the Opium War—the century of humiliation—has been one of imperialist plunder through foreign trade. Consequently, self-reliance has been China's guiding principle, although its interpretation has been the subject of debate in the councils of China's government. To Western businessmen, the real risk of conducting business with China isn't legal or economic, but political. And political support will be forthcoming, if foreign trade lies in China's interest and it is comfortable with foreign investors. As long as the factors that shape China's strategic interests persist—the drive toward modernity, the pressure of population, and the Soviet threat—China will continue to woo foreign businessmen. It's on the threshold of a new era. The door is open for those who wish to enter. Firms that enter now will be in the best position to reap future benefits. Westerners cannot ignore China's great potential as a materials and manufacturing base from which to attack Asian markets.

Forecasts concerning China's future are hazardous, reminding us of the words of St. Paul: "For we know in part, and we prophesy in part. . . . Now we see through a glass, darkly." But astute businessmen will want to know as much about the possibilities as they can. So, to the question—Will it last?—we answer with a qualified yes. China will continue to liberalize its economic system, but will undergo significant mutations, not all of which appeal to us. These will take the form of contractual failure, political flip-flops, managerial incompatibility, bureaucratic bottlenecks, and labor disputes. In the struggle to maturity, most societies without a deep-seated democratic tradition are caught in what seems a remorseless dilemma. Evidently, they can enjoy economic growth but only at the price of personal liberties. They may prosper under hard-fisted rule, but at the cost of fear, censorship, and imprisonment. While we must not draw analogies too explicitly, Chile of the early 1980s is a plausible model of China's shape of things to come. In 1787, Alexander Hamilton, one of America's founding fathers, wrote: "The spirit of commerce has a tendency to soften the manners of men, and to extinguish those inflammable humours which have so often kindled into war." It has been Chile's lot to enjoy the spirit of commerce, while suffering the humours of civil repression. Likewise, China has progressively liberated business from state control, while rigidly suppressing heresy. The party will cede more commercial authority to the consumer while re-asserting absolute control over the citizenry. The Chinese economy will move from highly centralized state planning to a system that embraces interest rates, tax incentives, negotiated wages and worker bonuses, expanded foreign trade, and foreign funds to finance internal development. In contrast to previous years, China has agreed to use customer-provided designs, materials, and equipment in producing export commodities. It has also accepted more flexible pricing, i.e., closer adherence to international terms and prices.

China describes itself as a developing country of the Third World, a term used to differentiate the superpowers of the First World and the developed, non-superpower nations of the Second World (Germany, Japan). Mao envisioned the Third World, led by China, uniting the Second World, which is bullied by the superpowers, to isolate and defeat the superpowers (the United States, the Soviet Union). In this way, superpower dominance and the bipolar system that reflects that dominance would be ended. It's in the Third World that capitalism has its greatest potential. Most new countries lack an entrepeneurial base, for they usually adopt some form of statism. Yet, developing countries that have pursued the strongest centralized economic planning have fared the worst. Those countries that accommodate the presence of capitalist enterprises, geared toward market demand and material incentives, have made impressive gains. Hong Kong and Singapore are examples. Karl Marx and Frederick Engels wrote in the *Communist Manifesto* that capitalism "during its rule of scarcely one-hundred years, has created more massive and colossal productive forces than all the preceding generations together." In 1980, Hu Qiaomu, director of the Academy of Social Science, admitted in the *People's Daily* that China had to adopt such capitalist principles as "the pricing system, the rule of value, and the advantage of material incentives." Slowly, perceptibly, China has accepted such capitalist tenets as the profit motive, open competition, the private ownership of production. We may yet hear the gong sound in the Shanghai Stock Exchange. China has sacrificed many taboos to get into the world's commercial system. It has borrowed from abroad, encouraged joint ventures, and allowed foreigners to roam the country in a way rarely allowed a century ago. The Chinese are awed by the clout of the Western market the same way Westerners are mesmerized by the size of the Chinese market.

China has instituted many reforms that constitute a significant departure from traditional command economy planning. But it would be premature to interpret these reforms as a trend toward capitalism as we know it. Central planners still determine major goals of the Chinese economy and the priorities attached to these goals. It's significant that plans of all enterprises working under the new system are reviewed by planning authorities to assure their compliance with overall national goals. Is China similar to Germany in 1935? Or to Japan in 1955? No one—perhaps least of all the Chinese—knows. And the most fascinating thing about China is that it faces a kaleidoscope of possibilities. "The worst possible way of predicting the future is viewing it as a continuation of the present," Zbigniew Brezinski said in 1975. "History is full of dramatic gaps and sudden changes." In the final analysis, the West stands to gain from China's more open stance. "We have a long-term, common strategic interest in the improvement of our relationship with the People's Republic," Carter's National Security Advisor said in 1978. "This is not motivated by some tactical 'China card.' It stems from an interest, jointly shared with China, in a world of many centers of power—what we call diversity, or what the Chinese occasionally call non-hegemony." Whatever its long-term policy, our medium-term interest is to continue doing exactly what we are doing: talking and trading.

China . . . scene of the greatest revolution of this century . . . the Celestial Middle Kingdom. Westerners might never understand it. No matter. Not even the Chinese profess to understand China. But tolerance and common sense can do what reams of polemics and prophecy cannot— bridge differences between East and West.

APPENDICES

1

PINYIN CONVERSION

The official Pinyin spelling for certain Chinese names of cities, provinces, geographical features, and people is listed in the left column. The spelling sometimes adopted in English is in the right column.

Cities

Anshan	An-shan
Aomen	Macao
Beijing	Peking (Pei-ching)
Changsha	Ch'ang-sha
Chengdu	Ch'eng-tu
Daqing	Ta-ch'eng
Fushun	Fu-shun
Fuzhou	Fu-chou
Guangzhou	Canton (Kuang-chou)
Guilin	Kuei-lin
Guizhou	Kuei-chow
Guiyang	Kuei-yang
Hangzhou	Hang-chou
Haerbin	Harbin
Hefei	Ho-fei
Jinan	Tsinan
Jinggang Shan	Ching-kan Shan
Kailuan	K'ai-luan
Kunming	Kunming
Lanzhou	Lan-chou
Lasa	Lhasa
Luoyang	Lo-yang
Nanchang	Nan-ch'ang

Nanjing	Nanking (Nan-ching)
Nanning	Nan-ning
Qingdao	Tsingtao
Shanghai	Shanghai (Shang-hai)
Shaoshan	Shao-shan
Shenyang	Shen-yang
Shenzhen	Shen-chen
Shijiazhuang	Shih-chia-chuang
Suzhou	Suchou
Taibei	T'ai-pai
Taiyuan	T'ai-yūan
Tangshan	T'ang-shan
Tianjin	Tientsin (T'ien-chin)
Wulumuqi	Urumchi
Wuhan	Wu-han
Wuxi	Wu-hsi
Xi'an	Sian (Hsi-an)
Xianggang	Hong Kong
Xining	Hsin-ning
Yan'an	Ye-nan
Yantai	Chefoo (Yen-t'ai)
Yinchuan	Yin-ch'uan
Zhengzhou	Cheng-chou

Provinces

Anhui	Anhwei
Fujian	Fukien
Gansu	Kansu
Guangdong	Kwangtung
Guangxi Zhuangzu Zizhiqu	Kwangsi Chuang Autonomous Region
Guizhou	Kweichow
Hebei	Hopei
Henan	Honan
Jiangsu	Kiangsu
Jiangxi	Kiangsi
Jilin	Kirin
Liaoning	Liaoning

Nei Monggol Zizhiqu	Inner Mongolia Autonomous Region
Ningxia Huizu Zizhiqu	Ninghsia Hui Autonomous Region
Qinghai	Tsinghai
Shaanxi	Shensi
Shandong	Shantung
Shanxi	Shansi
Sichuan	Szechwan
Taiwan	Taiwan
Xinjiang Weiwuer Zizhiqu	Sinkiang Uighur Autonomous Region
Xizang Zizhiqu	Tibetan Autonomous Region
Yunnan	Yunnan
Zhejiang	Chekiang

Geographical Names

Bohai Wan	Gulf of Chihli
Beibu Wan	Gulf of Tonkin
Chang Jiang	Yangtse River
Dong Hai	East China Sea
Gebi Shamo	Gobi Desert
Huang Hai	Yellow Sea
Huang He	Yellow River
Nan Hai	South China Sea
Nan Hai Zhudao	South China Sea Islands
Turpan Pendi	Turfan Depression
Wanli Changcheng	Great Wall
Wusuli Jiang	Ussuri River
Yalu Jiang	Yalu River
Yalu Zangbu Jiang	Brahmaputra River
Hong He	Red River
Zhu Jiang	Pearl River
Zhonghua Renmin Gongheguo Ditu	Map of the People's Republic of China
Shoudu	Capital
Sheng	Province
Zizhiqu	Autonomous Region
Zhixiashi, Shi	City
Xian	County
Cunzhen	Town

Hu, Po, Chi, Nor, Cuo	Lake
Jiang, He, Shui, Qu, Muran, Zangbo	River
Hai	Sea, Lake
Wan	Gulf, Bay
Haixia	Strait, Channel
Yang	Ocean
Shuiku	Reservoir
Yunhe, Qu	Canal
Jing, Kuduk	Well
Quan, Bulag, Bulak	Spring
Qundao, Liedao	Archipelago, Islands
Dao, Yu	Island
Gang	Harbor
Shan, Ling, Ula	Mountain, Range, Ridge
Shan, Feng	Mount, Peak
Shankou, Guan	Pass
Pendi	Basin
Shamo	Desert
Dong	East
Nan	South
Xi	West
Bei	North
Zhong	Central
Da	Great, Greater, Grand
Xiao	Little, Lesser
Zuo	Left
You	Right

People

Cixi	Tz'u-hsi
Deng Xiaoping	Teng Hsiao-p'ing
Guangxu	Kuang-hsü
Hua Guofeng	Hua Kuo-feng
Jiang Qing	Chiang Ch'ing
Jiang Zhongzheng	Chiang Kai-shek
Kongfuzi, Kongzi	Confucious
Laozi	Lao-tzu

Lin Biao	Lin Piao
Liu Shaoqi	Liu Shao-ch'i
Li Zhongyun	Li Chung-Yun
Mao Zedong	Mao Tse-tung
Sunzi	Sun Tzu
Sun Zhongshan	Sun Yat-sen
Xue Fucheng	Hsueh Fu-ch'eng
Yuan Shikai	Yuan Shih-k'i a
Zhou Enlai	Chou En-lai
Zhu De	Chu Teh

Miscellaneous

Dongfang Binguan	Tung Fang Hotel
Erligou Dongkou	Erh Li Kou Road
Guomindang	Kuomintang Party (KMT)
Manzhou	Manchuria
Qing	Ch'ing Dynasty
Taiping Tianguo	T'ai-p'ing Tien Kuo
Tian An Men	T'ien An Men Square

2

ABBREVIATIONS OF
CHINESE ORGANIZATIONS

ARTCHINA	China National Arts and Crafts Import and Export Corporation
BOC	Bank of China
CAAC	Civil Aviation Administration of China
CAS	China Association of Standardization
CCP	Chinese Communist Party
CCPIT	China Council for the Promotion of International Trade
CECF	China Export Commodities Fair
CEROILFOOD	China National Cereals, Oils, and Foodstuffs Import and Export Corporation
CHINAPACK	China National Export Commodities Packaging Corporation
CHINATEX	China National Textiles Import and Export Corporation
CHINATUHSU	China National Native Produce and Animal Byproducts Import and Export Corporation
CHINSPECT	China National Import and Export Commodities Inspection Corporation
CITIC	China International Trust Investment Corporation
CNOOC	China National Offshore Oil Corporation
CNOGEDC	China National Oil and Gas Exploration and Development Corporation
COMPLANT	China National Complete Plant Export Corporation
COSCO	China Ocean Shipping Company
CTS	China (International) Travel Service
EQUIPEX	China National Machinery and Equipment Import and Export Corporation
FETAC	Foreign Economic and Trading Arbitration Committee
FICC	Foreign Investment Control Commission
FTC	Foreign Trade Corporation
GPSB	Guangzhou Public Security Bureau

IECC	Import-Export Control Commission
INDUSTRY	China National Light Products Import and Export Corporation
INSTRIMPEX	China National Instruments Import and Export Corporation
MAC	Maritime Arbitration Commission
MACHIMPEX	China National Machinery Import and Export Corporation
MINMETALS	China National Metals and Minerals Import and Export Corporation
MOFERT	Ministry of Foreign Economic Relations and Trade
NPC	National Party Congress, National People's Congress
PICC	People's Insurance Company of China
PLA	People's Liberation Army
PRC	People's Republic of China
PUBIMPORT	China National Publications Import Corporation
S&T	Science & Technology Commission
SCCC	State Capital Construction Commission
SEC	State Economic Commission
SGAFEC	State General Administration of Foreign Exchange Control
SINOCHEM	China National Chemicals Import and Export Corporation
SINOTRANS	China National Foreign Trade Transportation Corporation
SMBC	State Machine Building Commission
SPC	State Planning Commission
TECHIMPORT	China National Technical Import Corporation
ZHONGZU	China National Chartering Corporation

3

METRIC CONVERSION

China uses both the metric system and its own system. You must clearly
state the type of hundredweight or ton in quotations and sales confirma-
tions. A hundredweight can be 100 pounds of the short ton or 112 pounds
of the long ton. A ton can be a short ton of 2,000 pounds, a metric ton of
2,204.6 pounds, or a long ton of 2,240 pounds. Also, clearly define and
agree on all terms referring to quantity, quality, volume, length, and surface.

When you know	Divide by	To find
Inches	.04	Millimeters
Inches	.39	Centimeters
Feet	3.28	Meters (*Chek*)
Miles (Statute)	.62	Kilometers (*Gung Li*)
Acres	2.47	Hectares (10,000 m²)
Square Miles	.39	Square Kilometers
Cubic Feet	35.3	Cubic Meters
Gallons	.26	Liters
Pounds (Avoirdupois)	2.2	Kilograms (*Gung Jin*)
Long Tons	.98	Metric Tons
Short Tons	1.1	Metric Tons
Pounds	2,204.6	Metric Tons

When you know	Multiply by	To find
Mou	.1647	Acres
Jin or Gun (Catty)	1.33	Pounds
	.604	Kilograms
Dan (Picul)	133	Pounds
	60.47	Kilograms
Li (Chinese Mile)	.3106	Miles
	.5	Kilometers

4

CHRONOLOGY

Before the revolution (1839–1948)

Forces that sparked Communist revolt. Imperial powers dominate foreign trade.

1839–42   The First Sino-British Opium War.

China cedes Hong Kong to Britain and opens Shanghai and other cities to European trade.

1844   The United States signs the Treaty of Wanghia with the Qing government, getting most favored nation status.

1851–64   The Taiping Rebellion.

1893   Mao Zedong is born in Hunan province.

France extends its Indochinese colonial power to Laos and Cambodia.

1894–95   Japan declares war on China and wins a quick victory.

China forced to cede Taiwan to Japan and abandon ancient claims to suzerainty over Korea in the Treaty of Shimonoseki.

1900   Boxers, an anti-foreign, anti-dynastic movement, besiege Beijing's diplomatic quarter. An eight-nation expedition of 19,000 troops suppresses the revolt.

1911–12   The Republican revolution starts as troops in Wuhan rebel against Manchu authorities.

Sun Zhongshan is inaugurated provisional president of the Republic of China.

1915   In an effort to reduce China to a vassal state, Japan imposes Twenty-one Demands and seizes Qingdao, a German concession in China.

1916   Overthrow of Yuan Shikai. Era of warlords begins.

1917   The Bolshevik Revolution in Russia.

1920   Gregory Voitinsky, the first Comintern agent to China, meets with Sun.

1921   Chinese Communist Party formally organized in Shanghai.

1923   Under Comintern pressure, the CCP decides to close ranks with Sun's Guomindang.

1925   Sun dies.

1926–27   Jiang Zhongzheng (Chiang Kai-shek) leads combined forces against warlord rule.

            Nationalists massacre Communists in Shanghai.

1928–29   Mao and Zhu De form the People's Army and conquer rural territories in Jiangxi, where a Soviet government is proclaimed.

1930   Jiang launches his first war of extermination against the Communists. Mao's wife and sister are executed in Changsha.

1931   Japan invades Manchuria.

            The Great Famine (1929–32) ends in Northwest China. Estimated dead: 10 million.

1934–35   The Long March.

1937–38   Japan massively invades China. Jiang takes command of Nationalist-Communist resistence.

1939   Hitler-Stalin pact. Germany invades Poland.

1940–41   Breakdown of cooperation between Communists and Nationalists follows Jiang's attack on New Fourth (Red) Army.

1945   Truman bombs Hiroshima.

1946   U.S. General George C. Marshall tries to mediate a coalition government between Jiang and Mao.

1947   Guomindang attacks rout Communists from their Yan'an headquarters.

1948   Lin Biao takes the last Guomindang stronghold in Manchuria.

Rehabilitation (1949–1952)

Imposition of strict government control. Switch to Communist trading partners.

1949   The People's Republic of China is established with Mao as Chairman and Zhou Enlai as Premier and Foreign Minister.

1950   China signs a Treaty of Friendship, Alliance, and Mutual Assistance with the Soviet Union.

            China enters the Korean War.

1952   Land reform—begun in 1946—is completed.

The first Five-year Plan (1953–1957)

Buildup of industrial base with Soviet aid. Growing trade, with basic products being exchanged for Soviet machinery.

1953   Stalin dies.

            Armistice in Korea.

1954	China approves a constitution and establishes the State Council and People's Bank.
	French defeated at Dien Bien Phu.
1956	Khruschev criticizes Stalin's "personality cult."
1957	The Hundred Flowers campaign—three weeks during which intellectuals were encouraged to speak out.

The Great Leap Forward (1958–1960)

Overstraining of economy in attempt to accelerate industrialization.

1958	China bombards Nationalist-held Quemoy.
1960	Russia withdraws its technicians from China.

Recovery (1961–1965)

Retreat from Great Leap policies. Shift to Japan and Western Europe as suppliers of grain, machinery, and industrial raw materials.

1961	Imports of food grains begin.
1962	Russia gives arms to India to help it fight India's border war with China.
	11,000 U.S. advisors in Viet Nam.
1964	China tests first nuclear bomb.
	China and France establish diplomatic ties.
1965	China achieves oil self-sufficiency.

The Cultural Revolution (1966–1969)

Political upheaval. Planning and production dislocations cause slump in trade.

1966	Mao becomes Red Guard.
	Deng Xiaoping purged.
1967	China produces transistorized computer.
1968	U.S. strength in South Viet Nam peaks at 543,000.
1969	Chinese and Soviet troops clash.

Readjustment (from 1970)

Attempt to restore orderly growth. Expansion of international ties and cautious use of credit.

1970	China agrees to build 1,000-mile Tan-Zam Railway in Africa.

1971   The People's Republic takes China seat in the UN General Assembly and Security Council.

Lin Biao dies in a plane crash after failing to seize power.

1972   Nixon visits China.

Japan, Britain, and the German Federal Republic normalize relations with China.

1973   China's first export sale of oil made to Japan.

North Viet Nam, South Viet Nam, and the U.S. sign the Paris Accords, "ending the war and restoring the peace."

1974   Japan and China sign a most favored nation trade agreement.

1975   Jiang Zhongzheng dies.

Saigon falls to North Vietnamese assault.

1976   Mao and Zhou die.

The Gang of Four arrested.

1978   The New Long March, setting guidelines for long-term development.

U.S. recognizes China.

1979   Chinese troops invade Viet Nam.

Soviet troops invade Afghanistan.

1980   The U.S. extends Most Favored Nation status to China.

1981   Jiang Qing, Mao's widow, gets suspended death sentence for role in Cultural Revolution.

1982   Foreign companies bid for offshore oil exploration and development rights.

China's population exceeds 1 billion.

5

OFFSHORE PETROLEUM REGULATIONS

February 10, 1982—Following is a tentative translation of the text of the Regulations of the People's Republic of China on the Exploitation of Offshore Petroleum Resources in Cooperation with Foreign Enterprises:

Chapter I—General Principles

Article 1

In the interest of developing the national economy, expanding international economic and technological cooperation, and safeguarding national sovereignty and economic interests, these regulations are formulated to permit foreign enterprises to participate in the cooperative exploitation of offshore petroleum resources of the People's Republic of China.

Article 2

All petroleum resources in the internal waters, territorial waters and continental shelf of the People's Republic of China, and the maritime resources in all waters within the limits of national jurisdiction of the People's Republic of China are owned by the People's Republic of China.

All buildings and structures installed in the aforementioned sea areas to exploit petroleum and vessels serving the petroleum operations, as well as the corresponding onshore oil and/or gas terminals and bases are under the jurisdiction of the People's Republic of China.

Article 3

The Government of the People's Republic of China protects, in accordance with the legislations in force, investments by foreign enterprises participating in the exploitation of offshore petroleum resources, their share of profit and other legitimate rights and interests, and their activities in cooperative exploitation.

All cooperative activities to exploit offshore petroleum resources within the scope of the regulations shall comply with the laws and decrees of the People's Republic of China and relevant state stipulations. All persons and enterprises taking part in the petroleum operations shall be bound by the laws of China and shall accept inspection and supervision by the competent authorities of the Chinese Government.

Article 4

The Ministry of Petroleum Industry of the People's Republic of China is the competent authority in charge of the exploitation of offshore petroleum resources in cooperation with foreign enterprises. The ministry determines forms of cooperation and demarcates areas for cooperative exploitation in accordance with the zones and surface area designated by the state. It works out plans for the exploitation of offshore petroleum resources in cooperation with foreign enterprises in accordance with the long-term state economic program, formulates operational and management policies, and examines and approves the overall development program for offshore oil and/or gas fields.

Article 5

The China National Offshore Oil Corporation (CNOOC) is in full charge of the work of exploiting offshore petroleum resources in the People's Republic of China in cooperation with foreign enterprises.

CNOOC is a state corporation with the qualification of a juridical person, which has the exclusive right to explore for petroleum within the areas of cooperation and to develop, produce and market it.

CNOOC may establish regional subsidiaries, specialized companies and overseas offices to carry out the tasks entrusted by the head office as the work requires.

Article 6

CNOOC shall, by calling for bids and entering into petroleum contracts with foreign enterprises, exploit offshore petroleum resources in cooperation with foreign enterprises in accordance with the zones, surface area and areas demarcated for cooperative exploitation.

Petroleum contracts referred to in the preceding paragraph shall come into force after approval by the Foreign Investment Commission of the People's Republic of China.

All documents signed by CNOOC in other forms of cooperative exploitation of petroleum resources utilizing technology and funds provided by foreign enterprises shall also be subject to approval by the Foreign Investment Commission of the People's Republic of China.

Chapter II—Rights and Obligations of the Parties to Petroleum Contracts

Article 7

CNOOC shall exploit offshore petroleum resources in cooperation with foreign enterprises by entering into petroleum contracts. Unless otherwise specified by the Ministry of Petroleum Industry or in the petroleum contract, the foreign enterprise that is one party to the contract (hereinafter "foreign contractor") shall provide exploration investment, undertake exploration operations, and bear all exploration risks. After a commercial oil and/or gas field is discovered, both the foreign contractor and CNOOC shall make investment in the cooperative development. The foreign contractor shall be responsible for the development and production operations until CNOOC takes over the production operations when conditions permit under the petroleum contract. The foreign contractor may recover its investment and expenses and receive remuneration out of the petroleum produced according to the provisions of the petroleum contract.

Article 8

The foreign contractor may export the petroleum it receives as its share and/or purchases and remit abroad the investment it recovers, its profit and other legitimate income according to law.

Article 9

All Chinese and foreign enterprises involved in the exploitation of offshore petroleum resources shall pay taxes in accordance with the tax laws of the People's Republic of China and pay royalties.

Any employee of the said enterprises in the preceding paragraph shall pay individual income tax according to law.

Article 10

The equipment and materials imported for the implementation of the petroleum contract shall be exempted from customs, or levied customs at a reduced rate, or given other preferential treatment in accordance with state regulations.

Article 11

The foreign contractor shall open a bank account in accordance with the stipulations of the provisional regulations for exchange control of the People's Republic of China.

Article 12

In implementing the petroleum contract, the foreign contractor shall use appropriate and advanced technology and managerial experience and is obliged to transfer the technology and pass on the experience to the personnel of the Chinese side involved in the implementation (hereinafter "Chinese personnel").

In the course of petroleum operations, the foreign contractor must give preference to the Chinese personnel in employment, keep the percentage of Chinese steadily rising, and train the Chinese personnel in a planned way.

Article 13

In the course of implementing the petroleum contract, the foreign contractor must accurately report the petroleum operations to CNOOC in due time; and during the operations it must acquire complete and accurate data, records, samples, vouchers, and other original data, and regularly submit to CNOOC the necessary data and samples as well as technological, economic, financing and accounting, and administrative reports.

Article 14

For the implementation of the petroleum contract, the foreign contractor shall establish its subsidiary or branch or representative office within the territory of the People's Republic of China and fulfill the registration formalities according to law.

The domiciles of the subsidiaries, branches, and representative offices mentioned in the preceding paragraph shall be determined through consultation with CNOOC.

Article 15

The provisions of Articles 3, 8, 9, 10 and 14 of the regulations shall apply to foreign subcontractors which render services to the petroleum operations.

Chapter III—Petroleum Operations

Article 16

In order to achieve the highest practicable ultimate oil recovery, the operator shall work out an overall development plan for each oil and/or gas field and conduct the production operations in accordance with the regulations and relevant rules promulgated by the Ministry of Petroleum Industry on exploitation of petroleum resources and with reference to international practice.

Article 17

For the implementation of the petroleum contract, the foreign contractor shall use the existing bases within the territory of the People's Republic of China. If a new base is needed, it shall be established within the territory of the People's Republic of China.

The location of the new base and such arrangements as may be necessary in special circumstances shall be subject to prior written approval from CNOOC.

Article 18

CNOOC has the right to send personnel to join the foreign operator in making master designs and engineering designs for the implementation of the petroleum contract. Design corporations within the territory of the People's Republic of China shall have priority in entering into subcontracts for the master designs and engineering designs, provided that the terms offered by these design corporations are competitive.

Article 19

The operator must give preference to manufacturers and engineering companies within the territory of the People's Republic of China in concluding subcontracts for all facilities to be built in implementing the petroleum contract, including artificial islands, platforms, buildings and structure, provided that they are competitive in quality, price, and terms of delivery and services.

Article 20

As for the equipment and materials required to implement the petroleum contract, the operator and subcontractors shall give preference to procuring and using equipment and materials manufactured and supplied by the People's Republic of China, provided that these are competitive.

Article 21

As for the services required to implement the petroleum contract, including services for geophysical prospecting, well drilling, diving, helicopter, vessels and onshore bases, the operator and subcontractors shall enter into subcontracts and service contracts with relevant enterprises within the territory of the People's Republic of China, provided that these services are competitive in price, efficiency and service quality.

Article 22

All assets purchased and built by the foreign contractor for implementation of the petroleum contract in accordance with the plan and budget shall be owned entirely by CNOOC when the foreign contractor has fully recovered its investment for those assets (but the rental equipment from any third party is excluded). Within the term of the petroleum contract, the foreign contractor may continue to use those assets in accordance with the provisions of the contract.

Article 23

CNOOC is the owner of all the data, records, samples, vouchers and other original data obtained in the course of the petroleum operations, as provided in Article 13 of the regulations.

The utilization, transfer, donation, exchange, sale and publication of the aforementioned data, records, samples, vouchers and other original data and their delivery and transmission to outside the People's Republic of China shall be conducted in accordance with the rules on the control of data and information formulated by the Ministry of Petroleum Industry.

Article 24

The operator and subcontractors shall carry out the petroleum operations in compliance with the laws and rules on environmental protection and safety of the People's Republic of China, and with reference to international practice to protect fishery and other natural resources and prevent the air, seas, rivers, lakes and the land from being polluted or damaged.

Article 25

The petroleum produced within the petroleum contract area shall be landed in the territory of the People's Republic of China or may be exported from oil and/or gas metering points of offshore terminals.

In case such petroleum has to be landed outside the territory of the People's Republic of China, the approval of the Ministry of Petroleum Industry must be obtained.

Article 26

In case of war, threat of war or other emergency circumstances, the Government of the People's Republic of China shall have the right to requisition a portion or all of the petroleum obtained and/or purchased by the foreign contractor.

Chapter IV—Supplementary Provisions

Article 27

Any dispute arising between foreign and Chinese enterprises during the cooperative exploitation of offshore petroleum resources shall be settled amicably through consultations.

If the parties to the dispute fail to arrive at a solution through consultation, the dispute may be settled through mediation or arbitration by an arbitration body of the People's Republic of China, or through arbitration by another arbitration body agreed upon by both parties.

Article 28

In case an operator or subcontractor violates the regulations in conducting petroleum operations, the Ministry of Petroleum Industry is authorized to warn the operator or subcontractor and demand remedy within a limited time. Should the operator or subcontractor fail to remedy the violation within the specified time, the ministry shall have the right to take necessary steps, even to the extent of suspending its right to conduct the petroleum operations. All economic losses so incurred shall be borne by the party responsible.

The party responsible for serious violation of the regulations shall be fined or even be sued before juridical authorities by the Ministry of Petroleum Industry.

Article 29

The terms used in the regulations shall be defined as follows:

1. Petroleum—crude oil or natural gas deposited underground and produced or being produced therefrom.

2. Exploitation—in general, activities related to exploration, development, production and marketing of petroleum as well as other related activities.

3. Petroleum contract—the contract for the exploration for, and development and production of petroleum signed, under the legislation in force, between CNOOC and foreign enterprises for the cooperative exploitation of offshore petroleum resources of the People's Republic of China.

4. Contract area—an offshore area demarcated by geographical coordinates for the exploitation of petroleum resources under the petroleum contract.

5. Petroleum operations—all exploration, development and production operations carried out in the implementation of the petroleum contract, and other related activities.

6. Exploration operations—means all the work done in locating the petroleum-bearing traps by means of geological, geophysical and geochemical methods and exploratory drilling, and all work to determine the commerciality of the discovered petroleum traps, including appraisal drilling, feasibility studies and preparation for the overall development plan of any oil and/or gas field.

7. Development operations—all the work of designing, construction, installation, drilling and other relevant research work carried out for petroleum production from the date of the approval of the overall development plan of an oil and/or gas field by the Ministry of Petroleum Industry, including production activities carried out before the commencement of commercial production.

8. Production operations—all the operations carried out after the date of commencement of the commercial production of an oil and/or gas field for producing petroleum, and related activities, such as extraction, injection, stimulation, processing, storage, transportation and lifting of petroleum, etc.

9. Foreign contractor—a foreign enterprise which may be a company or consortium entering into the petroleum contract with CNOOC.

10.   Operator—an entity, which is responsible for performing the operations under the petroleum contract.

11.   Subcontractor—an entity which renders services to the operator.

Article 30

The detailed rules and regulations for the implementation of the regulations shall be worked out by the Ministry of Petroleum Industry.

Article 31

The regulations shall come into force on the date of its promulgation.

6

JAPANESE AND EUROPEAN TRADE AGREEMENTS

The Japan–China Long-Term Trade Agreement

In accordance with the spirit of the Joint Statement issued by and the Trade Agreement reached between the governments of both Japan and China, the Japan–China Long-Term Trade Consultation Committee of Japan and the China–Japan Long-Term Trade Consultation Committee of China have consulted in a friendly manner in order to develop economic and trade relations between the two countries over a long period of time and in a stable manner, and with the backing of the respective governments, conclude, as a part of the trade between Japan and China, a long-term trade agreement wherein technology and industrial plants, as well as construction materials, machinery and equipment will be exported from Japan to China, while crude oil and coal will be exported from China to Japan as follows:

Article 1

The term of validity for this Agreement shall be eight years from 1978 to 1985.

The total value of exports by both parties during the term of validity for this Agreement shall be about U.S. $10 billion respectively.

Article 2

The value of technology and industrial plants to be exported from Japan to China from the first year (1978) of this Agreement to the fifth year (1982) thereof shall be about U.S. $7–8 billion and that of construction materials, machinery and equipment, about U.S. $2–3 billion.

Both parties agree that the contract value to be agreed upon each year constitutes the final value

Commodities and quantities thereof to be exported from China to Japan from the first year (1978) of this Agreement to the fifth year (1982) thereof are as follows:

Year	Unit	Crude Oil	Coking Coal	Ordinary Coal
1978	10,000 tons	700	15–30	15–20
1979	10,000 tons	760	50	15–20
1980	10,000 tons	800	100	50–60
1981	10,000 tons	950	150	100–120
1982	10,000 tons	1,500	200	150–170

Both parties agree to consult each other on and finalize in 1981 commodities and quantities thereof to be exported from China to Japan from the sixth year (1983) of this Agreement to the eighth year (1985) thereof. Quantities of crude oil and coal to be exported from China to Japan in the last three years of this Agreement shall increase year after year based on the quantities for the fifth year of this Agreement.

Article 3

Both parties agree in principle that technology and industrial plants as well as construction materials, machinery and equipment shall be exported from Japan to China on a deferred payment formula.

Article 4

Transactions based on this Agreement shall be conducted in accordance with individual contracts to be concluded between the Japanese parties concerned and the Export & Import Corporations concerned, of China.

Both parties agree that transactions shall be conducted on the basis of reasonable international prices and international trade practices.

Article 5

Both parties agree to extend technological cooperation to each other in necessary fields of scientific technology for the purpose of implementing this Agreement and expanding economic exchanges between Japan and China.

Article 6

Both parties agree to designate one authorized foreign exchange bank respectively and to place it in charge of the statistical compilation necessary in order to grasp the progress of settlements of transactions based on this Agreement.

The banks designated are the Bank of Tokyo for Japan and the Bank of China for China.

Both banks shall take necessary measures for compiling statistics and shall consult with each other on these measures.

Article 7

Written contracts for transactions, letters of credit, bills of exchange and letters of guarantee based on this Agreement shall carry the following designations: LT-1 for the first year, LT-2 for the second year, and so forth.

Article 8

Both parties shall respectively establish a secretariat, which handles liaison and relevant business matters, in order to implement this Agreement.

The Japanese side shall establish in Tokyo the Secretariat of the Japan–China Long-Term Trade Consultation Committee of Japan and the Chinese side shall establish in Beijing the Secretariat of the China–Japan Long-Term Trade Consultation Committee of China.

Article 9

Both parties agree that their respective representatives shall hold a conference alternatively in Tokyo and Beijing each year to deliberate on the implementation of and problems related to this Agreement.

Article 10

This Agreement shall not be annulled unless by mutual consent.

Contracts concluded based on this Agreement shall not be annulled unless by mutual consent of both parties concerned.

Article 11

This Agreement shall be valid on and after the date of signing until December 31, 1985.

This Agreement may be modified by mutual consent upon consultation.

Article 12

This Agreement was signed on the 16th day of February, 1978, in Beijing. The written Agreement has been made out in duplicate in Japanese and Chinese, and both parties shall retain one copy each.

Chairman   Chairman
The Japan–China Long-Term   The China–Japan Long-Term
Trade Consultation Committee,   Trade Consultation Committee,
Japan   China

Source: *Business Strategies for the People's Republic of China*, published by Business International Asia/Pacific Ltd., Hong Kong. Copyright © 1980.

The Trade Agreement between The European Economic Community and the People's Republic of China Signed April 3, 1978

The Council of the European Communities and the Government of the People's Republic of China, desiring to develop economic relations and trade between the European Economic Community and the People's Republic of China on the basis of equality and the mutual advantage of the two Contracting Parties and to give a new impetus to their relations, have decided to conclude this Agreement, the terms of which are as follows:

Article 1

The two Contracting Parties will endeavor, within the framework of their respective existing laws and regulations, to promote and intensify trade between them.
To this end they confirm their determination:

A. To take all appropriate measures to create favorable conditions for trade between them;

B.   To do all they can to improve the structure of their trade in order to diversify it further, and

C.   To examine in a spirit of good will any suggestions made by the other Party, in particular in the Joint Committee, for the purpose of facilitating trade between them.

Article 2

1.   In their trade relations the two Contracting Parties shall accord each other most-favored-nation treatment in all matters regarding:

A.   Customs duties and charges of any kind applied to the import, export, re-export or transit of products, including the rules for the collection of such duties or charges;

B.   Rules, procedures and formalities concerning customs clearance, transit, warehousing and transshipment of products imported or exported;

C.   Taxes and other internal charges levied directly or indirectly on products or services imported or exported;

D.   Administrative formalities for the issue of import or export licenses.

2.   Paragraph 1 of this Article shall not apply to:

A.   Advantages accorded by either Contracting Party to States which together with it are members of a customs union or free trade area;

B.   Advantages accorded by either Contracting Party to neighboring countries for the purpose of facilitating border trade;

C.   Measures which either Contracting Party may take in order to meet its obligations under international commodity agreements.

Article 3

The two Contracting Parties will make every effort to foster the harmonious expansion of their reciprocal trade and to help, each by its own means, to attain a balance in such trade.

Should an evident imbalance arise, the matter must be examined within the Joint Committee so that measures can be recommended in order to improve the situation.

Article 4

1.   The People's Republic of China will give favorable consideration to imports from the European Economic Community. To this
end the Chinese authorities will see to it that Community exporters have the possibility of participating fully in opportunities
for trade with China.

2.   The European Economic Community will accord increasing
liberalization of imports from the People's Republic of China. To
this end it will endeavor progressively to introduce measures extending the list of products for which imports from China have
been liberalized and to increase the amounts of quotas. The manner in which this is to be implemented will be examined within the
Joint Committee.

Article 5

1.   The two Contracting Parties shall provide each other with information on any problems that may arise in their trade and shall
undertake friendly consultations, with the desire to promote
trade, for the purpose of seeking mutually satisfactory solutions to
those problems. Each Contracting Party will see that no action is
taken before consultations are held.

2.   In an exceptional case, however, where the situation does not
admit any delay, either Contracting Party may take measures but
must endeavor as far as possible to undertake friendly consultations before doing so.

3.   Each Contracting Party will ensure that, when taking the
measures referred to in paragraph 2, the general objectives of the
Agreement are not prejudiced.

Article 6

The two Contracting Parties undertake to promote visits by persons,
groups and delegations from business, trade and industry, to facilitate industrial and technical exchanges and contacts connected with trade and to
foster the organization of fairs and exhibitions of mutual interest and the
provision of services pertaining thereto. As far as possible they must grant
each other facilities in connection with the above activities.

Article 7

Trade in goods and the provision of services between the two Contracting Parties shall be effected at market-related prices and rates.

Article 8

The Contracting Parties agree that payments for transactions shall be made, in accordance with their respective existing laws and regulations, in currencies of the Member States of the Community, Renminbi, or any convertible currency agreed by the two parties concerned in the transactions.

Article 9

1.   An EEC-China Joint Committee for Trade shall be set up, comprising representatives of the European Economic Community and representatives of the People's Republic of China.

2.   The tasks of the Joint Committee shall be as follows:

A.   To monitor and examine the functioning of this Agreement;

B.   To examine any questions that may arise in the application of this Agreement;

C.   To examine problems that could hinder the development of trade between the Parties;

D.   To examine means and new opportunities of developing trade between the Contracting Parties and other matters relating to their trade; and

E.   To make recommendations that may help attain the objectives of this Agreement.

3.   The Joint Committee shall meet once a year, in Brussels and Peking alternately. Special meetings may be convened by mutual agreement, at the request of either Contracting Party. The office of chairman of the Joint Committee shall be held by each of the two Contracting Parties in turn. Where both Parties consider it necessary, the Joint Committee may set up working parties to assist it in its work.

Article 10

As far as the European Economic Community is concerned, this Agreement shall apply to the territories in which the Treaty establishing the European Economic Community is applied, under the conditions laid down in that Treaty.

Article 11

This Agreement shall enter into force on the first day of the month following the date on which the Contracting Parties notify each other that the legal procedures necessary to this end have been completed. It is concluded for a period of five years. The period of validity of the Agreement shall be tacitly extended year by year provided that neither Contracting Party gives the other Party written notice of denunciation of the Agreement six months before it expires.

However, the Agreement may be amended by mutual consent of the two Contracting Parties in order to take account of new situations.

In witness whereof, the undersigned, being duly authorized for this purpose, have signed this Agreement.

Done at Brussels, February 3, 1978, in two copies in the Danish, Dutch, English, French, German, Italian and Chinese Languages, each text being equally authentic.

For the Government of the People's Republic of China.
For the Council of the European Communities.

Source: *Business Strategies for the People's Republic of China*, published by Business International Asia/Pacific Ltd., Hong Kong. Copyright © 1980.

7

U.S./CHINA AGREEMENTS

Shanghai Communiqué

Issued February 27, 1972, at the meetings between President Richard M. Nixon and Prime Minister Zhou Enlai.

. . . Progress toward the normalization of relations between China and the United States is in the interests of all countries;

Both wish to reduce the danger of international military conflict;

Neither should seek hegemony in the Asia Pacific region and each is opposed to efforts by any other country or group of countries to establish such hegemony; and

Neither is prepared to negotiate on behalf of any third party or to enter into agreements or understandings with the other directed at other states.

Both sides are of the view that it would be against the interests of the peoples of the world for any major country to collude with another against other countries, or for major countries to divide up the world into spheres of interest.

The two sides reviewed the long-standing serious disputes between China and the United States. The Chinese side reaffirmed its position: The Taiwan question is the crucial question obstructing the normalization of relations between China and the United States; the Government of the People's Republic of China is the sole legal government of China; Taiwan is a province of China which has long been returned to the motherland; the liberation of Taiwan is China's internal affair in which no other country has the right to interfere; and all U.S. forces and military installations must be withdrawn from Taiwan. The Chinese Government firmly opposes any activities which aim at the creation of "one China, one Taiwan," "one China, two governments," "two Chinas," and "independent Taiwan" or advocate that "the status of Taiwan remains to be determined."

The U.S. side declared: The United States acknowledges that all Chinese on either side of the Taiwan Strait maintain there is but one China and that Taiwan is a part of China. The United States Government does not challenge that position. It reaffirms its interest in a peaceful settlement of the Taiwan question by the Chinese themselves. With this prospect in mind, it affirms the ultimate objective of the withdrawal of all U.S. forces and military installations from Taiwan. In the meantime, it will progressively reduce its forces and military installations on Taiwan as the tension in the area diminishes. . . .

The two sides expressed the hope that the gains achieved during this visit would open up new prospects for the relations between the two countries. They believe that the normalization of relations between the two countries is not only in the interest of the Chinese and American peoples but also contributes to the relaxation of tension in Asia and the world. . . .

Joint Communiqué on the Establishment of Diplomatic Relations between the United States and the People's Republic of China

Issued simultaneously in Washington and Beijing, December 15/16, 1978.

The United States of America and the People's Republic of China have agreed to recognize each other and to establish diplomatic relations as of January 1, 1979.

The United States of America recognizes the Government of the People's Republic of China as the sole legal government of China. Within this context the people of the United States will maintain cultural, commercial, and other unofficial relations with the people of Taiwan.

The United States of America and the People's Republic of China reaffirm the principles agreed on by the two sides in the Shanghai communiqué and emphasize once again that:

- Both wish to reduce the danger of international military conflict.
- Neither should seek hegemony in the Asia Pacific region or in any other region of the world and each is opposed to efforts by any other country or group of countries to establish such hegemony.
- Neither is prepared to negotiate on behalf of any third party or to enter into agreements or understandings with the other directed at other states.
- The Government of the United States of America acknowledges the Chinese position that there is but one China and Taiwan is part of China.
- Both believe that normalization of Sino-American relations is not only in the interest of the Chinese and American peoples but also contributes to the cause of peace in Asia and the world.

The United States of America and the People's Republic of China will exchange ambassadors and establish embassies on March 1, 1979.

Statement of the Government
of the People's Republic of China
January 1, 1979

As of January 1, 1979, the People's Republic of China and the United States of America recognize each other and establish diplomatic relations, thereby ending the prolonged abnormal relationship between them. This is a historic event in Sino-U.S. relations.

As is known to all, the Government of the People's Republic of China is the sole legal government of China and Taiwan is a part of China. The question of Taiwan was the crucial issue obstructing the normalization of relations between China and the United States. It has now been resolved between the two countries in the spirit of the Shanghai Communique and through their joint efforts, thus enabling the normalization of relations so ardently desired by the people of the two countries. As for the way of bringing Taiwan back to the embrace of the motherland and reunifying the country, it is entirely China's internal affair.

At the invitation of the U.S. Government, Deng Xiaoping, Vice Premier of the State Council of the People's Republic of China, will pay an official visit to the United States in January 1979, with a view to further promoting the friendship between the two peoples and good relations between the two countries.

United States Statement

As of January 1, 1979, the United States of America recognizes the People's Republic of China as the sole legal government of China. On the same date, the People's Republic of China accords similar recognition to the United States of America. The United States thereby establishes diplomatic relations with the People's Republic of China.

On that same date, January 1, 1979, the United States of America will notify Taiwan that it is terminating diplomatic relations and that the Mutual Defense Treaty between the U.S. and the Republic of China is being terminated in accordance with the provisions of the Treaty. The United States also states that it will be withdrawing its remaining military personnel from Taiwan within four months.

In the future, the American people and the people of Taiwan will maintain commercial, cultural, and other relations without official government representation and without diplomatic relations.

The Administration will seek adjustments to our laws and regulations to permit the maintenance of commercial, cultural, and other non-governmental relationships in the new circumstances that will exist after normalization.

The United States is confident that the people of Taiwan face a peaceful and prosperous future. The United States continues to have an interest in the peaceful resolution of the Taiwan issue and expects that the Taiwan issue will be settled peacefully by the Chinese themselves.

The United States believes that the establishment of diplomatic relations with the People's Republic will contribute to the welfare of the American people, to the stability of Asia where the United States has major security and economic interest, and to the peace of the entire world.

Agreement on Trade Relations between the United States of America and the People's Republic of China

The Government of the United States of America and the Government of the People's Republic of China;

Acting in the spirit of the Joint Communique on the Establishment of Diplomatic Relations between the United States of America and the People's Republic of China;

Desiring to enhance friendship between both peoples;

Wishing to develop further economic and trade relations between both countries on the basis of the principles of equality and mutual benefit as well as nondiscriminatory treatment;

Have agreed as follows:

Article 1

1.   The Contracting Parties undertake to adopt all appropriate measures to create the most favorable conditions for strengthening, in all aspects, economic and trade relations between the two countries so as to promote the continuous, long-term development of trade between the two countries.

2.   In order to strive for a balance in their economic interests, the Contracting Parties shall make every effort to foster the mutual expansion of their reciprocal trade and to contribute, each by its own means, to attaining the harmonious development of such trade.

3.   Commercial transactions will be effected on the basis of contracts between firms, companies and corporations, and trading

organizations of the two countries. They will be concluded on the basis of customary international trade practice and commercial considerations such as price, quality, delivery and terms of payment.

Article 2

1.   With a view to establishing their trade relations on a non-discriminatory basis, the Contracting Parties shall accord each other most-favored-nation treatment with respect to products originating in or destined for the other Contracting Party, i.e., any advantage, favor, privilege, or immunity they grant to like products originating in or destined for any other country or region, in all matters regarding:

A.   Customs duties and charges of all kinds applied to the import, export, re-export or transit of products, including the rules, formalities and procedures for collection of such duties and charges;

B.   Rules, formalities and procedures concerning customs clearance, transit, warehousing and transshipment of imported and exported products;

C.   Taxes and other internal charges levied directly or indirectly on imported or exported products or services;

D.   All laws, regulations and requirements affecting all aspects of internal sale, purchase, transportation, distribution or use of imported products; and

E.   Administrative formalities for the issuance of import and export licenses.

2.   In the event either Contracting Party applies quantitative restrictions to certain products originating in or exported to any third country or region, it shall afford to all like products originating in or exported to the other country treatment which is equitable to that afforded to such third country or region.

3.   The Contracting Parties note, and shall take into consideration in the handling of their bilateral trade relations, that, at its current state of economic development, China is a developing country.

4.   The principles of Paragraph 1 of this Article will be applied by the Contracting Parties in the same way as they are applied under similar circumstances under any multilateral trade agreement to

which either Contracting Party is a party on the date of entry into force of this Agreement.

5.   The Contracting Parties agree to reciprocate satisfactorily concessions with regard to trade and services, particularly tariff and non-tariff barriers to trade, during the term of this Agreement.

Article 3

For the purpose of promoting economic and trade relations between their two countries, the Contracting Parties agree to:

A.   Accord firms, companies and corporations, and trading organizations of the other Party treatment no less favorable than is afforded to any third country or region;

B.   Promote visits by personnel, groups and delegations from economic, trade and industrial circles; encourage commercial exchanges and contacts; and support the holding of fairs, exhibitions and technical seminars in each other's country;

C.   Permit and facilitate, subject to their respective laws and regulations and in accordance with physical possibilities, the stationing of representatives, or the establishment of business offices, by firms, companies and corporations, and trading organizations of the other Party in its own territory; and

D.   Subject to their respective laws and regulations and physical possibilities, further support trade promotions and improve all conveniences, facilities and related services for the favorable conduct of business activities by firms, companies and corporations, and trading organizations of the two countries, including various facilities in respect of office space and residential housing, telecommunications, visa issuance, internal business travel, customs formalities for entry and re-export of personal effects, office articles and commercial samples, and observance of contracts.

Article 4

The Contracting Parties affirm that government trade offices contribute importantly to the development of their trade and economic relations. They agree to encourage and support the trade promotion activities of these offices. Each Party undertakes to provide facilities as favorable as possible for the operation of these offices in accordance with their respective physical possibilities.

Article 5

1. Payments for transactions between the United States of America and the People's Republic of China shall either be effected in freely convertible currencies mutually accepted by firms, companies and corporations, and trading organizations of the two countries, or made otherwise in accordance with agreements signed by and between the two parties to the transaction. Neither Contracting Party may impose restrictions on such payments except in time of declared national emergency.

2. The Contracting Parties agree, in accordance with their respective laws, regulations and procedures, to facilitate the availability of official export credits on the most favorable terms appropriate under the circumstances for transactions in support of economic and technological projects and products between firms, companies and corporations, and trading organizations of the two countries. Such credits will be the subject of separate arrangements by the concerned authorities of the two Contracting Parties.

3. Each Contracting Party shall provide, on the basis of most-favored-nation treatment, and subject to its respective laws and regulations, all necessary facilities for financial, currency and banking transactions by nationals, firms, companies and corporations, and trading organizations of the other Contracting Party on terms as favorable as possible. Such facilities shall include all required authorizations for international payments, remittances and transfers, and uniform application of rates of exchange.

4. Each Contracting Party will look with favor towards participation by financial institutions of the other country in appropriate aspects of banking services related to international trade and financial relations. Each Contracting Party will permit those financial institutions of the other country established in its territory to provide such services on a basis no less favorable than that accorded to financial institutions of other countries.

Article 6

1. Both Contracting Parties in their trade relations recognize the importance of effective protection of patents, trademarks and copyrights.

2. Both Contracting Parties agree that on the basis of reciprocity legal or natural persons of either Party may apply for registration of trademarks and acquire exclusive rights thereto in the territory of the other Party in accordance with its laws and regulations.

3.   Both Contracting Parties agree that each Party shall seek, under its laws and with due regard to international practice, to ensure to legal or natural persons of the other Party protection of patents and trademarks equivalent to the patent and trademark protection correspondingly accorded by the other Party.

4.   Both Contracting Parties shall permit and facilitate enforcement of provisions concerning protection of industrial property in contracts between firms, companies and corporations, and trading organizations of their respective countries, and shall provide means, in accordance with their respective laws, to restrict unfair competition involving unauthorized use of such rights.

5.   Both Contracting Parties agree that each Party shall take appropriate measures, under its laws and regulations and with due regard to international practice, to ensure to legal or natural persons of the other Party protection of copyrights equivalent to the copyright protection correspondingly accorded by the other Party.

Article 7

1.   The Contracting Parties shall exchange information on any problems that may arise from their bilateral trade, and shall promptly hold friendly consultations to seek mutually satisfactory solutions to such problems. No action shall be taken by either Contracting Party before such consultations are held.

2.   However, if consultations do not result in a mutually satisfactory solution within a reasonable period of time, either Contracting Party may take such measures as it deems appropriate. In an exceptional case where a situation does not admit any delay, either Contracting Party may take preventive or remedial action provisionally, on the condition that consultation shall be effected immediately after taking such action.

3.   When either Contracting Party takes measures under this Article, it shall ensure that the general objectives of this Agreement are not prejudiced.

Article 8

1.   The Contracting Parties encourage the prompt and equitable settlement of any disputes arising from or in relation to contracts between their respective firms, companies and corporations, and trading organizations, through friendly consultations, conciliation or other mutually acceptable means.

2. If such disputes cannot be settled promptly by any one of the above-mentioned means, the parties to the dispute may have recourse to arbitration for settlement in accordance with provisions specified in their contracts or other agreements to submit to arbitration. Such arbitration may be conducted by an arbitration institution in the United States of America, the People's Republic of China, or a third country. The arbitration rules of procedure of the relevant arbitration institution are applicable, and the arbitration rules of the United Nations Commission on International Trade Law recommended by the United Nations, or other international arbitration rules, may also be used where acceptable to the parties to the dispute and to the arbitration institution.

3. Each Contracting Party shall seek to ensure that arbitration awards are recognized and enforced by their competent authorities where enforcement is sought, in accordance with applicable laws and regulations.

Article 9

The provisions of this Agreement shall not limit the right of either Contracting Party to take any action for the protection of its security interests.

Article 10

1. This Agreement shall come into force on the date on which the Contracting Parties have exchanged notifications that each has completed the legal procedures necessary for this purpose, [February 1, 1980] and shall remain in force for three years.

2. This Agreement shall be extended for successive terms of three years if neither Contracting Party notifies the other of its intent to terminate this Agreement at least thirty (30) days before the end of a term.

3. If either Contracting Party does not have domestic legal authority to carry out its obligations under this Agreement, either Contracting Party may suspend application of this Agreement, or, with the agreement of the other Contracting Party, any part of this Agreement. In that event, the Parties will seek, to the fullest extent practicable in accordance with domestic law, to minimize unfavorable effects on existing trade relations between the two countries.

4. The Contracting Parties agree to consult at the request of either Contracting Party to review the operation of this Agree-

ment and other relevant aspects of the relations between the two Parties.

In witness whereof, the authorized representatives of the Contracting Parties have signed this Agreement.

Done at Beijing in two original copies this 7th day of July, 1979, in English and Chinese, both texts being equally authentic.

For the United States of America

Leonard Woodcock

For the People's Republic of China

Li Qiang

8

SAMPLE CONTRACTS

China National Cereals, Oils & Foodstuffs Import and Export Corporation Sales Contract

No. . . . .

Date . . . .

The China National Cereals, Oils & Foodstuffs Import and Export Corporation, hereinafter called the Sellers, agree to sell and Messrs.

. . . .

hereinafter called the Buyers, agree to buy the undermentioned goods subject to the terms and conditions stipulated below:

1. Name of Commodity & Specifications	2. Quantity	3. Unit Price	4. Amount

With   % more or less both in amount and quantity allowed at the Sellers' option.

    5.   Time of Shipment:

    6.   Packing:

7.   Loading Port and Destination:

8.   Insurance:

9.   Terms of Payment: To be made against sight draft drawn under an irrevocable, transferable, divisible Letter of Credit, without recourse, for the total value of the goods in . . . ., allowing 5% more or less both in amount and quantity at Sellers' option in favor of the China National Cereals, Oils & Foodstuffs Import and Export Corporation . . . .

. . . . Branch, established through . . . .

. . . .

. . . .

. . . . The Letter of Credit in due form must reach the Sellers 30 days before shipment and remain valid for at least 15 days in China after the last days of shipment.

10.   The General Terms and Conditions on the back page constitute an inseparable part of this Contract and shall be equally binding upon both parties.

The Sellers

China National Cereals, Oils & Foodstuffs Import and Export Corporation, Beijing, The People's Republic of China

The Buyers

General Terms and Conditions

1.   Documents to be submitted by the Sellers to the Bank for negotiation:

A.   Full set clean-on-board shipped Bill of Lading.

B.   Invoice.

C.   Inspection Certificate on Quality and Inspection Certificate on Weight issued by the China Commodity Inspection Bureau at the port of shipment.

D.   Insurance Policy.

2.   Quality and Weight:
Quality and Weight certified by the China Commodity Inspection

Bureau at the port of shipment as per their respective certificates are to be taken as final.

3.   Shipping Advice:
Immediately after loading is completed, the Sellers shall notify by cable the number of credit, quantity and name of vessel to the Buyers.

4.   Amendments of Letter of Credit:
The Buyer shall open Letter of Credit in accordance with the terms of this Contract. If any discrepancy is found, amendments of Letter of Credit should be made immediately by the Buyers upon receipt of the Sellers' advice, failing which the Buyers shall be held responsible for any losses thus incurred as well as for late shipment thus caused.

5.   Force Majeure:
Should the Sellers fail to deliver the contract goods or effect the shipment in time by reason of war, flood, fire, storm, heavy snow or any other causes beyond their control, the time of shipment might be duly extended, or alternatively a part or whole of the Contract might be cancelled without any liability attached to the Sellers, but the Sellers have to furnish the buyers with a certificate attesting such event or events.

6.   Arbitration:
Should there be any disputes between the contracting parties, they shall be settled through negotiation. In case no settlement can be reached, the case under dispute may then be referred to arbitration.

7.   Claims:
Should the quality, quantity and/or weight be found not in conformity with those stipulated in this Contract, aside from those usual natural changes of quality and weight in transit and losses within the responsibility of the shipping company and/or insurance companies, the Buyers shall have the right within 30 days after the arrival of the goods at the port of destination, to lodge claims concerning the quality, quantity or weight of the goods. (Claims for perishable goods are to be put forward immediately after arrival of the goods at destination), but the Buyers should provide the Sellers with the Certificates issued by the concerned Inspection Organization.

Source: *Business Strategies for the People's Republic of China*, published by Business International Asia/Pacific Ltd., Hong Kong. Copyright © 1980.

China National Textiles Import & Export Corporation, Shanghai Silk Branch

Sales Confirmation

Date:
To:

The undersigned Sellers and Buyers have agreed to close the following transactions according to the terms and conditions stipulated below:
by Buyers' cable/letter dated
Sellers' cable/letter dated

Quality No., Name of Commodity and Specification	Quantity	Unit Price	Amount	Time of Shipment

Both Amount and Quantity   % More or Less Allowed   Total Amount:

Loading Port and Destination:

Terms of Payment:

By 100% value confirmed irrevocable letter of credit with I/T reimbursement available by draft at sight with transshipment and partial shipments allowed, to reach the Sellers 30 days before the month of shipment, with shipment validity arranged till the 15th day after the month of shipment, and to remain valid for negotiation in the loading port until the 10th day after the shipment validity. A 10% more or less should be allowed in the quantity and amount of the credit, and the world "ABOUT" should be mentioned before the quantity and amount. The terms and conditions in the L/C should be strictly in accordance with those in this contract.

Insurance:

To be effected by Sellers covering All Risks and War Risks at 110% of invoice value as per Ocean Marine Cargo Clauses and War Risks Clauses (1/4/1972) of The People's Insurance Company of China (abbreviated as C.I.C.-All Risks & War Risks).

Remarks:

The Buyers

The Sellers

China National Textiles Import & Export Corporation, Shanghai Silk Branch.

Please sign and return one copy of this Confirmation.

Source: *Business Strategies for the People's Republic of China*, published by Business International Asia/Pacific Ltd., Hong Kong. Copyright © 1980.

Purchase Contract

The Buyers:

China National Machinery Import and Export Corporation

The Sellers:

This Contract is made by and between the Buyers and the Sellers; whereby the Buyers agree to buy and the Sellers agree to sell the under-mentioned commodity according to the terms and conditions stipulated below:

1. *Commodity, Specifications, Quantity and Unit Price:*

2. *Total Value:*

3. *Country of origin and Manufacturers:*

4. *Packing:* To be packed in strong wooden case(s) or in carton(s), suitable for long distance ocean parcel post air freight transportation and to change of climate, well protected against moisture and shocks. The Sellers shall be liable for any damage of

the commodity and expenses incurred on account of improper packing and for any rust attributable to inadequate or improper protective measures taken by the Sellers in regard to the packing. One full set of service instructions for each instrument shall be enclosed in the case(s).

5.   *Shipping Mark:* The Sellers shall mark on each package with fadeless paint the package number, gross weight, net weight measurement and the wordings: "Keep Away From Moisture", "Handle with Care", "This Side Up" etc., and the shipping mark:

6.   *Time of Shipment:*

7.   *Port of Shipment:*

8.   *Port of Destination:*

9.   *Insurance:* To be covered by the Buyers after shipment.

10.   *Payment: for/by*

(1) In case by L/C: The Buyers, upon receipt from the Sellers of the delivery advice specified in Clause 12(1)(a) hereof, shall 15–20 days prior to the date of delivery, open an irrevocable Letter of Credit with the Bank of China, Peking, in favour of the Sellers, for an amount equivalent to the total value of the shipment. The Credit shall be payable against the presentation of the draft drawn on the opening bank and the shipping documents specified in Clause 11 hereof. The Letter of Credit shall be valid until the 15th day after the shipment is effected.

(2) In case by Collection: After delivery is made, the Sellers shall send the shipping documents specified in Clause 11 hereof, from the Sellers' Bank through Bank of China, to the Buyers for collection.

(3) In case by M/T or T/T: Payment to be effected by the Buyers within seven days after receipt of the shipping documents specified in Clause 11 of this contract.

11.   *Documents:* The Sellers shall present to the paying bank the following documents for negotiation:

A.   In case by freight:
3 Negotiable copies of clean on board ocean Bill of Lading marked "Freight To Collect"/"Freight Prepaid", made out to order, blank endorsed, and notifying the China National Foreign Trade Transportation Corporation at the port of destination.
In case by air freight:
One copy of Airway Bill marked "Freight Prepaid" and consigned to the Buyers.

In case by post:
One copy of Parcel Receipt addressed to the Buyers.

B.   5 copies of Invoice with the insertion of Contract No. and the Shipping Mark. (In case of more than one shipping mark, the invoice shall be issued separately.)

C.   2 copies of Packing List issued by the Manufacturers.

D.   1 copy of Certificate of Quantity and Quality issued by the Manufacturers.

E.   Certified copy of cable/letter to the Buyers, advising shipment immediately after shipment is made.

F.   The Sellers shall, within 10 days after the shipment is effected, send by air-mail two sets of the abovementioned documents (except Item E)-One set to the Buyers and the other set to the China National Foreign Trade Transportation Corporation at the port of destination.

12.   *Shipment:*

A.   In case of FOB Terms:

1.   The Sellers shall, 30 days before the date of shipment stipulated in the Contract, advise the Buyers by cable/letter of the Contract No., commodity, quantity, value, number of package, gross weight and date of readiness at the port of shipment for the Buyers to book shipping space.

2.   Booking of shipping space shall be attended to by the Buyers' Shipping Agents Messrs. China National Chartering Corporation, Beijing, China. (Cable address: Zhongzu Beijing)

3.   China National Chartering Corporation, Beijing, China, or its Port Agents, (or Liners' Agents) shall send to the Sellers 10 days before the estimated date of arrival of the vessel at the port of shipment, a preliminary notice indicating the name of vessel, estimated date of loading, Contract No. for the Sellers to arrange shipment. The Sellers are requested to get in close contact with the shipping agents. When it becomes necessary to change the carrying vessel or in the event of her arrival having to be advanced or delayed the Buyers or the Shipping Agent shall advise the Sellers in time. Should the vessel fail to arrive at the port of loading within 30 days after the arrival date advised by the Buyers, the

Buyers shall bear the storage and insurance expenses incurred from the 31st day.

4.   The Sellers shall be liable for any dead freight or demurrage, should it happen that they have failed to have the commodity ready for loading after the carrying vessel has arrived at the port of shipment on time.

5.   The Sellers shall bear all expenses, risks of the commodity before it passes over the vessel's rail and is released from the tackle. After it has passed over the vessel's rail and been released from the tackle, all expenses of the commodity shall be for the Buyers' account.

B.   In case of C&F Terms:

1.   The Sellers shall ship the goods within the shipment time from the port of shipment to the port of destination. Transshipment is not allowed. The contracted goods shall not be carried by a vessel flying the flag of the country which the Buyers can not accept. The carrying vessel shall not call or stop over at the port/ports of Taiwan and/or the port/ports in the vicinities of Taiwan prior to her arrival at the port of destination as stipulated in Clause 8 of this Contract.

2.   In case the goods are to be dispatched by parcel post/air-freight, the Sellers shall, 30 days before the time of delivery as stipulated in Clause 6, inform the Buyers by cable/letter of the estimated date of delivery, Contract No., commodity, invoiced value, etc. The sellers shall, immediately after dispatch of the goods, advise the Buyers by cable/letter of the Contract No., commodity, invoiced value and date of dispatch for the Buyers to arrange insurance in time.

13.   *Shipping Advice:*
The Sellers shall, immediately upon the completion of the loading of the goods, advise by cable/letter the Buyers of the Contract No., commodity, quantity, invoiced value, gross weight, name of vessel and date of sailing, etc. In case the Buyers fail to arrange insurance in time due to the Sellers not having cabled in time, all losses shall be borne by the Sellers.

14.   *Guarantee of Quality:*
The Sellers guarantee that the commodity hereof is made of the best materials with first class workmanship, brand new and un-

used, and complies in all respects with the quality and specification stipulated in this Contract. The guarantee period shall be 12 months counting from the date on which the commodity arrives at the port of destination.

15. *Claims:*
Within 90 days after the arrival of the goods at destination, should the quality, specification, or quantity be found not in conformity with the stipulations of the Contract except those claims for which the insurance company or the owners of the vessel are liable, the Buyers shall, on the strength of the Inspection Certificate issued by the China Commodity Inspection Bureau, have the right to claim for replacement with new goods, or for compensation, and all the expenses (such as inspection charges, freight for returning the goods and for sending the replacement, insurance premium, storage and loading and unloading charges, etc.) shall be borne by the Sellers. Regarding quality, the Sellers shall guarantee that if, within 12 months from the date of arrival of the goods at destination, damages occur in the course of operation by reason of inferior quality, bad workmanship or the use of inferior materials, the Buyers shall immediately notify the Sellers in writing and put forward a claim supported by Inspection Certificate issued by the China Commodity Inspection Bureau. The Certificate so issued shall be accepted as the base of a claim. The Sellers, in accordance with the Buyers' claim shall be responsible for the immediate elimination of the defect(s), complete or partial replacement of the commodity or shall devaluate the commodity according to the State of defect(s). Where necessary, the Buyers shall be at liberty to eliminate the defect(s) themselves at the Sellers' expenses. If the Sellers fail to answer the Buyers within one month after receipt of the aforesaid claim the claim shall be reckoned as having been accepted by the Sellers.

16. *Force Majeure:*
The Sellers shall not be held responsible for the delay in shipment or nondelivery of the goods due to the Force Majeure, which might occur during the process of manufacturing or in the course of loading or transit. The Sellers shall advise the Buyers immediately of the occurrence mentioned above and within fourteen days thereafter, the Sellers shall send by airmail to the Buyers for their acceptance a certificate of the accident issued by the Competent Government Authorities where the accident occurs as evidence thereof.
Under such circumstances the Sellers, however, are still under the obligation to take all necessary measures to hasten the delivery of

the goods. In case the accident lasts for more than 10 weeks, the Buyers shall have the right to cancel the Contract.

17.   Late Delivery and Penalty:

Should the Sellers fail to make delivery on time as stipulated in the Contract, with exception of Force Majeure causes specified in Clause 16 of this Contract, the Buyers shall agree to postpone the delivery on condition that the Sellers agree to pay a penalty which shall be deducted by the paying bank from the payment under negotiation. The penalty, however, shall not exceed 5% of the total value of the goods involved in the late delivery. The rate of penalty is charged at 0.5% for every seven days, odd days less than seven days should be counted as seven days. In case the Sellers fail to make delivery ten weeks later than the time of shipment stipulated in the Contract, the Buyers shall have the right to cancel the contract and the Sellers, in spite of the cancellation, shall still pay the aforesaid penalty to the Buyers without delay.

18.   Arbitration:

All disputes in connection with this Contract or the execution thereof shall be settled through friendly negotiations. In case no settlement can be reached, the case may then be submitted for arbitration to the Arbitration Committee of the China Council for the Promotion of International Trade in accordance with the Provisional Rules of Procedures promulgated by the said Arbitration Committee. The Arbitration shall take place in Beijing and the decision of the Arbitration Committee shall be final and binding upon both parties; neither party shall seek recourse to a law court or other authorities to appeal for revision of the decision. Arbitration fee shall be borne by the losing party. Or the Arbitration may be settled in the third country mutually agreed upon by both parties.

19.   Special Provisions:

In Witness Thereof, this Contract is signed by both parties in two original copies; each party holds one copy.

The Buyers:

China National Machinery Import and Export Corporation

The Sellers:

Insurance
The People's Insurance Company of
China, Beijing

Invoice No.   Policy No.
INSURANCE POLICY

This Policy of Insurance witnesses that The People's Insurance Company of China (hereinafter called "The Company"), at the request of . . . (hereinafter called the "Insured") and in consideration of the agreed premium paying to the Company by the Insured, undertakes to insure the undermentioned goods in transportation subject to the conditions of this Policy as per the Clauses printed overleaf and other special clauses attached hereon.

Marks & Nos.	Quantity	Description of Goods	Amount Insured

Total amount Insured: . . . .

Premium . . . . *as arranged* . . . .

Rate . . . . *as arranged* . . . .

Per conveyance S.S. . . . .

Slg. on or abt . . . .

From . . . . to . . . .

Conditions:

. . . .

. . . .

Claims, if any, payable on surrender of this Policy together with other relevant documents. In the event of accident whereby loss or damage may result in a claim under this Policy immediate notice applying for survey must be given to the Company's Agent as mentioned hereunder:

Claim payable at . . . .

Date . . . .

General Terms
and Conditions of Insurance

1. Scope of Cover

This insurance is classifed into three forms—Total Loss Only (T.L.O.), With Average (W.A.) and All Risks. Where the insured goods sustain loss or damage, this Company shall undertake to indemnify therefore according to the risks insured and the Provisions of these Clauses.

(1) Total Loss Only (T.L.O)

This Company shall be liable for

A.   total loss of the insured goods caused in the course of transit by natural calamities—heavy weather, lightning, floating ice, seaquake, earthquake, flood, etc. or by accidents—grounding, stranding, sinking, collision or derailment of the carrying conveyance, fire, explosion and falling of entire package or packages of the insured goods into sea during loading or discharge, etc.;

B.   Sacrifice in and contribution to General Average and Salvage Expenses arising from the foregoing events.

(2) With Average (W.A.)

This Company shall be liable for

A.   total or partial loss of the insured goods caused in the course of transit by natural calamities—heavy weather, lightning, floating ice, seaquake, earthquake, flood, etc. or by accidents—grounding, stranding, sinking, collision or derailment of the carrying conveyance, fire, explosion and falling of entire package or packages of the insured goods into sea during loading or discharge, etc.;

B.   Sacrifice in and contribution to General Average and Salvage Expenses arising from the foregoing events.

(3) All Risks

In addition to the liability covered under the aforesaid Total Loss Only and With Average insurance, this Company shall also be liable for total or partial loss of the insured goods caused by shortage, shortage in weight, leakage, contact with other substance, breakage, hook, rainwater, rust, wetting, heating, mould, tainting by odour, contamination, etc. arising from external causes in the course of transit.

Goods may be insured on Total Loss Only or With Average or All Risks conditions and may also be insured against additional risks upon consultation.

2. Exclusions

This Company shall not be liable for

A. Loss or damage caused by the intentional act or fault of the Insured;

B. Loss or damage falling under the liability of the Consignor or arising from normal losses of the insured goods;

C. Loss or damage caused by strikes of workers or delay in transit;

D. Risks covered and excluded in the Ocean Marine Cargo War Risk Clauses of this Company.

3. Commencement and Termination of Cover

This insurance shall take effect from the time the insured goods leave the Consignor's warehouse at the place of shipment named in the Policy and shall continue in force in the ordinary course of transit including sea and land transit until the insured goods are delivered to the Consignee's warehouse at the destination named in the Policy. The Cover shall, however, be limited to sixty days upon discharge of the insured goods from the sea-going vessel at the final port of discharge.

4. Survey of Damage to Goods and Presentation of Claim

A. The Insured shall take delivery of the insured goods in good time upon arrival thereof at the destination or port of destination named in the Policy and shall undertake to:

apply immediately for survey to the surveying agent of the claims settling agent stipulated in the Policy should the insured goods be found to have sustained loss or damage. In case this Company has no surveying agent or claims settling locally, a local competent surveyor may be applied to for survey;

obtain forthwith from the Carrier or relevant Authorities (Customs and Port Authorities, etc.) Certificate of Loss or Damage and/or Short-landed Memo and lodge a claim with the Carrier or the party concerned in writing should the insured goods be found short in entire package or packages or to show apparent traces of damage.

B.   The Insured shall submit the following documents when presenting a claim to this Company:

Original Policy or Certificate of Insurance, original or copy of Bill of Lading, Invoice, Packing List and Tally Sheet;

Certificate of Loss or Damage and/or Short-landed Memo, Survey Report and Statement of Claims.

When third party liability is involved, the letters and cables relative to pursuing of recovery to and from the third party and the other essential certificates or documents shall be submitted in addition.

C.   The time of validity of a claim under this insurance shall not exceed a period of nine months counting from the time of completion of discharge of the insured goods from the sea-going vessel at the final port of discharge.

This Company shall undertake to indemnify the Insured for the reasonable expenses incurred by him for having immediately taken effective measures in salving and preventing further loss of the insured goods after damage was sustained but the amount of such indemnity together with the amount of the claim shall not exceed the insured amount of the damaged goods.

5.   Treatment of Disputes

All disputes arising between the Insured and this Company shall be settled by friendly negotiation on the principles of seeking truth from facts and of fairness and reasonableness. Where a settlement fails after negotiation and it is necessary to submit to arbitration or take legal actions, such arbitration or legal actions shall be carried out at the place where the defendant is domiciled.

War Risk Clauses

1.   Scope of Cover

This Company shall undertake to indemnify for the loss of or damage to the insured goods consequent upon the undermentioned causes:

A.   Loss or damage caused by war, hostile acts or armed conflicts;

B.   Loss or damage caused by seizure, detainment, confiscation or blockade arising from the events in (A.) hereinabove, but such loss or damage shall be dealt with only on expiry of six months from the day when the loss or damage arises;

C.   Loss or damage caused by conventional weapons of war, including mines, torpedoes and bombs.
This Company shall further be liable for:
Sacrifice in and contribution to General Average and Salvage Expenses arising from the events enumerated in (A.) and (C.) hereinabove.

2.   Exclusion

This Company shall not be liable for loss or damage caused by atomic or hydrogen bombs or nuclear weapons of war.

3.   Commencement and Termination of Cover

This insurance shall attach from the time the insured goods are loaded on the sea-going vessel or lighter at the port of shipment named in the Policy until the insured goods are discharged from the sea-going vessel or lighter at the port of destination named in the Policy, but in case the insured goods are not discharged from the sea-going vessel or lighter the longest duration of this insurance allowable on the insured goods upon arrival at the port of destination shall be limited to 15 days counting from midnight of the day of their arrival at such port.

This insurance shall cease to attach when the insured goods are discharged from the seagoing vessel or lighter at the port of transhipment, but in case the insured goods are not discharged from the sea-going vessel, the longest duration of the insurance allowable on the insured goods upon arrival at such port shall be limited to 15 days counting from midnight of the day of their arrival at such port. The insurance shall reattach when the insured goods are loaded on the on-carrying sea-going vessel at the port of transhipment.

4.   Automatic Termination of Cover

Should the insured goods be used for serving a war of aggression launched by imperialism, this insurance shall terminate automatically from the time of the outbreak of such war.

Note: These Clauses are the clauses of an additional insurance to the Ocean Marine Cargo Insurance. In case of conflict between any clauses of these Clauses and the Ocean Marine Cargo Clauses, these Clauses shall prevail.

9

FOREIGN EXCHANGE REGULATIONS

Provisional Regulations for Exchange Control of the People's Republic of China

Promulgated by the State Council on December 18, 1980.

Chapter I. General provisions

Article 1

These provisional regulations are formulated for the purpose of strengthening exchange control, increasing national foreign exchange income and economizing on foreign exchange expenditure so as to expedite the national economic growth and safeguard the rights and interests of the country.

All foreign exchange income and expenditure, the issuance and circulation of all kinds of payment instruments in foreign currency, dispatch and carriage into and out of the People's Republic of China of foreign exchange, precious metals and payment instruments in foreign currency shall be governed by these regulations.

Article 2

Foreign exchange herein mentioned refers to:

A. Foreign currencies, including banknotes, coins, etc.

B. Securities in foreign currency, including government bonds, treasury bills, corporate bonds and debentures, shares, interest and dividend coupons, etc.

C.   Instruments payable in foreign currency, including bills, drafts, cheques, bank deposit certificates, postal savings certificates, etc.

D.   Other foreign exchange funds.

Article 3

The People's Republic of China pursues the policy of centralized control and unified management of foreign exchange by the state. The administrative organ in charge of exchange control of the People's Republic of China is the State General Administration of Exchange Control (SGAEC) and its branch offices. The specialized foreign exchange bank of the People's Republic of China is the Bank of China. No other financial institution shall engage in foreign exchange business, unless approved by the SGAEC.

Article 4

All Chinese and foreign organizations and individuals in the People's Republic of China must, unless otherwise stipulated by law or decree or in these regulations, sell their foreign exchange proceeds to the Bank of China. Any foreign exchange required is to be sold to them by the Bank of China in accordance with the quota approved by the state or with relevant regulations.

The circulation, use and mortgage of foreign currency in the People's Republic of China are prohibited. Unauthorized sales and purchases of foreign exchange and unlawfully seizing possession of foreign exchange in whatever ways and by whatever means are prohibited.

Chapter II. Exchange control relating to state organizations and collective economic units

Article 5

Foreign exchange income and expenditure of state organs, armed force units, non-governmental bodies, educational institutions, state enterprises, government establishments, and urban and rural collective economic units in China (hereinafter referred to as domestic organizations) are all subject to control according to plan.

Domestic organizations are permitted to retain a proportion of their foreign exchange receipts in accordance with relevant regulations.

Article 6

Unless approved by the SGAEC or its branch offices, domestic organizations shall not:

Possess foreign exchange; deposit foreign exchange abroad; offset foreign exchange expenditure against foreign exchange income; or use the foreign exchange belonging to state organs stationed abroad or Chinese enterprises and establishments resident in foreign countries or in the Hong Kong and Macao regions, by way of borrowing or acquisition.

Article 7

Unless approved by the State Council, domestic organizations shall not issue securities with foreign exchange value inside or outside China.

Article 8

Departments under the State Council and people's governments of various provinces, municipalities and autonomous regions shall compile annual overall plans for domestic organizations under their respective jurisdiction whereby loans may be accepted from banks or enterprises in foreign countries or in the Hong Kong and Macao regions. These plans shall be submitted to the SGAEC and the Foreign Investment Control Commission for examination and forwarding to the State Council for approval.

The procedure for examining and approving individual borrowings shall be prescribed separately.

Article 9

The portion of foreign exchange retained by domestic organizations, non-trade foreign exchange and foreign exchange under compensatory trade received in advance for later payments, funds borrowed in convertible foreign currency, and other foreign exchange held with the approval of the SGAEC or its branch offices, must be placed in foreign currency deposit accounts or foreign currency quota accounts to be opened with the Bank of China, and must be used within the prescribed scope and be subject to the supervision of the Bank of China. When domestic organizations import or export goods, the banks handling the transactions shall check their foreign exchange recipts and payments either against the import or export licenses duly verified by the customs or against the customs declaration form for imports or exports.

Article 10

When domestic organizations import or export goods, the banks handling the transactions shall check their foreign exchange receipts and payments either against the import or export licenses duly verified by the customs or against the customs declaration forms for imports or exports.

Article 11

State organs stationed abroad must use foreign exchange according to the plan approved by the state.

The operating profits of enterprises and establishments in foreign countries or in the Hong Kong and Macao regions must, except the portion kept locally as working funds according to the plan approved by the state, be transferred back on scheduled time and be sold to the Bank of China.

No Chinese organization stationed abroad is permitted to keep foreign exchange for domestic organizations without authorization.

Article 12

Delegations and work-groups sent temporarily to foreign countries or to the Hong Kong and Macao regions must use foreign exchange according to their respective specific plans, and must, upon their return, promptly transfer back to China their surplus foreign exchange to be checked by and sold to the Bank of China.

Foreign exchange earned in their various business activities by the delegations and work-groups referred to in the above paragraph and by members thereof, must be promptly transferred back to China and must not be kept abroad without the approval of the SGAEC or its branch offices.

Chapter III. Exchange control relating to individuals

Article 13

Foreign exchange remitted from foreign countries or from the Hong Kong and Macao regions to Chinese or foreign nationals or stateless persons residing in China must be sold to the Bank of China, except the portion retained as permitted by the state.

Article 14

Chinese and foreign nationals and stateless persons residing in China are permitted to keep in their own possession foreign exchange already in China.

The foreign exchange referred to in the above paragraph shall not, without authorization, be carried or sent out of China either in person or by others or by post. If the owners wish to sell the foreign exchange, they must sell it to the Bank of China and are permitted to retain a portion thereof as convertible foreign currency according to the percentage prescribed by the state.

Article 15

When foreign exchange that has been kept in foreign countries or in the Hong Kong and Macao regions by Chinese residents in China prior to the founding of the People's Republic of China, by Overseas Chinese prior to their returning to and settling down in their home places, is transferred to China, the owners are permitted to retain a portion thereof as convertible foreign currency according to the percentage prescribed by the state.

Article 16

When foreign exchange belonging personally to individuals sent to work or study in foreign countries or in the Hong Kong and Macao regions is remitted or brought back to China, the owners returning after completion of their missions are permitted to retain the entire amount as convertible foreign currency.

Article 17

The percentages of foreign exchange retention permitted under Articles 13, 14 and 15 of these regulations shall be prescribed separately.

Foreign exchange retained by individuals as permitted under Articles 13, 14, 15 and 16 of these regulations must be deposited with the Bank of China. These foreign exchange deposits may be sold to the Bank of China or remitted out of China through the Bank of China, or taken out of China against certification by the Bank of China. It is however, not permitted, without authorization, to carry or send deposit certificates out of China either in person or by others or by post.

Article 18

Foreign exchange remitted or brought into China from foreign countries or from the Hong Kong and Macao regions by foreign nationals coming to China, by Overseas Chinese and Hong Kong and Macao compatriots returning for a short stay, by foreign experts, technicians, staff members and workers engaged to work in domestic organizations, and by foreign students and trainees, may be kept in their own possession, or sold to or deposited with the Bank of China, or remitted or taken out of China.

Article 19

Chinese and foreign nationals and stateless persons residing in China may apply to the local branch offices of the SGAEC for the purchase of foreign exchange to be remitted or taken out of China. When approved, the required foreign exchange will be sold to the applicants by the Bank of China.

When foreign experts, technicians, staff members and workers engaged to work in domestic organizations require foreign exchange to be remitted or taken out of China, the Bank of China will deal with their applications in accordance with the stipulations in the contracts or agreements.

Chapter IV. Exchange control relating to foreign representations in China and their personnel

Article 20

Foreign exchange remitted or brought into China from foreign countries or from the Hong Kong and Macao regions by foreign diplomatic missions, consulates, official commercial offices, offices of international organizations and non-governmental bodies resident in China, diplomatic officials and consuls as well as members of the permanent staff of the above units, may be kept in their own possession, or sold to or deposited with the Bank of China, or remitted or taken out of China.

Article 21

The conversion into foreign currency, if required, of visa and certification fees received in renminbi from Chinese citizens by foreign diplomatic missions and consulates in China, is subject to approval by the SGAEC or its branch offices.

Chapter V. Exchange control relating to enterprises with overseas Chinese capital, enterprises with foreign capital, and Chinese and foreign joint ventures and their personnel

Article 22

All foreign exchange receipts of enterprises with Overseas Chinese capital, enterprises with foreign capital and Chinese and foreign joint ventures, must be deposited with the Bank of China, and all their foreign exchange disbursements must be paid from their foreign exchange deposit accounts.

The enterprises referred to in the above paragraph must submit periodic reports and statements of their foreign exchange receipts and payments.

Article 23

Except where otherwise approved by the SGAEC or its branch offices, renminbi should in all cases be used in the settlement of accounts between enterprises with Overseas Chinese capital, enterprises with foreign capital, Chinese and foreign joint ventures and other enterprises and individuals residing in the People's Republic of China.

Article 24

Enterprises with Overseas Chinese capital, enterprises with foreign capital and foreign partners in Chinese and foreign joint ventures may apply to the Bank of China for remitting abroad their net profits after tax as well as other legitimate earnings by debiting the foreign exchange deposit accounts of the enterprises concerned.

The enterprises and foreign partners referred to in the above paragraph should apply to the SGAEC or its branch offices for transferring foreign exchange capital abroad by debiting the foreign exchange deposit accounts of the enterprises concerned.

Article 25

An amount not exceeding 50 percent of their net wages and other legitimate earnings after tax may be remitted or taken out of China in foreign currency by staff members and workers of foreign nationality and those from the Hong Kong and Macao regions employed by enterprises with Overseas Chinese capital, enterprises with foreign capital and Chinese and foreign joint ventures.

Article 26

Enterprises with Overseas Chinese capital, enterprises with foreign capital and Chinese and foreign joint ventures which wind up operations in accordance with legal procedure, should be responsible for the liquidation within the scheduled period of their outstanding liabilities and taxes due in China, under the joint supervision of the relevant departments in charge and the SGAEC or its branch offices.

Chapter VI. Control relating to carrying foreign exchange, precious metals and payment instruments in foreign currency into and out of China

Article 27

No restriction as to the amount is imposed on the carrying into China of foreign exchange, precious metals and objects made from them, but declaration to the customs is required at the place of entry. To carry foreign exchange out of China or to carry out of China the foreign exchange previously brought in shall be permitted by the customs against certification by the Bank of China or against the original declaration form at the time of entry.

To carry out of China precious metals and objects made from them or to carry out of China precious metals and objects made from them previously brought in shall be permitted by the customs according to the specific circumstances as prescribed by government regulations or against the original declaration form at the time of entry.

Article 28

Renminbi traveller's cheques, traveller's letters of credit and other renminbi payment instruments convertible into foreign currency may be brought into China against declaration to the customs, and taken out of China against certification by the Bank of China or against the original declaration form at the time of entry.

Article 29

Unless otherwise approved by the SGAEC or its branch offices, the carrying or sending out of China either in person or by others or by post of the following documents and securities held by Chinese residing in China is not permitted; bonds, debentures, share certificates issued abroad; title deeds for real estate abroad; documents or deeds necessary in dealing with creditor's right or owner's right to possession regarding inheritance, real estate and other foreign exchange assets abroad.

Article 30

The carrying or sending out of China of renminbi cheques, drafts, passbooks, deposit certificates and other renminbi instruments held by Chinese or foreign nationals or stateless persons residing in China, is not permitted, either in person or by others or by post.

Chapter VII. Supplementary provisions

Article 31

All units and individuals have the right to report any violation of these regulations. Reward shall be given to such units or individuals according to the merit of the report. Violators shall be penalized by the SGAEC, its branch offices or by the departments of public security, or by the departments of Administration of Industry and Commerce, or by the customs. According to the seriousness of the offense, the penalties may take the form of compulsory exchange of the foreign currency for renminbi, or fine or confiscation of the properties or both, or punishment by judicial authorities according to law.

Article 32

The exchange control regulations for special economic zones, for trade in border areas, and for personal dealings between inhabitants across the border shall be formulated by the people's governments of the provinces, municipalities and autonomous regions concerned in the spirit of these regulations and in the light of specific local conditions, and shall be enforced upon the approval of the State Council.

Article 33

Detailed provisions for the enforcement of these regulations shall be formulated by the SGAEC.

Article 34

These regulations shall come into force on March 1, 1981.

Regulations on Foreign Exchange Control

With the approval of the State Council, the State General Administration of Exchange Control has promulgated "detailed rules and regulations on exchange control relating to individuals" which took effect on 1 January 1982.

Following are the "detailed rules and regulations on exchange control relating to individuals:" Chinese, foreign nationals, or stateless persons residing in China shall sell foreign exchange remitted to them from foreign countries, or from the Hong Kong and Macao regions, to the Bank of China. The receiver is permitted to retain 10 percent of a single remittance of large amounts equivalent to 3,000 yuan or more.

The Renminbi obtained from the sale of the above-mentioned foreign exchange to the Bank of China is entitled to the relevant preferential treatment given to overseas remittances.

Chinese residing within the boundaries of China are permitted to retain a portion of 30 percent of the foreign exchange they had deposited or inherited in foreign countries before the founding of the People's Republic of China and Overseas Chinese, as well as compatriots from Hong Kong and Macao, are permitted to retain 30 percent of the foreign exchange they had deposited or inherited in foreign countries, or in the Hong Kong and Macao regions, before returning to China and settling down in their native homes, provided that the Bank of China is entrusted with the remittance of foreign exchange back to China. The Renminbi obtained from the sale of the remaining portion of 70 percent of the foreign exchange is entitled to the relevant preferential treatment given to overseas remittances.

Foreign nationals or stateless persons residing within the boundaries of China are permitted to retain the same portion of foreign exchange as mentioned in the above article which they have deposited or inherited outside the boundaries of China and they have entrusted the Bank of China for the remittance in China.

Overseas Chinese and compatriots from Hong Kong and Macao are permitted to retain a portion of 30 percent of the foreign exchange which they bring in or which is remitted to them when they return to China or settle down in their native homes, provided that they apply to the bank for retaining the portion within 2 months of their entry to China. The Renminbi obtained from the sale of the remaining portion of 70 percent of the foreign exchange is entitled to the relevant preferential treatment given to overseas remittance.

The application for retaining the above-mentioned foreign exchange that has been brought into China can be made only when a declaration is submitted to customs.

The personnel who have been sent by the state to work in foreign countries, or in the Hong Kong and Macao regions, must either remit, in due time, or bring back to China the remaining portion of foreign exchange, including wages and allowances for individuals, when they return to China upon completion of their assignments. The remaining portion should not be deposited outside the boundaries of China but may be kept by individuals in accordance with the certificates issued by Chinese organs stationed in foreign countries.

Students, trainees, graduate students, scholars, teachers, coaches and other personnel who have been sent by the state to study in foreign countries or in the Hong Kong and Macao regions must either remit in due time or bring back to China the remaining portion of their income in foreign exchange obtained during their stay abroad when returning to China. The remaining portion should not be deposited outside the boundaries of China and the portion due to each individual may be kept by them in accordance with the certificates issued by Chinese organs stationed in foreign countries.

The foreign exchange obtained in the forms of publication fees, copyright fees, awards, subsidies or remuneration by individuals from publishing their inventions, creative works or books outside the boundaries of China, or from delivering speeches or giving lectures in their capacity as individuals outside the boundaries of China, or from contributing to foreign papers, magazines or professional journals should be remitted back to China in due time and should not be deposited outside the boundaries of China. The portion that is due to individuals may be kept in accordance with the relevant regulations approved by the State Council and the ministries and commissions concerned or in accordance with the agreement of the State General Administration of Exchange Control.

The portion of foreign exchange permitted to be kept by individuals as mentioned above in various articles must be deposited in the Bank of China. The deposit in foreign currency may be sent or carried out of China against the certification by the Bank of China. When the deposit is converted into renminbi, the relevant preferential treatment given to overseas remittance will be applied. However, the carrying or sending out of China in person, by others, or by post of deposit certificates is not permitted.

In handling foreign exchange kept by individuals, item 2 of article 4 of the "provisional regulations for exchange control of the PRC" should not be violated.

Chinese, foreign nationals, or stateless persons residing in China are permitted to individually possess foreign exchange kept in China. However, it is not permitted to carry or send foreign exchange out of the country whether in person, by others, or by post. If foreign exchange has to be sold, it should be sold to the Bank of China in accordance with the regulations prescribed in article 2 of these detailed regulations.

Foreigners visiting China, Overseas Chinese returning to China for a short time, compatriots from Hong Kong and Macao visiting their native homes, foreign experts, technical personnel, workers and staff members invited to work at various organs in China and foreign students and trainees are free to keep for themselves, as well as sell to or deposit in the Bank of China, foreign exchange which is remitted to them from foreign countries or Hong Kong and Macao regions or which they bring in. They may also send or carry it out of China against the original declaration form issued by customs at the time of entry.

The carrying or sending out of foreign exchange by foreign experts, technical personnel and workers and staff members who have been invited to work at various organs in China will be handled by the Bank of China in accordance with the relevant regulations prescribed in contracts or agreements.

Foreign exchange applications

The State General Administration of Exchange Control has issued a "detailed ruling on the examination and approval of applications for foreign exchange by individuals," which took effect on 1 January 1982.

The "individuals" in the "detailed ruling on the examination and approval of applications for foreign exchange by individuals" refers to Chinese, foreign nationals and stateless persons residing in China. As prescribed by the "detailed ruling," individuals are allowed to apply for foreign exchange when they make provisional remittances to places outside China, when they need foreign exchange to pay travel and miscellaneous expenses at the time of departure from the country, when Overseas Chinese transfer their investments and deposits out of China and when emigrants departing China transfer their money out of China.

It is prescribed by the "detailed ruling" that when extraordinary events (such as serious illness, death, accidents, disasters, etc.) occur to an individual's parents, spouse or children outside China and if the individual can produce a certificate of his working unit and other related certificates from places of residence of parents, spouse and children, the individual's application for provisional foreign exchange may be approved, as deemed fit.

Individuals whose departure from China has been approved by public security departments and who have secured valid entrance visas to the countries of destination (Chinese should secure an "exit permit" from public security departments) may be offered foreign exchange to pay travel and miscellaneous expenses needed for the shortest possible route between China's port of departure and their destination.

For individuals departing China on single-trip exit visa passports, in addition to foreign exchange approved to them for paying travel and miscellaneous expenses, the remainder will be handled according to the following stipulations:

> 1. Retirement pay, living expenses after discharge from work, allowances for leaving office and pensions for the disabled or bereaved families paid by organizations in China can be remitted out of China in their entirety, provided the individuals concerned can produce working units' certificates approved by responsible departments at the next higher level and examined, verified and approved by the Bank of China.
>
> 2. Individuals without retirement pay, living expenses after discharge from work, allowances for leaving office and pension for the disabled and bereaved families may be offered foreign exchange, as deemed fit, after taking the specific circumstances into account.

Individuals who hold approved round-trip exit-entrance visas and who apply for remitting out of China their retirement pay, living expenses after discharge from work, allowances for leaving office and the pension for the disabled or bereaved families will not be offered foreign exchange.

Individuals whose departures have been approved by public security departments and who have received foreign exchange remitted from outside China to pay travel and miscellaneous expenses at the time of departure, may retain the originally remitted currencies if they declare their intention to do so before the bank makes payments to them. These foreign exchanges may be remitted or hand-carried out of China at the time of departure.

For Overseas Chinese and Hong Kong and Macao compatriots outside China who have used foreign exchange in investing in national and local Overseas Chinese investment corporations, the payments for matured shares and the dividends they receive will be handled according to regulations. Those who are repaid in foreign exchange by investment corporations can remit the foreign exchange out of China. Those who are repaid in Renminbi will not be offered foreign exchange.

Overseas Chinese and Hong Kong and Macao compatriots outside China, who put their money in Overseas Chinese Renminbi deposits of banks in China under their personal titles, may be offered foreign exchange, as deemed fit, if they apply to remit their money out of China.

Individuals who have emigrated with their whole families with the approval of public security departments and who have entrusted banks in China to take care of their Overseas Chinese Renminbi deposits are not allowed to remit these deposits out of China, as stipulated in the regulations for depositing. Depositors who can prove themselves to be in financial difficulties and ask to remit their deposits out of China may be offered foreign exchange, as deemed fit.

Application for foreign exchange in the above cases should be made at the subbureaus of foreign exchange control or the authorized Bank of China at the applicant's place of residence. The foreign exchange approved after examination can be remitted or hand-carried out of China.

Rules Governing the Carrying of Foreign Exchange, Precious Metals, and Payment Instruments in Convertible Currency Into or Out of China (August 10, 1981)

Article 1

These rules are formulated for implementing the stipulations in articles 27, 28, 29 and 30 of the Provisional Regulations for Exchange Control of the People's Republic of China.

Article 2

No restriction is imposed on the quantity of foreign exchange, payment instruments in convertible Renminbi, gold, silver, platinum and other precious metals and objects made from them which may be carried into China by persons entering the country, but they must be declared to the customs at the place of entry.

Article 3

The carrying out of China of foreign exchange, payment instruments in convertible Renminbi, gold, silver, platinum and other precious metals and objects made from them previously brought in shall be permitted by the customs against the original declaration form issued at the time of entry.

Article 4

The unused portion of the Renminbi which has been converted either from foreign exchange and payment instruments in convertible Renminbi brought in or from foreign exchange remitted in by persons entering the country may be converted back into foreign exchange before their departure from China and the customs shall permit the taking out of China of the foreign exchange so obtained against the exchange memo issued by the Bank of China.

Article 5

The carrying out of China of objects made from gold, silver, platinum and other precious metals bought in the country shall be permitted by the customs against certification by the sellers within the limit as prescribed by the state.

Article 6

The carrying out of China of foreign exchange and payment instruments in convertible Renminbi shall be permitted by the customs against certification by the Bank of China.

The carrying out of China of drafts, traveller's cheques and traveller's letters of credit in foreign currency, and Renminbi banknote and passbook custodian certificates issued or sold by the Bank of China shall be permitted by the customs after examination, and no certification by the Bank of China is required.

Article 7

Chinese, or foreign nationals, or stateless persons residing in China shall, when emigrating from the country, be permitted by the customs to carry out of China gold, silver, platinum and other precious metals and objects made from them within the limit as prescribed by the state.

Article 8

The carrying or sending out of China in person, or by others, or by post of Renminbi cheques, drafts, passbooks and deposit certificates and other Renminbi payment instruments held by Chinese, or foreign nationals, or stateless persons residing in the country is not permitted.

Article 9

Unless otherwise approved by the State General Administration of Exchange Control or its branch offices, it is not permitted to carry or send out of China in person, or by others, or by post documents and securities held by Chinese residing in the country, such as foreign bonds, debentures, shares and title deeds; certification and agreements relating to the settlement of creditor's rights, inheritances, real estates and other foreign exchange assets abroad; and letters and instruments containing instructions of payment abroad.

Article 10

Where foreign enterprises which have terminated their business in China and foreign nationals who have left China wish to carry out of China foreign securities kept in the country, they shall be permitted to do so by the customs on the approval of the State General Administration of Exchange Control or its branch offices, but it is not permitted to carry out of the country Chinese securities and shares whether in person, or by others, or by post.

Article 11

Where bilateral agreements have been signed between China and foreign countries on the carrying of currencies into and out of each other's boundary, matters will be handled in accordance with the provisions thereof.

Article 12

These rules shall also apply where foreign exchange, payment instruments in convertible Renminbi, gold, silver, platinum and other precious metals and objects made from them are carried into or out of the country by compatriots from HongKong and Macao.

Article 13

These rules are promulgated by the State General Administration of Exchange Control.

10

TAX LAWS

The Income Tax Law of the People's Republic of China Concerning Foreign Enterprises

Following is an unofficial translation of the full text of the Income Tax Law of the People's Republic of China Concerning Foreign Enterprises which came into force on January 1, 1982. The law was adopted at the Fourth Session of the Fifth National People's Congress on December 13 and promulgated by an order of Ye Jianying; Chairman of the NPC Standing Committee, on the same day.

Article 1

Income tax shall be levied in accordance with this law on the income derived from production, business and other sources by any foreign enterprise operating in the People's Republic of China.

"Foreign enterprises" mentioned in this law refer, with the exception of those for whom separate provisions are stipulated in Article 11, to foreign companies, enterprises and other economic organizations which have establishments in the People's Republic of China engaged in independent business operation or co-operative production or joint business operation with Chinese enterprises.

Article 2

The taxable income of a foreign enterprise shall be the net income in a tax year after deduction of costs, expenses and losses in that year.

Article 3

Income tax on foreign enterprises shall be assessed at progressive rates for the parts in excess of a specific amount of taxable income. The tax rates are as follow:

Range of income	Tax rate (per cent)
Annual income below 250,000 yuan	20
That part of annual income from 250,000 to 500,000 yuan	25
That part of annual income from 500,000 to 750,000 yuan	30
That part of annual income from 750,000 to 1 million yuan	35
That part of annual income above 1 million yuan	40

Article 4

In addition to the income tax levied on foreign enterprises in accordance with the provisions of the preceding article, a local income tax of 10 per cent of the same taxable income shall be levied.

Where a foreign enterprise needs reduction in or exemption from local income tax on account of the small scale of its production or business, or its rate of profit, this shall be decided by the people's government of the province, municipality or autonomous region in which that enterprise is located.

Article 5

A foreign enterprise scheduled to operate for a period of 10 years or more in farming, forestry, animal husbandry or other low profit occupations may, upon approval by the tax authorities of an application filed by the enterprise, be exempted from income tax in the first profit-making year and allowed a 50 per cent reduction in the second and third years.

With the approval of the Ministry of Finance, a 15–30 per cent reduction in income tax may be allowed for a period of 10 years following the expiration of the term for exemptions and reductions specified in the preceding paragraph.

Article 6

Losses incurred by a foreign enterprise in a tax year may be carried over to the next year and made up with a matching amount drawn from that year's income. Should the income in the subsequent tax year be insufficient to make up for the said losses, the balance may be made up with further deductions against income year by year over a period not exceeding five years.

Article 7

Income tax on foreign enterprises shall be levied on an annual basis and paid in quarterly instalments. Such provisional payments shall be made within 15 days after the end of each quarter. The final settlement shall be made within five months after the end of a tax year. Excess payments shall be refunded by the tax authorities or deficiencies made good by the taxpayer.

Article 8

Foreign enterprises shall file their provisional income tax returns with the local tax authorities within the period prescribed for provisional payments. The taxpayer shall file its final annual income tax return together with its final accounts within four months after the end of the tax year.

Article 9

The method of financial management and the system of accounting of foreign enterprises shall be submitted to local tax authorities for reference.

Where the method of financial management and the system of accounting of foreign enterprises are in contradiction with the provisions of the tax law, tax payments shall be assessed according to the provisions of the tax law.

Article 10

Foreign enterprises shall present relevant certificates to the local tax authorities for tax registration when they go into operation or close down in accordance with law.

Article 11

A 20 per cent income tax shall be levied on the income obtained from dividends, interest, rentals, royalties and other sources in China by foreign companies, enterprises and other economic organizations which have no establishments in China. Such tax shall be withheld by the paying unit in each of its payments.

For the payment of income tax according to the provisions in the preceding paragraph, the foreign companies, enterprises and other economic organizations which earn the income shall be the taxpayer, and the paying unit shall be the withholding agent. Taxes withheld on each payment by a withholding agent shall, within five days, be turned over to the State Treasury and the income tax return submitted to the tax authorities.

Income from interest on loans given to the Chinese Government or China's State banks by international finance organizations shall be exempted from income tax. Income from interest on loans given at a preferential interest rate by foreign banks to China's State banks shall also be exempted from income tax.

Income derived from interest on deposits of foreign banks in China's State banks and on loans given at a normal interest rate by foreign banks to China's State banks shall be taxed. However, exemption from income tax shall be granted to those foreign banks in whose countries income from interest on deposits and loans of China's State banks is exempted from income tax.

Article 12

The tax authorities have the right to investigate the financial affairs, account books and tax situation of any foreign enterprise, and have the right to investigate the withholding situation of any withholding agent. Such foreign enterprises and withholding agents must make reports on facts and provide all relevant information and shall not refuse to cooperate or conceal any facts.

Article 13

Income tax levied on foreign enterprises shall be computed in terms of Renminbi. Income in foreign currency shall be assessed according to the exchange rates quoted by the State General Administration of Exchange Control of the People's Republic of China and taxes in Renminbi.

Article 14

Foreign enterprises and withholding agents must pay their tax within the prescribed time limit. In case of failure to pay within the prescribed time limit, the appropriate tax authorities, in addition to setting a new time limit for tax payment, shall surcharge overdue payments at one half of one per cent of the overdue tax for every day in arrears, starting from the first day of default.

Article 15

The tax authorities may, acting at their discretion, impose a penalty on any foreign enterprise which has violated the provisions of Articles 8, 9, 10 and 12 of this law.

In dealing with those withholding agents who have violated the provisions of Article 11 of this law, the tax authorities may in addition set a new time limit for the payment of the part of tax that should have been withheld and, at their discretion, impose a penalty of not more than the amount that should have been withheld.

In dealing with foreign enterprises which have evaded or refused to pay income tax, the tax authorities may, in addition to pursuing the tax, impose a fine of not more than five times the amount of tax underpaid or not paid, according to how serious the offence is. Cases of gross violation shall be handled by the local people's courts according to law.

Article 16

In case of disputes with tax authorities about tax payment, foreign enterprises must pay tax according to the relevant regulations first before applying to higher tax authorities for reconsideration. If they do not accept the decisions made after such reconsideration, they can bring the matter before the local people's courts.

Article 17

Where agreements on tax payment have been concluded between the Government of the People's Republic of China and the government of another country, matters concerning tax payment shall be handled in accordance with the provisions of these agreements.

Article 18

Detailed rules and regulations for the implementation of this law shall be formulated by the Ministry of Finance of the People's Republic of China.

Article 19

This law shall come into force as of January 1, 1982.

Regulations on Income Tax for Foreign Enterprises

Detailed rules and regulations for the implementation of the income tax law of the PRC concerning foreign enterprises (approved by the State Council on 17th February 1982 and promulgated by the Ministry of Finance on 21st February 1982)

Article 1

The detailed rules and regulations are formulated in accordance with the provisions of Article 18 of the income tax law of the PRC concerning foreign enterprises (hereinafter referred to as tax law for short).

Article 2

The establishments mentioned in Article 1 of the tax law refer to organizations, places or business agents established by foreign enterprises in China engaged in production or business operations.

The organizations and places mentioned in the previous section mainly include management organizations, branch organizations, representative organizations, factories, places where natural resources are being exploited and places where building, installation, assembling, exploration and other projects are being undertaken under contracts.

Article 3

Foreign enterprises and Chinese enterprises engaged in co-operative production or joint business operations should each pay their income taxes separately.

Article 4

Income derived from production and business mentioned in Article 1 of the tax law means income of foreign enterprises from production and business operations in industry, mining, communications, transportation, agriculture, forestry, animal husbandry, fisheries, poultry farming, commerce, services and other trades.

Income derived from other sources mentioned in Article 1 of the tax law covers dividends, interest, income from lease or transfer of property, patent right, proprietary technology, ownership of trademarks, copyright and so forth and other non-operating earnings.

Article 5

The taxable income for the purpose of levying local income tax mentioned in Article 4 of the tax law is the same as the taxable income mentioned in Article 3 of the tax law, both being the income calculated according to the formulas listed in Article 9 of these rules and regulations.

Article 6

Enterprises mentioned in Section 2 of Article 4 of the tax law, which are engaged in small-scale production or business, or which have a low rate of profit, refer to foreign enterprises whose annual income is under 1,000,000 yuan.

Article 7

Enterprises with a low rate of profit mentioned in Article 5 of the tax law include foreign enterprises in low-profit deep-mining operations for coal resources.

Article 8

The tax year for foreign enterprises starts from 1st January and ends 31st December on the Gregorian calendar.

Foreign enterprises which have difficulty in computing according to the tax year stipulated in the previous section may ask for approval by local tax offices to use the enterprises' own 12-month fiscal year for tax computation.

Article 9

The following are formulas for the computation of taxable incomes:

    1.   Industry:

        A.   Cost of production of the year equals direct material used in production of the year plus direct wages plus manufacturing expenses.

B.   Cost of product of the year equals cost of production of the year plus inventory of semi-finished product at the beginning of the year and in-production product plus inventory of semi-finished product at the end of the year and in-production product.

C.   Cost of sale of product equals cost of product of the year plus inventory of product at the beginning of the year minus inventory of product at the end of the year.

D.   Net volume of sale of product equals total volume of sale of product minus (sales returns plus sales allowance).

E.   Profit from sale of product equals net volume of sale of product minus cost of sale of product minus taxes on sales minus (selling expenses plus administrative expenses).

F.   Amount of taxable income equals profit from sale of product plus profit from other operations plus non-operating income minus non-operating expenditure.

2.   Commerce:

A.   Net volume of sales equals total volume of sales minus (sales returns plus sales allowance).

B.   Cost of sales equals inventory of merchandise at the beginning of the year plus (purchase of the year minus [purchase returned plus purchase discount] plus purchase expenses) minus inventory of merchandise at the end of the year.

C.   Sales profit equals net volume of sales minus cost of sales minus sales tax minus (selling expenses plus overhead expenses).

D.   Amount of taxable income equals sales profit plus profit from other operations plus non-operating income minus non-operating expenditure.

3.   Service trades:

A.   net business income equals gross business income minus (business tax plus operating expenses plus overhead expenses);

B.   amount of taxable income equals business income plus non-operating income minus non-operating expenditure.

4.   Other lines of operation: Refer to the above-mentioned formula for calculation.

Article 10

The following items shall not be counted as cost, expense or loss in computing the amount of taxable income:

1. Expenditure for the purchase or construction of machinery, equipment, buildings, facilities and other fixed assets.

2. Expenditure for the purchase of intangible assets.

3. Interest on capital.

4. Income tax payments and local surtax payments.

5. Penalties for illegal operations and losses in the form of confiscated property.

6. Overdue tax payments and tax penalties.

7. Losses from windstorms, floods and fire risks covered by insurance indemnity.

8. Donations and contributions other than those for public welfare and relief purposes in China.

9. Royalties paid to head offices.

10. Other expenses that are not relevant to production and operation.

Article 11

Reasonable administrative expenses paid by a foreign enterprise to its head office in connection with production and business operations and actual expenses paid to the head office for services directly provided may be listed as expenditures, which should be backed up by certifying documents from the head office, receipts and vouchers, together with a financial report signed by a registered accountant, and examined and approved by the local tax office where the enterprise is located.

If agreement on sharing of administrative expenses paid to its head office is included in the contract signed by a foreign enterprise with a Chinese enterprise for co-operative production or joint business operations, such payments may be listed as expenditures according to the method defined in the contract, after examination and approval by the local tax office.

Article 12

Foreign enterprises are permitted to list as expenditures interests paid on loans at reasonable rates, which should be backed up by certifying documents on the loans and interest payments and examined and verified by the local tax offices as being normal loans.

Article 13

Reasonable entertainment expenses paid by a foreign enterprise for the purpose of production and business operation, which should be backed up by certifying documents, receipts and vouchers, may be listed as expenditures within the following limits:

1. Entertainment expenses of a foreign enterprise whose annual net volume of sale of products is less than 15,000,000 yuan shall be no more than three per thousand of its annual net volume of sale of products; if its annual net volume of sale of products exceeds 15,000,000 yuan, its entertainment expenses for that portion above 15,000,000 yuan shall be no more than one per thousand of that portion.

2. Entertainment expenses of a foreign enterprise whose annual total business income is less than 5,000,000 yuan shall be no more than 10 per thousand of its total business income; if its annual total business income exceeds 5,000,000 yuan, its entertainment expenses for that portion above 5,000,000 yuan shall be no more than three per thousand of that portion.

Article 14

Depreciation of a foreign enterprise's fixed assets in use shall be calculated on an annual basis. A foreign enterprise's fixed assets cover houses, buildings, machinery and other mechanical apparatuses, means of transport and other equipment used for the purpose of production and operation with a useful life of more than one year. Items with a per-unit value of less than 500 yuan and a short useful life, and which are not major equipment used for the purpose of production and operation, may be listed as expenses according to the actual number in use.

Article 15

Fixed assets shall be assessed according to the original price.

For fixed assets used as investment by a foreign enterprise and a Chinese enterprise engaged in joint production or business operation, the original price shall be the price agreed upon by the participants.

For purchased fixed assets, the original price shall be the purchase price plus transport fees, installation expenses and other related expenses incurred before they are put to use.

For self-made and self-built fixed assets, the original price shall be the actual expenditures incurred in the course of manufacture or construction.

For used fixed assets that are shipped in from abroad, the price shall be reassessed according to documents certifying their original price, the number of years in use, data on their market price and their actual value. For fixed assets without certifiable documents, the price shall be assessed by the enterprise and reported to the local tax office for reassessment according to their actual value.

Article 16

Depreciation of fixed assets shall be calculated beginning from the month when they are put to use. When fixed assets cease to be used within a certain tax year, their depreciation shall no longer be calculated beginning from the month following that in which they are no longer used.

The investment of an enterprise engaged in petroleum prospecting in the sea shall be calculated using the oilfield (or gasfield) prospected as a unit; the entire investment shall be regarded as capital expenditure. Depreciation shall be calculated beginning for the month when the oilfield (or gasfield) is put into production for commercial purposes.

Article 17

In the depreciation of fixed assets, the residual value shall be assessed first and deducted from the original price, the principle being that of setting the residual value at 10% of the original price; those cases that call for the retention of a small or no residual value at all shall be submitted to the local tax authorities for approval. If the depreciation of fixed assets is calculated in a comprehensive way, the residual value may not be retained.

The depreciation of fixed assets shall generally be computed on average by the straight line method.

Article 18

Useful life for the purpose of computing depreciation of fixed assets is defined as follows:

1.   The minimum useful life for houses and building is 20 years.

2.   The minimum useful life for trains, ships, machines and equipment and other facilities for the purpose of production is 10 years.

3.   The minimum useful life for electronic equipment, means of transport, other trains and ships as well as appliances, apparatus and furniture relevant to production and operation is five years.

For the cases where the fixed assets of a foreign enterprise, owing to special reasons, need to accelerate depreciation or where methods of depreciation need to be modified, applications shall be submitted by the said enterprise to the local tax authorities for examination and then relayed level by level to the Ministry of Finance for approval.

The depreciation of fixed assets resulting from investment by a foreign enterprise engaged in petroleum prospecting in the sea during and after the period of prospecting may be calculated in a comprehensive way; the time for depreciation shall be no less than six years.

The above provision applies to enterprises engaged in coal mining.

Article 19

Expenditure arising from increase of value and from prolongation of the useful life of fixed assets in use as a result of expansion, replacement, rebuilding or technical reform shall be regarded as capital expenditure and shall not be listed as expense.

Fixed assets continuing to be in use after full depreciation shall no longer be depreciated.

Article 20

The balance of the gain of a foreign enterprise, derived from the transfer of ownership of its fixed assets or from their sale at current prices after deduction by the net sum of non-depreciated assets or the residual value, shall be entered in the year's loss and gain account.

Article 21

Intangible assets such as patent rights, technical know-how, owner-ship of sites and other royalties the possession of which has been trans-ferred to a foreign enterprise shall be assessed by amortization according to the payment of a reasonable price from the month they begin to be in use.

The above-mentioned intangible assets used as investment by a foreign enterprise and a Chinese enterprise engaged in joint production and business operation shall be assessed by amortization according to the sums provided in the agreements or contracts from the month they begin to be in use.

As for those intangible assets with a time limit provision on their use, if they are transferred or used as investment, they shall be assessed by amortization according to the provision of the time limit; those without the provision shall be assessed by amortization in no less than 10 years.

Article 22

Expenses arising during the period of preparation for a foreign enterprise shall be amortized after it goes into production or business, with the time of amortization being no less than five years.

Reasonable prospecting expenses incurred by a foreign enterprise engaged in petroleum prospecting in the sea may be amortized from the income from its oilfield (or gasfield) which has gone into production for commercial purposes, with the time of amortization being no less than one year.

Article 23

Inventory or merchandise, raw materials, in-production products, semi-finished products, finished products and byproducts shall be computed according to the cost price. As for the method of computation, the enterprise may choose one of the following: First-in first-out, shifting average and weighted average. In those cases where a change in the method of computation is necessary, it shall be submitted for approval to the local tax authorities.

Article 24

When a foreign enterprise cannot provide evidence of accurate costs and expenses, and so it is impossible to calculate accurately its taxable income amount, local tax authorities shall determine its profit rate and taxable income on the basis of its net amount of sales or its total amount of business income and according to the profit level of other enterprises of the same or similar trade.

For engineering projects undertaken by foreign enterprises under contract for the exploration and exploitation of seabed oil resources the profit rate and the taxable income amount shall be determined on the basis of the total income from the project undertaken.

Article 25

For foreign air and maritime transport enterprises engaged in international transport business, the taxable income amount shall be 5 % of the total income earned from transport service for passengers and cargoes loaded within the territory of China.

Article 26

For foreign enterprises which co-operate with Chinese enterprises in production and which prorate the products with Chinese enterprises, they are considered as having income when such products are distributed, and the amount of the income shall be calculated on the basis of the prices at which the products are sold to the third party or according to the prevailing market prices of the products.

Foreign enterprises engaged in co-operative projects for the exploitation of seabed oil resources are considered as having income when they receive their share of crude oil, and the amount of the income shall be calculated on the basis of a price which is adjusted periodically according to the international market price of crude oil of equal quality.

Article 27

The income obtained from dividends, interest, rentals, royalties and other sources in China mentioned in Article 11 of the tax law is explained as follows:

Dividends mean dividends obtained from or profits shared with enterprises in China.

Interest means interest earned from deposits or loans, interest on various bonds purchased and interest earned from payment made for others and from deferred payment in China.

Rentals mean rentals on property rented to others in China.

Royalties mean the income obtained from patent right, special technical know-how, copyright and ownership of trademarks provided for use in China.

Income from other sources means the income which is decided by the Ministry of Finance to be taxable other than the above.

Article 28

With regard to the income obtained from dividends, interest, rentals, royalties and other sources in China referred to in the preceding article, unless otherwise stipulated, the total amount of the income shall be used for the purpose of assessing the amount of tax to be paid, and such tax shall be withheld by the paying units from each payment.

Article 29

The international finance organizations mentioned in Article 11 of the tax law mean the International Monetary Fund, the World Bank, the International Development Association, the International Fund for

Agricultural Development, and other finance organizations of the United Nations. The preferential interest rate mentioned therein means an interest rate which is at least 10 % less than the general interest rate in the international monetary market.

Article 30

China's state banks mentioned in Article 11 of the tax law include the People's Bank of China, the Bank of China, the Agricultural Bank of China, the People's Construction Bank of China, the Investment Bank of China, and the International Trust and Investment Corporation which is authorized by the State Council to do foreign exchange deposit, loan and credit business with foreign firms.

Article 31

The income derived from interest on deposits mentioned in paragraph four of Article 11 of the tax law does not include the interest obtained from the deposits of foreign banks in China's state banks at a rate lower than the interest rate prevailing in the international monetary market. Income derived from interest on deposits at a rate lower than the interest rate in the international monetary market is exempted from income tax.

Article 32

The payments mentioned in Article 11 of the tax law include the amounts paid in cash, by remittance and through transfers and the equivalent amounts paid with negotiable securities or material objects.

Article 33

The income tax to be paid in quarterly instalments prescribed in Article 7 of the tax law may be paid according to the actual quarterly profit or it may be paid in the amount equivalent to one-fourth of the annual tax computed on the basis of the current year's planned profit or the preceding year's actual income.

Article 34

For foreign enterprises which have operated less than a year, the income tax to be paid shall be assessed on the basis of the actual income earned during the period of operation at the applicable tax rate stipulated by the tax law.

Article 35

When foreign enterprises go into operation or close down, they shall, within 30 days prior to starting operation or closing down, go to the local tax authorities for tax registration in connection with their opening or closing business in accordance with Article 10 of the tax law.

Article 36

Foreign enterprises shall file their income tax returns and their final accounting statements with the local tax authorities within the prescribed period irrespective of profit or loss of the tax year and, unless otherwise stipulated, shall send the audit reports by chartered public accountants registered in the People's Republic of China.

Article 37

When foreign enterprises are unable to file tax returns within the prescribed time limit because of special circumstances, they shall submit an application within the said time limit, and upon approval of the local tax authorities, the time limit for filing tax returns and for final settlement may be extended appropriately.

The final day of the time limit for tax payment and filing tax returns may be extended if it falls on an official holiday.

Article 38

Accounting on the accrual basis shall be practiced for revenue and expenditure of foreign enterprises. All accounting records shall be accurate and perfect and shall have lawful vouchers as the basis for entry account.

Article 39

Vouchers for accounting, accounting books and reports used by foreign enterprises shall be recorded in the Chinese language or in both Chinese and foreign languages.

Accounting vouchers, accounting books and reports shall be kept for at least 15 years.

Article 40

Sales invoices and business receipts shall be submitted for approval to the local tax authorities before they are used.

Article 41

Officials sent by tax authorities shall produce identification cards when investigating the financial affairs, accounting books and tax situation of a foreign enterprise and undertake to keep the investigations secret.

Article 42

Foreign enterprises with income in foreign currency shall pay income tax in quarterly instalments. The income shall be assessed according to the exchange rate quoted by the State General Administration of Foreign Exchange Control on the day when the tax payment certificates are made out and shall be taxed in RMB. The final settlement shall be made after the end of the tax year to determine the amount to be refunded by the tax authorities or made up by the taxpayer. Refunds or makeup payments shall be made in RMB according to the exchange rate quoted by the State General Administration of Foreign Exchange Control on the last day of the tax year.

Article 43

Tax authorities may impose a penalty of not more than 5,000 yuan on a foreign enterprise which has violated the provisions of Article 8, paragraph 2 of Article 9, Article 10 or Article 12 of the tax law according to the gravity of the case.

Article 44

Tax authorities may impose a penalty of not more than 5,000 yuan on a foreign enterprise which has violated the provisions of paragraph 2 of Article 39 or Article 40 of these detailed rules and regulations.

Article 45

"Evasion of income tax" and "refusal to pay income tax" as stated in paragraph 3 of Article 15 of the tax law are hereby explained:

"Evasion of income tax" refers to the taxpayer's deliberate violation of the provisions of the tax law by forging, altering or destroying ledgers, receipts or vouchers for entry account, misrepresenting and overstating costs and expenditures, concealing or understating the amount of taxable income or earnings, avoiding taxes, or by other illegal actions.

"Refusal to pay income tax" refers to the taxpayer's resistance to the provisions of the tax law by refusing to file tax returns and produce certificates, receipts and vouchers for tax purposes, refusing to be investigated by tax authorities on financial affairs, accounting books and tax situations, refusing to pay taxes and fines according to the law, or by other illegal actions.

Article 46

Tax authorities shall serve notices on cases involving penalties in accordance with the relevant provisions of the tax law and these detailed rules and regulations.

Article 47

When a foreign enterprise applies for reconsideration in accordance with the provisions of Article 16 of the tax law, the tax authorities concerned are required to make decision within three months after receiving the application.

Article 48

Income tax returns and tax payment certificates used by foreign enterprises are to be printed by the General Taxation Bureau of the PRC Ministry of Finance.

Article 49

The right of interpreting the provisions of these detailed rules and regulations resides in the PRC Ministry of Finance.

Article 50

These detailed rules and regulations come into force on the same date as the publication and enforcement of the income tax law of the PRC concerning foreign enterprises.

SELECTED
BIBLIOGRAPHY

These books and articles expand on topics discussed in each chapter.

1—China in Transition

Books

Chang, Chun-Shu. *The Making of China: Main Themes in Pre-modern Chinese History*. Englewood Cliffs: Prentice-Hall, 1975.

Cheng, Peter. *A Chronology of the People's Republic of China from October 1, 1949 [to December 31, 1969]*. Totowa, NJ: Rowan and Littlefield, 1972.

Davies, John Paton, Jr. *Dragon by the Tail: American, British, Japanese, and Russian Encounters With China and One Another*. New York: Norton, 1972.

Hucker, Charles O. *China's Imperial Past: An Introduction to Chinese History and Culture*. Stanford: Stanford University Press, 1975.

_____. *China to 1850: A Short History*. Stanford: Stanford University Press, 1978.

Mao, Tse-tung. *Quotations from Chairman Mao Tse-tung*. New York: Bantam, 1967.

Meisner, Maurice. *Mao's China: A History of the People's Republic*. New York: Free Press, 1967.

Shinn, Rinn-Sup. [Chapter 1, "Historical Setting"] *China: A Country Guide*. Washington, D.C.: Foreign Area Studies, The American University, 1981.

Snow, Edgar. *The Other Side of the River*. New York: Random House, 1961.

————. *Red Star Over China*. New York: Grove, 1968.

Articles

Michael, Franz. "China After the Cultural Revolution: The Unresolved Succession Crisis," *Orbis*, Summer 1973, pp. 315–333.

Starr, John Bryan. "Chinese Politics 1973–76: From the 10th Party Congress to the Premiership of Hua Kuo-feng: The Significance of the Color of the Cat," *China Quarterly*, September 1976, pp. 457–488.

"Red China's Economic Planner Li Fu-chun: Behind the China Debate: Hunger and Hate," *TIME [cover story]*, December 1, 1961.

"Visionary of a New China: Teng Hsiao-p'ing Opens the Middle Kingdom to the World," *TIME [Man of the Year cover story]*, January 1, 1979.

2—The Four Modernizations

Overviews

Books

Baum, Richard. *China's Four Modernizations: The New Technological Revolution*. Boulder: Westview Press, 1980.

Chen, Nai-Ruenn, and Walter Galenson. *The Chinese Economy Under Communism*. Chicago: Aldine, 1969.

Dernberger, Robert F. *China's Development Experience in Comparative Perspective*. Cambridge: Harvard University Press, 1980.

Donnithorne, Audry. *China's Economic System*. London: Allen and Unwin, 1967.

Eckstein, Alexander. *China's Economic Revolution*. London: Cambridge University Press, 1977.

————, and Robert F. Dernberger. *Quantitative Measures of China's Economic Output*. Ann Arbor: University of Michigan Press, 1979.

Howe, Christopher. *China's Economy: A Basic Guide*. New York: Basic Books, 1978.

Ramski, Thomas G. *Economic Growth and Employment in China*. New York: Oxford University Press, 1979.

Rozman, Gilbert. *The Modernization of China*. New York: The Free Press, 1981.

Lardy, Nicholas R. *Economic Growth and Distribution in China.* New York: Cambridge University Press, 1978.

Government publications

The People's Republic of China. State Statistical Bureau. *Ten Great Years.* Beijing: Foreign Languages Press, 1960.

U.S. Central Intelligence Agency. National Foreign Assessment Center. *China: The Continuing Search for a Modernization Strategy.* (Research Paper, No. ER 80–10248.) Washington: GPO, April 1890.

_____. *China: In Pursuit of Economic Modernization.* (Research Paper, No. ER 78–10680.) Washington: GPO, December 1978.

_____. *China: A Statistical Compendium.* (Research Paper, No. ER 79–10374.) Washington: GPO, July 1979.

_____. *China: Economic Indicators.* (Research Paper, No. ER 78–10750.) Washington: GPO, December 1978.

_____. *Handbook of Economic Statistics: 1979.* (Research Paper, No. ER 79–10274.) Washington: GPO, 1979.

_____. *China: International Trade Quarterly Review, Fourth Quarter, 1979.* (Research Paper, No. ER CIT 80–003.) Washington: GPO, May 1980.

U.S. Department of Commerce. *China's Economy and Foreign Trade, 1977–78.* Washington: GPO, September 1978.

_____. *China's Economy and Foreign Trade, 1978–79.* Washington: GPO, September 1979.

U.S. Congress. 90th, 1st Session. Joint Economic Committee. *An Economic Profile of Mainland China.* Washington: GPO, 1967.

_____. 92nd, 2nd Session. Joint Economic Committee. *People's Republic of China: An Economic Assessment.* Washington: GPO, 1972.

_____. 94th, 1st Session. Joint Economic Committee. *China: A Reassessment of the Economy.* Washington: GPO, 1975.

_____. 95th, 2nd Session. Joint Economic Committee. *Chinese Economy Post-Mao: Policy and Performance.* Washington: GPO, 1978.

Agriculture

Articles

Broder, Jonathan. "Cycles of Drought, Rain Ruin China Breadbasket," *Chicago Tribune,* February 27, 1983, sec. 3, p. 6.

Walker, Tony. "Dismantling China's Communes: A 'Quiet Revolution' in the Chinese Countryside," *World Press Review*, June 1982, p. 55.

Wang, Zaizong. "Solving China's Population Problem," *China Reconstructs*, April 1980, pp. 5–9.

Government publications

U.S. Department of Agriculture. *Agricultural Situation Review of 1979 and Outlook for 1980: People's Republic of China.* Washington: GPO, June 1980.

U.S. Central Intelligence Agency. *China: Demand for Foreign Grain.* (Research Paper, No. ER 79–10073.) Washington: GPO, January 1979.

National Academy of Science. *Plant Studies in the People's Republic of China.* Washington: GPO, 1975.

————. *Insect Control in the People's Republic of China.* Washington: GPO, 1977.

Industry

Books

Harrison, Selig. *China, Oil, and Asia.* New York: Columbia University Press, 1977.

Szuprowicz, Bohden, and Maria Szuprowicz. *Doing Business With the People's Republic of China: Industries and Markets.* New York: John Wiley & Sons, 1978.

Articles

Clarke, William. "China's Electric Power Industry," *Chinese Economy Post-Mao.* Washington: GPO, 1978, pp. 403–435.

Craig, Jack, Jim Lewek, and Gordon Cole. "A Survey of China's Modern Machine-Building Industry," *Chinese Economy Post-Mao.* Washington: GPO, 1978, pp. 284–322.

Government publications

U.S. Department of State. *Offshore Oil and Gas Exploration by the People's Republic of China.* Washington: GPO, January 1980.

U.S. Congress. 96th, 1st Session. Hearings before Subcommittee on Priorities and Economy in Government. Joint Economic Committee. Executive Session, June 26 and July 9, 1979. *Allocation of Resources in the Soviet Union and China, 1979.* Washington: GPO, July 1980.

U.S. Central Intelligence Agency. *Coal Mine Equipment: A Market Assessment for the People's Republic of China.* Washington: GPO, March 1977.

_____. *Electric Power for China's Modernization: The Hydroelectric Option.* (Research Paper, No. ER–10089U.) Washington: GPO, May 1980.

_____. *Chinese Coal Industry: Prospects Over the Next Decade.* (Research Paper, No. ER 79–10092.) Washington: GPO, February 1979.

_____. *China: the Steel Industry in the 1970s and 1980s.* (Research Paper, No. ER 79–10245.) Washington: GPO, May 1979.

Science

Books

Ludlow, Nicholas H. *Selling Technology to China. Washington: National* Council for U.S.-China Trade, 1979.

Needham, Joseph. *Science and Civilization in China.* New York: Cambridge University Press, 1954–80.

Sutlmeier, Richard P. *Science, Technology, and China's Drive for Modernization.* Stanford: Hoover Institution Press, 1980.

Articles

"China's Use of DP Expected to Triple by 1985," *Computerworld*, November 12, 1979, p. 16.

"A New Long March for China: Mobilizing to Try to Catch Up in Science and Technology," *TIME*, October 15, 1979, pp. 115–116.

Szuprowicz, Bohden O. "China's Computer Industry," *Datamation*, June 1975, pp. 83–88.

Government publications

U.S. Central Intelligence Agency. *The Electronics and Computer Establishment in the People's Republic of China.* Washington: GPO, January 1980.

_____. *The Telecommunications Establishment in the People's Republic of China.* Washington: GPO, 1980.

U.S. Congress. 96th, 2nd Session. Hearings before Subcommittee on Science, Research, and Technology and the Subcommittee on Investigations and Oversight. Committee on Science and Technology. November 13 and November 15, 1979. *Technology Transfer to China.* Washington: GPO, July 1980.

Defense

Books

Clubb, O. Edmund. *China and Russia, The Great Game.* New York: Columbia University Press, 1970.

Ellison, Herbert J. *The Sino-Soviet Conflict: A Global Perspective.* Seattle: University of Washington Press, 1982.

Articles

Eiland, Michael D. "Military Modernization and China's Economy," *Asian Survey*, December 1977, pp. 1143–1157.

"The Sino-Soviet Border Dispute: Chinese and Russian Arguments," *China News Analysis*, August 31, 1979, pp. 1–9.

Government publications

U.S. Central Intelligence Agency. *Chinese Defense Spending: 1965–79.* (Research Paper, No. SR 80–100091.) Washington: GPO, July 1980.

U.S. Defense Intelligence Agency. *Handbook on the Chinese Armed Forces.* Washington: GPO, 1979.

3—Trading Blocks

Japan

Articles

"A 'Reagan Doctrine' in Asia Takes Shape," *U.S. News & World Report*, August 10, 1981, p. 36.

Larkin, Bruce D. "Sino-Japanese Relations: Economic Priorities," *Current History*, September 1982, pp. 268–271.

Europe

Articles

"Chairman Hua Comes to See How Europe Works," *Financial Times*, October 15, 1979, p. 18.

Broadbent, K. P. "China and the EEC: The Politics of a New Trade Relationship," *World Today*, May 1976, pp. 190–198.

The United States

Books

Fairbank, John K. *The United States and China*. Cambridge: Harvard University Press, 1979.

Kinter, William R. *A Matter of Two Chinas: The China-Taiwan Issue in U.S. Foreign Policy*. Philadelphia: Foreign Policy Institute, 1979.

Articles

"Taiwan Faces Reality," *World Press Review*, October 1980, pp. 32–37.

Cohen, Jerome Alan. "U.S.-China Relations," *Far Eastern Economic Review*, March 7, 1980, pp. 45–52.

4—Making Contact

Books on trade

Bloch, Carolyn. *Exporting: Basics for the Small Firm*. Silver Springs: Contax, 1978.

Fayerweather, John. *International Marketing*. Englewood Cliffs: Prentice-Hall, 1965.

Goldsmith, Howard R. *How to Make a Fortune in Import/Export*. Reston: Reston Publishing Company, 1980.

Marjaro, Simon. *A Strategic Approach to World Markets*. New York: John Wiley & Sons, 1977.

Schultz, George J. *Foreign Trade Marketplace*. Detroit: Gale Research, 1977.

Stanley, A. O. *Handbook of International Marketing*. New York: McGraw-Hill, 1963.

U.S. Small Business Administration. *Export Marketing for Smaller Firms*. Washington: GPO, 1979.

Books on trading with China

Azif, Herbert B. *China Trade: A Guide to Doing Business With the People's Republic of China*. Coral Springs: Intraworld Trade News, 1981.

Business Strategies for the People's Republic of China. Hong Kong: Business International Asia/Pacific Ltd., 1980.

Fung, Lawrence. *China Trade Handbook*. Hong Kong: The Arsdale People, 1980.

McDougall, Corlina. *Trading With China*. New York: McGraw-Hill, 1980.

U.S. Department of Commerce. *Doing Business With the People's Republic of China*. Washington: GPO, November 1980.

Articles

Roby, Jerry L. "Is the China Market for You?" *Harvard Business Review*, January-February 1980, pp. 150–158.

Winski, Joseph. "China Trade Means Wealth—for Patient Trader," *Chicago Tribune*, September 19, 1979, sec. 4, p. 1, 12.

5—Negotiating the Contract

Books

De Pauw, John W. *U.S.-Chinese Trade Negotiations*. New York: Praeger, 1981.

Fisher, Rodger, and William Ury. *Getting to Yes: Negotiating Agreement Without Giving In*. Boston: Houghton Mifflin Company, 1981.

Lall, Arthur. *How Communist China Negotiates*. New York: Columbia University Press, 1968.

Young, Kenneth T. *Negotiating With the Chinese Communists: The United States Experience, 1953–67*. New York: McGraw-Hill, 1968.

6—Navigating the Bureaucracy

Books

Gorman, Tom, and Jeffrey S. Muir. *Advertising in the People's Republic of China.* Hong Kong: China Consultants International, 1979.

Harding, Harry. *Organizing China: The Problem of Bureaucracy, 1949–1976.* Stanford: Stanford University Press, 1981.

Schultz, Jeffrey. *China's Foreign Trade Corporations: Organization and Personnel.* Washington: National Council for U.S.-China Trade, 1979.

Willmott, W. E. *Economic Organization in Chinese Society.* Stanford: Stanford University Press, 1972.

U.S. Central Intelligence Agency. *Directory of Chinese Officials: National Level Organizations.* (Research Paper, No. CR 80–12651.) Washington: GPO, July 1980.

Articles

Xue, Mundo. "Combating Bureaucracy," *Beijing Review,* June 30, 1980, pp. 26–28.

"Decentralizing Foreign Trade," *China Sources,* March 1980, pp. 8–9.

7—Law

Books

Cohen, Jerome Alan, and Hungdah Chiu. *People's Republic of China and International Law, A Documentary Study.* Princeton: Princeton University Press, 1974.

Holtzman, Howard M. *Legal Aspects of Doing Business With China.* New York: Practising Law Institute, 1976.

Hsiao, Gene T. *The Foreign Trade of China—Policy, Law, and Practice.* Berkeley: University of California Press, 1977.

Li, Victor H. *Law Without Lawyers.* Stanford: Stanford University Press, 1977.

Articles

Edwards, Rangle. "Formal Law Beginning a Comeback in Post-Mao China," *Contemporary China*, Summer 1978, pp. 92–102.

Liu, Yiu-chu. "Disputes and Arbitration," *China Sources*, March 1980, pp. 33–34.

8—Finance

Books

Bornstein, Morris. *Comparative Economic Systems: Models and Cases.* Homewood, Ill: Richard D. Irwin, 1965.

Hsiao, Katherine H. *Money and Monetary Policy in Communist China.* New York: Columbia University Press, 1971.

Articles

"China Data," *China Business Review*, May-June 1982, pp. 56–57.

"Lessons of U.S.-China Hotel Venture," *Wall Street Journal*, August 11, 1982, p. 27.

Government publications

U.S. Department of Commerce. *Prospects for People's Republic of China Hard Currency Trade Through 1985.* Washington: GPO, 1979.

———. *East-West Countertrade Practices: An Introductory Guide for Business.* Washington: GPO, August 1978.

9—China Profile

Books

DeKeijzer, Arne J., and Frederic Kaplan. *The China Guidebook, 1982–83.* New York: Eurasia Press, 1982.

Felber, John E. *The American's Tourist Manual: People's Republic of China.* Newark: International Intertrade, 1980.

Fisher, Robert C. *Fodor's People's Republic of China.* New York: David McKay, 1979.

Garside, Evelyne. *China Companion: A Guide to 100 Cities, Resorts, and Places of Interest in the People's Republic of China.* New York: Farrar, Straus, Giroux, 1982.

Malloy, Ruth. *Travel Guide to the People's Republic of China.* New York: William Morrow, 1975.

Articles

"China to Begin a Census of Its 1 Billion People," *Philadelphia Inquirer,* June 30, 1982, p. 3.

"China Today and Us." *East Asia Millions,* November 1982, pp. 250–263.

Government publications

U.S. Central Intelligence Agency. *People's Republic of China Atlas.* (Stock No. 4115–0001.) Washington: GPO, November 1971.

U.S. Department of Interior. *Gazetteer of the People's Republic of China: Pinyin to Wade-Giles, Wade-Giles to Pinyin.* Washington: Defense Mapping Agency, July 1979.

Conclusions—Problems and Prospects

Books

Butterfield, Fox. *China: Alive in the Bitter Sea.* ["Epilogue: China, the West, and the Future," pp. 446–457.] New York: Times Books, 1982.

Eckstein, Alexander. *China's Economic Revolution.* ["The Chinese Development Model: Prospects and Dilemmas," pp. 112–114.] London: Cambridge University Press, 1977.

Articles

Alsop, Stewart. "Does China Matter Much?" *Newsweek,* January 26, 1970, p. 84.

Hu, Jiwei. "Report on a Series of Struggles in the Top Echelons of the CCP," *Cheng Ming,* August 1, 1980, pp. 55–63.

Smith, Ray. "China Revisited," *Wheaton Alumni,* May 1979, pp. 8–11.

"Deng Solidifies Control, Hua Ousted from New Politburo," *Chicago Sun-Times,* September 13, 1982, p. 6.

"China: A Decade of Measured Progress," *TIME,* March 15, 1982, p. 27.

INDEX

A

ABI/Inform, 74
Academy of Sciences, 33
Academy of Social Science, 35
Acheson, Dean, 55
Administration Bureau for Industry and
    Commerce, 140, 148
Aeroflot, 31, 95
Agricultural Bank of China, 16, 155
Agriculture, modernizing, 16–20,
    48–49, 61, 202
    fertilizer, 17, 19–20
    grain, 16–17, 31
    irrigation, 17–19
    mechanization, 20
Air France, 31, 95
Air transportation, 31–32, 94–95,
    196–197
Aircraft, 60, 61
American Arbitration Association, 152
American Industrial Report, 109
American Institute of Marine Under-
    writers, 170
Aramco Steel Company, 61
Arbitration, 150–154
Asahi Glass, 52
Atlantic Alliance, 53
AUGUST 1, 35

B

Baker Tool Company, 61
Bank of China, the, 68, 70, 156, 158,
    159, 163, 165, 166, 167, 168, 173,
    184, 195
Banking, 155–158
Banks
    American banks with China ties,
        71–72
    Chinese, 70–71
Barre, M. Raymond, Prime Minister of
    France, 47
Barter, 179–181
Beijing
    airport, 32
    Hotel, 192
Beijing Review, 65, 77
Bethelehem Steel, 27
Bill of lading, 165
Biochemical Institute of Shanghai, 33

Bohai Sea Oil Company, 25
Books concerned with China, 75,
    305–315
Boxer Protocol of 1901, 3
Boxer Rebellion (1900), 3, 223
Brezhnev, Leonid, 41, 53
Brezinski, Zbigniew, 209
British Petroleum, 24
British Steel Corporation, 28
Brown, Harold, U.S. Defense Minister,
    48
Bureaucracy, 105–111
    China's actions, 107–108
    individuals' actions, 108–111

C

Callagan, James, British Prime
    Minister, 48
Cars, 197
Carter, Jimmy, 57, 159
Caterpillar Tractor, 193
Cathay Pacific Airways, 31
Ceasescu, Nicolae, President of
    Rumania, 53
Central Intelligence Agency, National
    Foreign Assessment Center, 79–80
Certificate of origin, 165
Chemical Society of China, 140
Chen Yun, 8, 13
Cheng Ming, 22
China, see People's Republic of China
China Business Review, 68, 76
China Daily, 74–75
China Reconstructs, 77
China's Foreign Trade, 77, 121, 140
Chinese Export Commodities Fair
    (CECF), 68, 98, 141–143
Chinese National Publications Import
    Corporation, 150
Chinese organizations, abbreviation of,
    219–220
Chinese Trade Organization (CTO),
    180, 183
Civil Aviation Administration of China
    (CAAC), 31, 95
Civil Aviation Administration of Korea,
    31
Civil Engineering Society of China, 140
Cohen, Herb, 108–109
Cohen, Jerome Alan, 153
Commercial invoice, 165
Commodity Credit Corporation, U.S.
    Department of Agriculture, 161
Common Market, the, 53

Communist Manifesto, The, 52, 208
Compensation, 54, 179, 181
Computers, 34, 35–39, 60, 61, 132
Conference Service Bureau, 92
Congressional Information Service
    (CIS), 78
Construction Bank of China, 155
Consultants, 91–92
Consultative Group Coordinating Com-
    mittee Alliance, 39
Contracts, 145–148
    forms, 255–269
    negotiating, 97–104
Control Data Corporation, 36
Corporate Intelligence Agency, 80–85
Counterpurchase transaction, 181
Countertrade, 179–184
Credit, 158–161
Cultural Revolution, 5, 9–10, 13, 19,
    33, 34, 40, 45, 105, 108, 142, 188,
    201, 202, 203, 205, 225
Customs, 93–94
Customs Import and Export Tariff, 164

D

Daqing Oil Field, 35
Deere, John & Company, 61
Defense, modernizing, 39–48, 50
    capabilities, 45–47
    in Viet Nam, 43–44, 45, 47
    intentions, 40–44
    needs, 47–48
Deng Xiaoping, 8, 12, 15, 44, 58, 108,
    201, 202, 203
Department of Commerce, 48, 79
*Directory of Online Information
    Resources*, 74
Drafts, 164–165
Dresser Industries, 61

E

East Asiatic, 162
Eastern South China Sea Company,
    25
East-West Market, 71
Education, 34–35
Electricity, 22
Elf Aquitaine Societe National, 24
Embassies, 88–91
End-users, 109, 118–120
Ethiopian Airlines, 31
European Economic Community
    (EEC), 11, 53, 240–244

Eximbank, 60, 159–161. 170
Expoconsul, 92
Export Industrial Committees (EICs),
    68
Exxon, 61

F

Fang Yi, 33, 34
Feasibility study, 65–67
Fertilizer, 14, 17, 19–20, 54, 61
Fiat, 141
Financial Times, 74
First National Bank of Chicago, 71–72,
    156
Five Emphases, 188
Five Golden Blossoms, 34
Five Ones Program, 34
Five-Year-Plan, 114
    first, 6–7, 11, 19, 203, 224–225
    second, 7
    fifth, 12
    sixth, 13
Fluor, 29, 193
Foreign Corrupt Practices Act (1977),
    104
Foreign Credit Insurance Association
    (FCIA), 170
Foreign Economic and Trade Arbitra-
    tion Committee (FETAC), 150
Foreign Exchange Certificates (FXC),
    195
Foreign exchange control, 167, 271–286
Foreign Investment Control Commis-
    sion of China (FICC), 115–116, 173
Foreign Trade Arbitration Commission,
    140
Foreign Trade Corporations (FTCs),
    86, 88, 90, 93, 114, 118, 120–137,
    139, 140, 141–144, 146, 147, 164,
    166, 169, 176, 192
Freedom of Information Act, 82
Friendship Store, 197, 199–200
Frost & Sullivan, 81
Fujian Investment Enterprise Corpora-
    tion, 156

G

Gang of Four, 12, 34, 40, 202, 203
Globe Physic Petroleum Company, 24
Grain 12, 14, 16–17, 31, 56
Grand Canal, 18, 30
Great Leap Forward, 7–8, 9, 40, 51,
    108, 142, 203, 225

Great Wall Hotel, 106
Gross National Product, 11, 203–204, 207
Guangzhou Foreign Trade Center, 141
Guangzhou Trade Fair, see Chinese Export Commodities Fair

H

Haig, Alexander, 41
Han dynasty, 187
Hitachi, 36, 84, 141
Honeywell, 36
Hong Kong, 16, 31, 39, 94, 137, 156–160, 183, 188, 193, 198, 208
    ceded to Great Britain, 2, 223
    lease expiration negotiations, 44, 157–159
Huo Guofeng, 12, 53

I

IBM, 36, 84
Import-Export Control Commission (IECC), 115
Industry, modernizing, 20–32, 49
    coal, 22–24
    electricity, 22
    iron and steel, 27–28
    light, 16, 21–22
    nonferrous metals, 28–30
    petroleum, 24–27
    transportation, 30–32
Institutional Investor, 161
Insurance, 169–170
    certificate, 166
    companies, 169–170
    contract, 265–269
International Chamber of Commerce, 152
International Club, 197, 199
International Harvester, 61
International Monetary Fund (IMF), 158, 159
Iran Air, 31
Iron and steel, 27–28, 33
Irrigation, 17–19, 22
Itoman, 184

J

Japan Airlines, 31, 95, 98
Japan-China Long Term Agreement, 52, 237–240

Japan-China Petroleum Development Company, 24
Japan Petroleum, 27
Japan Petroleum Group, 24
Jiang Qing, 11, 12, 226
Jiang Zhongzheng (Chiang Kai-shek), 4, 5, 15, 58, 105, 191, 224
Johnson Debt Default Act, 158
Joint ventures with China, 170–179

K

Kennedy, John F., 55
Kissinger, Henry A., 62, 99
Komatsu, 52
Kongfuzi (Confucious), 1, 2, 188
Kremlin, 41
Krupp, 162

L

Laws, see Regulations
Legal issues
    arbitration, 150–154
    contracts, 145–148
    copyrights, 150
    patents, 149
    trademarks, 148–149
Letter of credit (L/C), 165, 166, 167
Li Qiang, 149, 254
Lin Biao, 9, 45, 224
Liu Shaoqi, 8, 10
Lloyd's of London, 170
London Mining Journal, 29
Long March, 4, 15, 224
Long Term Trade Agreement (LTTA), 54
Lufthansa, 95

M

Macao, 31, 137, 157–158, 183
Macy's, 141
Manchu dynasty, 2, 105
Mao Zedong, 1, 4, 5, 7, 8, 9, 10, 13, 14, 15, 19, 45, 53, 101, 105, 107, 110, 112, 201, 202, 203, 223
    Hundred Flowers Movement, 7, 205, 225
    meeting with Nixon, 11, 56
    "Ten Principles of Military Operations", 65
Maritime Arbitration Commission, 140, 151

Market in China, entering, 85–96
    consultants, 91–92
    customs, 93–94
    proposal, the, 86–91
    transportation, 94–96
    visas, 92–93
Marshall, George C., General, 4
Marx, Karl, 52, 201, 208
Metric conversion, 221
Ming dynasty, 2
Mining, 22–24, 54
Ministries, 115-118
    Coal Industry, 24
    Communications, 137
    Finance, 13, 155
    Foreign Economic Relations and
       Trade (MOFERT), 68, 115,
       118, 120, 138, 173
    Public Health, 149
    Railways, 35
Mitsubishi Electric Corporation, 36, 80,
    84
Mobil Oil, 24
Moscow Declaration of Unity, 9
Most Favored Nation, 57, 223, 226
Multiple cropping, 16–17, 20
Mutual Defense Treaty with Taiwan,
    59

N

National Council for U.S.-China Trade,
    67–69
National Cash Register (NCR), 36
National Foreign Trade Council, 73,
    162
National Party Congress, 111–112
National People's Congress, 45, 112,
    115, 177, 178
National Science Conference, 33
National Textile Import and Export
    Corporation, 126, 184
Nationalist China, see Taiwan
NATO, 41
Negotiating contracts, 97–104
Neiman-Marcus, 141
New York Times, The, 74, 104
Nippon Electric Company of Japan, 39
Nippon Steel, 52
Nixon, Richard M., 56, 245
Nonferrous metals, 28–30, 54, 134
Northern Electric Company of Canada,
    39
Norwegian National Oil Company, 24
Nuclear defense capabilities, 46–47
Nuclear plants, 22, 54

O

Oil, see Petroleum
Online databases, 73–74
OPEC, 52, 162
Opium War (1839), 2, 100, 223

P

Packing list, 165
Pan American World Airlines, 94
Paris Convention for the Protection of
    Industrial Property, 149
Patents, 149
Payment, 164–168
Pennzoil, 24
People's Bank of China, 155–156
People's Insurance Company of China
    (PICC), 169
People's Liberation Army, 44, 45
People's Republic of China
    Administration Bureau for In-
       dustry and Commerce, 140,
       148
    Chemical Society, 140
    China Aviation Administration
       Corporation (CAAC), 196,
       197
    China Council for Promotion of
       International Trade (CCPIT),
       68, 88, 93, 97, 116, 121, 140,
       141, 148, 150, 151
    Civil Engineering Society, 140
    Climate, 186–187
    Constitution of, 112, 203
    establishment of, 5, 55, 224
    Food, 193–194
    Foreign Economic and Trade Ar-
       bitration Committee
       (FETAC), 150
    Foreign Investment Control
       Commission (FICC), 115, 116,
       173
    Foreign Affairs Ministry, 106, 192
    from 1970, 10–14, 225–226
    geography, 185–186
    history, 1–14, 223–226
    housing, 192–193
    International Travel Service,
       94–96, 192, 194
    International Trust and Invest-
       ment Corporation, 116, 139–140,
       144, 169, 172
    joint ventures with, 170–179
    language, 189–192

Ministry of Coal Industry, 24
Ministry of Communications, 137
Ministry of Finance, 13, 155
Ministry of Foreign Economic Relations and Trade (MOFERT), 68, 115, 118, 120, 138, 173
Ministry of Public Health, 149
Ministry of Railways, 35
money, 194–196
National Chartering Corporation (CNCC), 138, 163
National Chemical Import and Export Corporation, 168

People's Republic of China (cont'd)
National Foreign Trade Transportation Corporation, 138
National Import and Export Commodities Inspection Corporation (CHINSPECT), 138–139
National Offshore Oil Corporation (CNOOC), 25
National Oil and Gas Exploration and Development Corporation (CNOGEDC), 25
National Textile Import and Export Corporation, 126–127, 184
Ocean Shipping Company, 137–138
people, 187–188
pleasure, 199–200
pre-Revolutionary, 2–5, 223–224
Public Security Bureau, 106, 142, 196
relationship with Japan, 51–52, 141
relationship with the U.S., 54–63, 245–254
relationship with Western Europe, 52–54
religion, 188–189
Resource Company, 156
State Agricultural Commission, 115
State Capital Construction Commission, 115
State Council, 112–113
State Economic Commission, 68, 114
State Finance and Economic Commission, 115
State General Administration of Foreign Exchange Control (SGAFEC), 167
State Machine Building Commission, (SMBC), 115
State Planning Commission (SPC), 114
State Science and Technology Commission, 33, 114
State Statistical Bureau, 8, 77
telecommunications, 197–199
trading establishment, 111–144
transportation, 30–32, 196–197
Periodicals, 75–78, 150
Petroleum, 11, 24–27, 60–61, 136, 171, 227–235
Petroleum News Southeast Asia, 27
Pinyin, 190–191, 213–217
Politburo, 5, 41, 111, 112, 202, 206
Pricing, 162–164
Prime Computer, 36
Private Export Funding Corporation, 161
Probe International, 81

Q

Qing dynasty, 2–3

R

Radio Factory Number Three, 36
Radio receivers, 38, 132
Railways, 31, 54, 197
Reagan, Ronald, 59–60
Red Guards, 5, 9, 10, 33
Regulations
Customs, 164
Foreign exchange control, 167, 271–286
Joint ventures, 151, 170–179
Lawyers, 150–151
Offshore petroleum, 25, 227–235
Taxes, 175, 287–304
Research centers, 69–70
Return on investment, 66
Rusk, Dean, 55

S

Safire, William, 104
Science, modernizing, 32–39, 49–50
computers, 35–39
education, 34–35
telecommunications, 35–39, 54, 61, 132, 197–198

Semiconductor chip, 39
Shanghai Communique, 56–58,
    245–246
Shell Oil, 24
Shipping, 30–31, 54
Snow, Edgar, 1, 204
Solzhenitsyn, Alexander, 40
South China Morning Post, 74
South Yellow Sea Oil Company, 25
Standing Committee, 112
Steel, see Iron and Steel
Sun Zhongshan (Sun Yat-sen), 3–4, 105,
    191, 223, 224
Sunzi, (Sun Tzu), 39–40
Swiss Air, 31, 95

T

Taiping Rebellion, 2, 223
Taiwan, 16, 44, 52, 93, 94, 157
    American recognition of, 55,
        58–60
    Nationalist, 5
    surrender of, 3, 56
Taxation, 287–304
    on joint ventures, 171
Technical Exchange Department of the
    China Council for the Promotion of
    International Trade, 97
Technology, see Science
Telegraph, 39, 198
Telephones, 38, 198–199
Television, 38, 39, 132
Telex, 39, 198
Ten-Year Plan, 13, 21
Theroux, Eugene, 151, 154
Thatcher, Margaret, British Prime
    Minister, 157
Tianjing Massacre, 2
Tito, Josip, Marshal, 53
Total Petroleum Company of France,
    24
Trade Agreement Extension Act of
    1951, 57
Trade Expansion Act (1962), 57
Trade organizations, 72–73
Trademark Registration Agency, 148
Trademarks, 148–149
Transportation, 16, 94–96, 196–197,
    203
Trucking, 31
Truman, Harry S, 56

U

Union Oil of California, 24
United League, the, 3
United Nations, People's Republic of
    China admitted to, 11, 226
United States Chamber of Commerce,
    72, 162
United States Department of Com-
    merce, 48, 79
United States Embassy in Beijing, 89
United States government organizations
    concerned with China, 78–80
    United States Office of Manage-
        ment and Budget, 114
United States Overseas Private In-
    surance Corporation (OPIC),
    169–170
United States Trade Act of 1974, 149
United States Export-Import Bank, 60,
    170
United States Steel, 61
United States
    recognition of the People's
        Republic of China, 57, 59
    relationship with China, 54–63,
        141, 245–254
    trade with China, 60–63
Universal Copyright Convention, 150

V

Visas, 88, 92–93

W

Wade-Giles system of transliteration,
    190, 213–217
Warsaw Pact, 41, 53
Western South China Sea Oil Company,
    25
Woodcock, Leonard, 201, 254
World Bank, the, 158–159

Y

Ye Jianying, 59

Z

Zhang Zhingfu, 45
Zhao Ziyang, 13
Zhou Enlai, 5, 11, 12, 15, 56, 99, 224,
    226, 245